IDENTITY AND DEVELOPMENT

OTHER RECENT VOLUMES IN THE SAGE FOCUS EDITIONS

8. **Controversy (Third Edition)**
   Dorothy Nelkin
41. **Black Families (Second Edition)**
   Harriette Pipes McAdoo
64. **Family Relationships in Later Life (Second Edition)**
   Timothy H. Brubaker
89. **Popular Music and Communication (Second Edition)**
   James Lull
133. **Social Research on Children and Adolescents**
   Barbara Stanley and Joan E. Sieber
134. **The Politics of Life in Schools**
   Joseph Blase
135. **Applied Impression Management**
   Robert A. Giacalone and Paul Rosenfeld
136. **The Sense of Justice**
   Roger D. Masters and Margaret Gruter
137. **Families and Retirement**
   Maximiliane Szinovacz, David J. Ekerdt, and Barbara H. Vinick
138. **Gender, Families, and Elder Care**
   Jeffrey W. Dwyer and Raymond T. Coward
139. **Investigating Subjectivity**
   Carolyn Ellis and Michael G. Flaherty
140. **Preventing Adolescent Pregnancy**
   Brent C. Miller, Josefina J. Card, Roberta L. Paikoff, and James L. Peterson.
141. **Hidden Conflict in Organizations**
   Deborah M. Kolb and Jean M. Bartunek
142. **Hispanics in the Workplace**
   Stephen B. Knouse, Paul Rosenfeld, and Amy L. Culbertson
143. **Psychotherapy Process Research**
   Shaké G. Toukmanian and David L. Rennie
144. **Educating Homeless Children and Adolescents**
   James H. Stronge
145. **Family Care of the Elderly**
   Jordan I. Kosberg
146. **Growth Management**
   Jay M. Stein
147. **Substance Abuse and Gang Violence**
   Richard E. Cervantes
148. **Third World Cities**
   John D. Kasarda and Allan M. Parnell
149. **Independent Consulting for Evaluators**
   Alan Vaux, Margaret S. Stockdale, and Michael J. Schwerin
150. **Advancing Family Preservation Practice**
   E. Susan Morton and R. Kevin Grigsby
151. **A Future for Religion?**
   William H. Swatos, Jr.
152. **Researching Sensitive Topics**
   Claire M. Renzetti and Raymond M. Lee
153. **Women as National Leaders**
   Michael A. Genovese
154. **Testing Structural Equation Models**
   Kenneth A. Bollen and J. Scott Long
155. **Nonresidential Parenting**
   Charlene E. Depner and James H. Bray
156. **Successful Focus Groups**
   David L. Morgan
157. **Race and Ethnicity in Research Methods**
   John H. Stanfield II and Rutledge M. Dennis
158. **Improving Organizational Surveys**
   Paul Rosenfeld, Jack E. Edwards, and Marie D. Thomas
159. **A History of Race Relations Research**
   John H. Stanfield II
160. **The Elderly Caregiver**
   Karen A. Roberto
161. **Activity and Aging**
   John R. Kelly
162. **Aging in Rural America**
   C. Neil Bull
163. **Corporate Political Agency**
   Barry M. Mitnick
164. **The New Localism**
   Edward G. Goetz and Susan E. Clarke
165. **Providing Community-Based Services to the Rural Elderly**
   John A. Krout
166. **Religion in Aging and Health**
   Jeffrey S. Levin
167. **Clinical Case Management**
   Robert W. Surber
168. **Qualitative Methods in Aging Research**
   Jaber F. Gubrium and Andrea Sankar
169. **Interventions for Adolescent Identity Development**
   Sally L. Archer
170. **Destructive Behavior in Developmental Disabilities**
   Travis Thompson and David B. Gray
171. **Advances in Social Network Analysis**
   Stanley Wasserman and Joseph Galaskiewicz
172. **Identity and Development**
   Harke A. Bosma, Tobi L. G. Graafsma, Harold D. Grotevant, and David J. de Levita
173. **Interpersonal Communication in Older Adulthood**
   Mary Lee Hummert, John M. Wiemann, and Jon F. Nussbaum
174. **Gender Inequality at Work**
   Gerry A. Jacobs

IDENTITY AND DEVELOPMENT

An Interdisciplinary Approach

Harke A. Bosma
Tobi L. G. Graafsma
Harold D. Grotevant
David J. de Levita
editors

SAGE Publications
International Educational and Professional Publisher
Thousand Oaks London New Delhi

For information address:

SAGE Publications, Inc.
2455 Teller Road
Thousand Oaks, California 91320

SAGE Publications Ltd.
6 Bonhill Street
London EC2A 4PU
United Kingdom

SAGE Publications India Pvt. Ltd.
M-32 Market
Greater Kailash I
New Delhi 110 048 India

Printed in the United States of America

Library of Congress Cataloging-in-Publication Data

Main entry under title:
Identity and development: an interdisciplinary approach / edited by
Harke A. Bosma . . . [et al.].
p. cm — (Sage focus editions; vol 172)
Includes bibliographical references and index.
ISBN 0-8039-5189-2. — ISBN 0-8039-5190-6 (pbk.)
1. Identity (Psychology) 2. Identity (Psychology)—History.
3. Identity (Psychology) in literature. 4. Developmental psychology. I. Bosma, Harke, 1945-
BF697.I347 1994
155.2—dc20 94-22128

94 95 96 97 98 10 9 8 7 6 5 4 3 2 1

Sage Production Editor: Susan McElroy

This volume is respectfully dedicated to the memory of Erik H. Erikson (1902-1994), whose pioneering scholarship on identity and development inspired much of the work represented in this book.

Contents

Preface

In September 1990 a multidisciplinary conference on *Identity and Development* was held in Amsterdam in the Netherlands. The conference was visited by scholars from disciplines such as psychology, psychoanalysis, psychiatry, philosophy, sociology, history, comparative literature. It was organized to inform researchers and practitioners about recent research, theory, and clinical perspectives with regard to the study of identity and development. Since this work is taking place in different disciplines, another aim was to inform the participants about the use of both concepts in these disciplines. It was the hope of the organizers that the discussions at the conference would stimulate reflection on the theoretical meaning and scientific and practical use of the central concepts.

The need for such reflection had become evident from a research project of Graafsma and Bosma on identity development of adolescents with more or less serious emotional and behavioral problems. In this project researchers and practitioners worked together in a joint attempt to come to grips with the complexities of the nature and dynamics of the developmental process in clinical groups.

The cooperation and theoretical discussions with de Levita formed a strong impetus to broaden the scope of the reflection on identity and development to a multidisciplinary level. "Identity" and "development"

1

Introduction

HAROLD D. GROTEVANT
HARKE A. BOSMA
DAVID J. DE LEVITA
TOBI L. G. GRAAFSMA

Moderator: So, an issue that I'd like to pose is one that involves identity and choice. To what degree does choice play a role in the development of identity? Is identity something that is freely self-constructed, are there limitations, are there many restrictions, and when might we find more restrictions or fewer restrictions?

Rangell [psychoanalysis]: One of the main preoccupations of mine for many years has been unconscious choice. Nothing can be farther from an analyst's total concept and from understanding human nature than to think that the only choices that we make are conscious ones. Most of the choices we make are unconscious and then we rationalize them in conscious life. So, the question you asked: How much choice in the identity? How much choice depends upon how much is psychically determined that is automatic, imperative, driven, without choice, and how much above that is the individual able to assimilate his drives, his automatisms, his imperative needs, his uncontrollable nature and then choose, direct, guide? And there is even a third factor involved, the role of chance. Identity is both made and determined. Determined by our parents, then unconsciously chosen, and furthered and elaborated by ourselves. But we shouldn't overlook the role of fortuitous circumstances that happen in spite of any of us: political climate, physical climate, social climate, death, illness, love, loss.

Neubauer [comparative literature]: I've deliberately chosen a story (see Chapter 7) in which the choice was limited, in fact the identity was stamped upon the protagonist. I want to call your attention to another passage from *A Portrait of the Artist as a Young Man* (Joyce). That passage is one of choice: If you remember, the book ends with his deliberate rejection of family, church, country, and going to the continent and the affirmation of a kind of a joyous creativity, by choice, it seems.

Marcia [clinical/developmental psychology]: Just briefly, I think there are what the existentialists called conditions of "thrown-ness." It refers to one's gender, the time in which one is born, one's ethnic background, and especially being Jewish, which is a kind of double identity dose. I think that these conditions of thrown-ness are things with which one has to come to terms, so it's not as if one can choose to be male or female, or short or tall, but one has some room for decision making around what one makes of those things.

Mitzman [history]: My first reaction to the question is that it is totally ahistorical, because it assumes that everybody throughout history has had choices, whereas we know that there are many historical situations where there were none, at least in the sense that we know choice to exist today. People born into medieval villages, people born, even today, in various tribes in Africa or in other parts of the world, had none of the choices that we know now: to break away from families or not to break away from families, to strive for a certain kind of education or not. Everything was laid out. Yet, when I think about it a little further, then it occurs to me that that's actually a false interpretation. If I transpose your question now into any historical situation, then I have to realize that of course everybody has some kind of choice. It's not our kind of choice, but it's nevertheless a choice and probably crucial for their own development within that particular social constellation, so that even in a condition of serfdom people have choices as to how they are going to react to somebody being particularly beastly in their environment, somebody who may even be breaking the rather thin layer of morality that is generally accepted in that village. So I think there are always choices in any historical situation, but you have to transpose the question. If you're thinking about personality in the 16th century, you have to accept the conditions of life in the 16th century.

de Levita [child psychiatry]: I think choices are always choices out of what is available. Identity comes in at the point where you talk about what the society has available for the individual.

Josselson [psychology]: One is nevertheless choosing, all the time. And I would submit that even in the jungle, where everyone is very clear about what their occupational role is, nevertheless there are the people who everyone knows is a good person to take your troubles to, because they will be sympathetic and listen and that person will then know that that is their uniqueness within that society. . . . But what does one look at? Does one look at the ruling elite and what they do, or does one look at the common people and their history? In social history there is now a lot of interest in those people who are always left out and what was going on with them. They also had an identity.

Grotevant [developmental/family psychology]: Yes, I agree and I think for me one of the most attractive things about the notion of identity is that it looks at the individual in context and so, whether it be the historical context or the decision-making context, or the family context, the concept by itself begs the question of context, which is just a critical part of the whole term.

Widdershoven [philosophy/developmental psychology]: I would like to stress that choice has to be seen in historical context. I differentiate between psychological theories that leave more or less choice, and what I call the radical open variant of identity (see Chapter 6), a variant in which there is very much choice, in which we choose every moment, our life is constantly a process of choosing. I would like to stress that some psychological theories have brought this idea of choice to the surface, at this historical moment. Those theories were impossible, I think, 50 years ago, so these psychological theories about identity and about choice are themselves theories that have a historical background.

Rangell [psychoanalysis]: I think that every question picks one out of a duality in which only the duality will work. Is there any debate about friendship, not peer group—the kids don't talk about peers

> or parental input, they talk about "my mommy and daddy," they talk about friends. But is there any question here whether peer groups influence identity? It would be an absurd question. Every human being starts with a mother, then notices there's a father somewhere around, then has siblings, and then has friends. In the same way we talked about choices, and then the historian said that it's ahistorical, but a moment later he said, no, that's not true, because in any phase of history there are choices, and yet wherever there are choices there is history. It isn't one or the other, it's always both. Every speaker has spoken about two sides of a dichotomy. Dr. Marcia gave empirical scientific research, but on the other hand, he never eliminated intuitive, clinical, hunch research and conclusions and discoveries. We do both. We quantify and we qualify. There isn't "versus." We have generational conflicts, we have horizontal conflicts, or internal versus external or preoedipal versus oedipal. It's always a fusion and integration of both.

Conversations such as this illustrate attempts on the part of different disciplines to understand the human condition. Two interrelated features of human existence involve sameness and change. Thus, an important challenge is to understand the tension that arises when we consider ways in which humans exhibit both continuity and change across the life span.

The issues of change and sameness have been debated in philosophy since ancient Greek times, but they also have great contemporary relevance. Issues such as individual change and development, growing up in a changing society, adoption within families, migration and disputes among ethnic groups can be more effectively understood when concepts such as identity and development are available. Actually, both concepts are used within different disciplines and perspectives. Because one perspective alone is often not enough to fully understand the social problems of this scope, and a multidisciplinary approach is needed, questions arise about how these concepts are defined and used in the different disciplines, and what these disciplines can learn from each other in this respect.

Goals of the Volume

This volume developed from a conference that took place in Amsterdam during September 1990, bringing together academics and practitioners from several disciplines in the social sciences and humanities to explore the concepts of identity and development and the relations between them. The first day of the conference featured the presentations of seven papers followed by general discussion among the presenters and those in attendance. The second day was highly interactive, beginning with the presentation of a few brief position statements and building on these for interchange among those in the audience. Chapters 1 and 9 in this volume include segments of dialogue taken from the discussions at the conference. These passages have been lightly edited (with the speakers' assent) so that they lend to the coherence of the two chapters and the volume as a whole. Although most of the chapters discuss identity and development from one disciplinary perspective at a time, we have organized the book in such a way that it can capitalize on the multiple disciplines represented and the connections among them. In the concluding chapter, we have attempted to move beyond monodisciplinary and multidisciplinary views to an interdisciplinary perspective on identity and development.

In this volume, the concepts of identity and development are explored through the windows offered by psychoanalysis, psychology, history, and literary criticism. Although it was not possible to include full-length treatments of them, perspectives of philosophy and psychiatry are also discussed. All these disciplines were selected because they each explicitly address both concepts of identity and development with well-differentiated points of view. However, we make no claim that these perspectives exhaust all possible viewpoints within the social sciences and humanities.

The book includes introductory and concluding chapters that provide context for and summation of this multidisciplinary venture, and three major sections representing psychoanalysis, psychology, history and literary criticism. In introducing each section, we hope to inform readers about what they can expect in each chapter, describe the place that section plays in the volume as a whole, and briefly note the roles that the concepts of identity and development play in the section.

One could predict different outcomes from an undertaking of this sort. For some, there might be a hope that this multidisciplinary exchange would yield a shared understanding of the central concepts. Others might more pessimistically predict that this project would fail, with scholars hopelessly caught up in their own Tower of Babel, unable to communicate with one another.

We hope that this volume can illustrate how the inclusion of each specific perspective should force scholars to think more broadly than their own discipline might require. The goal is not to ask: "Who knows best?", but rather to see how the perspective offered by one discipline can inform another. Our view is that each discipline has its own limitations, and that openness to other disciplines allows consideration of alternative models. Moreover, this more expansive approach should bring into the foreground certain issues or questions that must be considered within each discipline. For example, the inclusion of the historical perspective in this volume presents the challenge of viewing all questions within their historical contexts. As Mitzman observed during the conference, "The entire contemporary discourse on identity occurs at a specific moment in Western history and under very specific conditions."

Thus, the perspectives highlighted in this volume speak not only to the state of knowledge within each discipline, but more importantly, to the value of reaching across disciplines in order to understand identity and development within their fullest meanings.

The usefulness of this approach was richly illustrated during the conference by the art historian Van de Wetering. His work involves the authentication of paintings attributed to Rembrandt:

> As an art historian I am one of the countless people who daily work with the concept of identity without ever using the word. The art historian who is reconstructing an artist's oeuvre unconsciously bases himself on the idea of a somehow coherent and stable identity of the artist under concern. The artist, therefore, is presumed to be "knowable" from the core of his oeuvre, and from that knowledge one considers oneself able to draw conclusions with respect to the autographness of other works. If we observe a certain evolution in the work of that artist, we tend to take that as the result of some natural force that transforms the products of that person in such a way that we even believe the identity is subject to certain changes. When we talk about Beethoven's "Alters-Stil," we implicitly think in terms of a natural evolution in the style and content of his works, and consider that evolution as a process the artist himself does not have control of.
>
> In a recent study of Rembrandt's "Alters-Stil" (see the first essay in the exhibition catalogue "The Master and his Workshop, Berlin/Amsterdam/London 1990/91"), I have tried to show that one of the prominent properties of that style, the broader brushwork, is not necessarily the result of such natural evolution, although a more or less gradual change from a finer to a broader *peinture* is to be observed. Both the 16th-century writer on art, Vasari, and his early 17th-century Dutch counterpart, Van Mander, describe such change from fine to broad in the production of Titian. Titian in Rembrandt's days was

> one of the legendary, and thus exemplary, artists from the past. Vasari and Van Mander emphasise that the broad manner is, though seemingly more easy, much more difficult than the finer manner. They therefore advise that only the older, experienced artist should use that manner.
>
> One could on the basis of these considerations hypothesize that the extremely ambitious Rembrandt consciously shaped his "evolution" on the changes in style of Titian. As long as one takes the character of the brushstroke of an artist as the manifestation of his identity—as, since the rise of Expressionism, we tend to do—one is tempted to think that here is a case of "manipulatable identity," the concept Professor Neubauer was just discussing. One wonders what implications the idea of "manipulatable identity" could have for the work of the art historian involved in reconstructing the oeuvre of an artist from the past. So I just wanted to reflect my enthusiasm about what's going on here from the perspective of an outsider. I've learned a lot!

Thus, the concept of identity evokes consideration both of how something remains constant over time (Which painting is a "real" Rembrandt?) and of how the techniques used in these paintings could have changed over time. In addition, the concept of identity also has a historical dimension in that it locates biographies in era-bound systems of social ideology. To become, with the advancing years, a wise man who knows life, is not only the outcome of the personal history of this or that person but also a general model of the attribution of meaning to certain biographies by a certain society. Although it has not been mentioned here what the historical origin is of this connection between wisdom and old age, it certainly seems Greek and in the case of Rembrandt prevails to the present day. During a guided tour of Rembrandt's self-portraits in the National Gallery in London, it was said in front of the next-to-last portrait: "These are eyes which have seen nearly everything." Then, in front of the last portrait: "These are eyes which have seen all."

The Central Concepts

Identity

There is no consensus about the phenomena that *identity* refers to. Though it is widely used by different scientists, others, because of its supposed vagueness, reject it as a useful scientific concept. When we restrict ourselves to psychology, it appears that various definitions of identity are used, and each of these is linked with its own operationalization. This situation has led to different schools with their own theoretical and empirical traditions, and the researchers within each school hardly seem to be aware of (or prefer to ignore?) what is going on outside their own school. Cross-references are scarce.

How is identity defined in general dictionaries? According to *The Concise Oxford Dictionary* (7th ed., 1982) identity is:

- absolute sameness; individuality, personality; condition of being a specified person;
- (Algebra) equality of two expressions for all values of the literal quantities; expression of this, e.g. $(x + 1)^2 = (\text{or} \equiv)\ x^2 + 2x + 1$;
- (Mathematics) transformation that leaves an object unchanged.

With regard to the human individual, the Oxford dictionary stresses elements like sameness, character, and being an identifiable person. And next to the equality of mathematical expressions, the Oxford dictionary also defines identity as a "transformation that leaves an object unchanged." This definition, together with the definition of sameness, character, and being an identifiable person, form the main elements of the meaning of the concept of identity in connection to human individuals. Both meanings are related and can go together. For example, an individual can try to achieve a clear identity and, at the same time, try to maintain that identity despite growth and change. Compare the example of a fruit tree during the four seasons: In winter it has no leaves, in spring it blossoms and produces new green leaves, in summer it bears fruit, and in autumn its leaves turn red and ultimately fall off. Nevertheless, there is no doubt that it remains the same tree. Or take a human being: Despite the tremendous changes between conception and death, it remains the same, unique person. However, despite these self-evident examples it is not at all clear what exactly the identity of the tree or that person is. And, on second thought, there is a paradox in the sense that something cannot change if it does not, in a certain respect, remain the same. Otherwise it would be a sequence.

The "characteristic and distinctive features of a subject" forms the key element of definitions of identity in the various approaches within psychology. Van der Werff, in his glossary of *self* and related terms, for example, defines identity as "the combination of essential psychic qualities which characterize and differentiate the person" (1985, p. 176). He made some further conceptual distinctions that clarify the meaning of identity and related concepts, such as personality, self, and self-concept, in a more recent paper titled "Identity and Development: Identity Scientists Build Their own Babel Tower" (Van der Werff, 1991). This paper was stimulated by the conference discussions. First a primary distinction between a person's objective and subjective identity is suggested. Individuals can be objectively identified by all kinds of data: physical characteristics (including fingerprints and DNA profile), name, date of birth, biographical descriptions, and so on. The same goes for psychological characteristics that can be objectively assessed: IQ, attitudes, personality traits, and such. According to Van der Werff, this identity variant could also be called personality. In his view subjective identity is the experiential side of objective identity. He distinguishes between a global and a more articulated sense of identity. Globally a sense of identity refers to "the awareness of continuously being one and the same person, distinct from all others"; more articulated, it refers to "the individual's mental representation of the objective identifiers just mentioned" (Van der Werff, 1991, p. 2): A person's image of his or her physical and psychological characteristics, a person's autobiography.

The concept of self has different connotations in psychology. For the most part these connotations are linked to specific theoretical schools (for further details, see Glossary). In general, however, self-psychology is a personality psychology from a specific theoretical perspective, and accordingly the self is interchangeable with the personality component of objective identity (Van der Werff, 1991, p. 3). Thus, *personality* and *self* in general can be used as synonyms. A similar line of reasoning holds for the subjective side of identity: With regard to a global sense of identity, it is hard to find any substantial difference with a sense of self. And with regard to the more articulated sense of identity, the person's concept or image of his or her characteristics usually is studied under the label self-concept (Van der Werff, 1991; Glossary).

All of the definitions given above only implicitly refer to the aspect of "remaining the same, despite changes." More explicit attention to this aspect was given by Erik H. Erikson (1950, 1968). Under the influence of his work, the concept of identity has become popular, especially within developmental psychology. In Erikson's theory, the human life cycle is described in eight developmental stages. (A more elaborated discussion of Erikson's theory follows in Chapter 4.) The fifth stage, in adolescence, comprises the crisis of identity versus identity diffusion. Normatively the adolescent faces the task of achieving a sense of identity, that is, "a sense of personal sameness and historical continuity" (Erikson, 1968, p. 17). Or, more explicitly: "The conscious feeling of having a personal identity is based on two simultaneous observations: the perception of the selfsameness and continuity of one's existence in time and space and the perception of the fact that others recognize one's sameness and continuity" (1968, p. 50). In his definition of a sense of identity, Erikson follows the general definition, continuously being one and the same person, but he adds a social aspect, namely the recognition of this sameness and continuity by others. Instead of others, he also tends to refer to the wider sociocultural context the person lives in (cf. Erikson, 1950). In that sense Erikson's conception of identity concerns the interplay between individual and context: A person can feel embedded in his or her context. In contrast, Erikson (1964) also has discussed the feelings of "uprootedness" of migrants. They are missing that sense of embeddedness.

There is a fundamental ambiguity in the concept of identity that seems to have been there right from the beginning. In modern history the term turns up in the work of the English empiricists Locke, Berkeley, and Hume as *personal identity,* in the double meaning of the essence of individuality on the one hand and the means by which an individual can be identified on the other. A good illustration of this double meaning is formed by Taylor's metaphor of a melody that is transposed into another key: It preserves its identity (its essence as well as its identifiability) even if no note of the first version exists in the second. For purposes of recognition by a listener, the key it is presented in is of no importance. You might not be impressed by this example, but in fact the question, "Is this a real Rembrandt or not?" deals with the same problem. "For the identity of plants and animals," says Locke (Frondizi, 1954, p. 36), "the substance they are made of is of no importance, it consists in the continuity of the same organization of parts in one coherent body, partaking of one common life." Personal identity, according to Locke, is due not to the identity of substance but merely to the identity of consciousness: I feel that I am the same person as I was yesterday.

It is remarkable how every word of Locke's discussion, now 300 years old, has become the center of current discussions of identity. At the turn of the century, psychiatry took an interest in some curious phenomena of identity disorder, subsumed by the concept of multiple personality. Preceded, as usual, by literature (*The Strange Case of Dr. Jekyll and Mr. Hyde* was published by R. L. Stevenson in 1886), it discovered quite a number of such strange cases in which people could present either with simultaneous multiple personalities or with successive multiple personalities mutually cognizant of each other or mutually amnesic. Morton Prince's (1906) book on this matter is currently acknowledged as the first extensive publication on the subject. This subject in its development curiously reflects the vicissitudes of the concept of identity itself. It started with some rare phenomenon like the fugue, a state in which a person has suddenly lost the knowledge of who he or she is and where he or she belongs, in other words, has lost the awareness of his personal identity. It has currently come back as one of the forms of splitting within the personality, a much more general concept by which a whole range of phenomena is subsumed. So the concept of identity in modern psychiatry covers many different phenomena whose differentiation from other diagnostic entities is not as easy as it originally was. For instance, a thoughtful handling of the DSM-IIIR handbook (American Psychiatric Association, 1987) is required to differentiate between identity diffusion and depression in an adolescent.

Locke's philosophical digressions about human identity thus provided the origin of two new lines of development in the meaning of the concept of identity. First is the one mentioned above, in which psychiatry investigates phenomena of consciousness, particularly after its discovery that in some disorders the sense of being the same person as yesterday can be disturbed. This inner feeling that cannot be shared by anyone and that belongs to the most individual part of a person has been called *inner core* by Rangell (see Chapter 2). All emphasis is on the feeling of the individual, a feeling that he or she can have also, as it were, on an uninhabited isle.

The second line of development in the meaning of the concept of identity received a strong impetus from Erikson's work. Here the starting point is not in "feeling to be the same as I was" but in the way one can be identified as such by his or her environment. The fact that others regard the person as the same in time and place takes on a metaphorical meaning and provides building blocks for his or her self-esteem and sense of identity. In Erikson's work identity always involves mutuality between the individual and his or her world. In contrast to what Erikson suggests in a number of places, however, there is no simple mutuality between the way in which individuals experience themselves and the way in which they are experienced by people around them. A whole range of systems exists dealing with the fundamental way in which the inner experience of the individual can be linked to structures in the outside world. They range from solipsistic systems in which the outer world is conceived of as nothing more than what the individual is projecting, to social systems in which individual and society are both seen as separately existing and measurable structures.

Thus the many definitions of identity can be ordered along a dimension that ranges from inner to outer. Some definitions (like those positing an inner core) focus on the interior of the person's being as the source of sameness and perhaps even the person's identifiability over time. At the other end of the dimension, cultural and social psychological conceptions of identity focus instead on the cultural and social structures and conventions that constrain who we appear to be to others and ourselves. Somewhere in the middle are conceptualizations that are more interactive, examining the interplay between the psychological interior and the sociocultural context.

The fact that three different areas can be highlighted, according to the function the concept of identity has to fulfill, makes it suitable to serve bridging functions. Erikson strongly underscored this function in almost every paper or publication on identity. In still another effort to verbalize the threefold meaning of identity in order to provide a basis to its bridge function, we would like to point to a qualification of Man once created by Clyde Kluckhohn: "Man is like all other men, like some other men and like no other man" (Erikson, 1956). Kluckhohn here seems to point to a fundamental property of all things existing (e.g., a conference is like all other conferences, like some other conferences, and like no other conference.)

The first point of Kluckhohn's definition means that things exist under names and are equal on the point of name-bearing to all other things that bear the same name. This point brings name-giving to the center of our interest. The second point means that things can be identified as having properties, and thus can be identified by means of these properties. The statement that things are like some other things means that they have properties in common. It makes them amenable to being classified. To identify the properties of things, we have to process them, whether by the simple actions of observation, by the senses, or by more complicated ways of observation. For example, to identify a mineral we can look at it, feel its surface, try to scratch that surface, submit parts of it to chemical reactions, make X-rays, and so on. According to these ways of processing the mineral, it will display its color, durability, percentage of water, calcium, and the like. Because the number of procedures one can apply is infinite, the number of properties one can identify is infinite as well. Each description of an entity and its properties contains the outcome of the processing of the entity by the author or others. It has to leave apart the possible outcomes of possible procedures that one could apply to the entity if one could invent them. This refers to the third point: No entity is like another entity because, in an infinite series of procedures, the chance that all outcomes are equal is zero. Returning to Humankind: We are unique because the number of procedures pertaining to identifying our qualities is infinite. Every individual therefore transcends all classification.

This classification uniqueness is, however, not the only kind of uniqueness we possess. There is a spatial uniqueness in the sense that "you cannot be where I am." Nobody else can sense my body, think my thoughts, feel my emotions and compose my fantasies as I can. This is my inner core.

As stated above, the definitions of identity can be ordered along a dimension that ranges from inner to outer. The interactive aspect of identity, which seems at the same time to be its most characteristic quality, is already present in the inner core, its most internal phenomenon, in that no inner core exists without traces of the presence of others or the environment. However, in Erikson's conceptualization, identity starts only where an environment makes perceptible efforts to identify, that is, to classify an individual. A person's identity consists of the efforts of the world around him or her to classify the person, the outcomes of this processing, and the person's own processing of these outcomes. Ways of processing someone to classify him or her can themselves be classified. These classifications are called the sciences. In psychology, sociology, history, literature, and the others, modes of processing human data are clustered into methods. The interdisciplinary function of the concept of identity, its potential to build bridges among the sciences, is based on the fact that the processing of the environment by the individual, and the processing of the individual by the environment, are by no means congruent processes. To understand what is happening on both sides of the bridge, we need at least two disciplines. The following example of identity themes in Bosnian refugee children may help make this clear. In this example the psychiatric study of the children and the study of the sociocultural history of the Bosnian people have to be combined to understand the lack of posttraumatic stress disorders.

The way we look at other people is not simply the regard we aim at ourselves, turned outward. One would be inclined to put the reflexive look at oneself at the beginning because this function belongs to the inner core. Ontogenetically, however, the reflexive function has its inception rather late in development, and it seems appropriate to consider the parents and their way of looking at the child as standing at the start of the process of mutual assignment of identity. This means that the very young child already has to undergo a most complicated processing by the parents, whose observations are colored by many memories, wishes, and expectations for the future. For the greater part, these belong to the domain of psychological functioning: for instance, when parents assign narcissistic value to their child, hoping that he or she will once contribute to the welfare and glory of the family. For quite another part the wishes and expectations are embedded in a narrative tradition insofar as parents tell their story to their children, a story often containing an identity theme that is silently handed down to the next generation. Whoever has seen Bosnian refugee children, playing war and soldier in a camp, knows how powerful these identity themes are. They may for instance prohibit the outbreak of posttraumatic stress disorders in children who seemed predetermined to present them, having been witnesses to atrocities that at first sight surpass everything that has hitherto been mentioned in the literature. Incorporating the future revenge of the nation on its enemies elicits in these children resiliencies that cannot be explained from other sources.

It is a strange paradox, which is nonetheless characteristic of identity, that the individual regards its environment with a subtle and sensitive gaze in which a wealth of psychic systems cooperate to refine this regard, enabling the person to distinguish the most delicate shades; and yet at the same time, the environment classifies the individual with the gross, shadeless platitudes of stereotypes. These have historical, sociocultural roots, and they are told to the individual like books are revealed to their readers, according to laws that belong to another realm than psychology. When we limit our gaze to the family, it could be stated that a child has there no identity to the extent that healthy parents are willing and able to freely observe their child and take him or her for what he or she is. A child in these happy circumstances is left to develop his or her own identity instead of being forced into one. If an identity theme is conveyed to the child, all the more when the theme existed before the child itself, it functions as a procrustean bed that obliges the child to certain behaviors irrespective of his or her talents, weak spots, or inclinations. Mitzman's contribution to this book (Chapter 8) includes a good example of this process.

Development

Like identity, the concept of development has been used in many different ways. Unlike identity, in which the core of the concept concerns sameness, the essence of development is change. However, the type of change differs dramatically in scale across different disciplinary points of view. Change may be considered across a phylogenetic time dimension, focusing on gradual yet clearly discernible adaptations of species to their ecological niches. The anthropogenetic scale concerns the development of the human species. Historical and cultural changes may be thought of on a somewhat smaller time scale, the sociogenetic scale. Ontogenetic development occurs on an even smaller scale, within the life span of an individual person. The microgenetic scale concerns short time changes, on the level of actual human behavior, such as information processing or classical and operant conditioning. These scales form different levels of generalization and correspond with different scientific disciplines, respectively biology, anthropology, history and sociology, developmental and experimental psychology. This book focuses on the sociogenetic and ontogenetic levels, though microgenetic identity is also of concern (e.g., intrapsychic processes, social-psychological processes).

In general, *development* has referred to organized change or change in organization. Collins (1982) cited Nagel's definition of development, which assumes a system with a definite structure and a set of changes in the structure, and thus in its modes of operation. Likewise, Schneirla's definition involved "progressive change in organized adaptive function through ontogeny" (Collins, 1982, p. xi). For our purposes a workable definition, at least from the perspective of psychology, has been stated by Ford and Lerner (1992, p. 49):

> Individual human development involves incremental and transformational processes that, through a flow of interactions among current characteristics of the person and his or her current contexts, produces a succession of relatively enduring changes that elaborate or increase the diversity of the person's structural and functional characteristics and the patterns of their environmental interactions while maintaining coherent organization and structural-functional unity of the person as a whole.

Different viewpoints on development have been advanced, many of them revolving around models that might be called either mechanistic or organismic. Widdershoven (Chapter 6) reviews the key differences between these approaches and highlights a contemporary narrative viewpoint to understanding development.

Multidisciplinary Perspectives

The challenge undertaken in this volume is to examine the intersection of the concepts of identity and development. This is obviously not a simple task, because these constructs are defined differently across and sometimes even within disciplines. In the concluding chapter, we present a model that can place the concepts into an interdisciplinary framework.

The value of broadening perspectives on both identity and development is illustrated by the following exchange between Professors Rangell (a psychoanalyst) and Mitzman (a historian) during the conference. Using their own disciplines' styles of analysis, they consider the complex interrelations among one specific historical figure (Hitler), the voters who elected him and made his rise to power possible, and the historical and cultural forces within Germany that contextualized it all. This discussion highlights how the concepts of identity and development can be used in different ways in different disciplines, and how fuller understanding of these phenomena can be attained through scholarly interchange.

Rangell: Dr. Mitzman, a historian, is talking about history, how it was, how it develops and how it might have been. He pointed to a crucial moment more than 50 years ago when a man named Hitler made a decision that changed the history of the world. I would go back 5 years before that, when a people made a decision to accept the man, which then led to his being supported and supported until he set the world on fire. Erik Erikson once made a very powerful statement about psychohistory. He said: Times meet the man. The leader alone is not enough. The followers alone are not enough. But you have to have a chemistry, a receptivity, a fusion between the two that makes an atomic reaction, if you will. I always remember: Hitler did not come in with a "putsch," he was elected at the end. The free German person, casting the free ballot in the electoral system where he could say yes or no, said yes to this man. And that's a datum. How do we explain that? Here we have the interface between individual psychology and group psychology. That's one of the most important interfaces in this conference, not only between disciplines but between the leader and the led. There are all kinds of theories about what makes behavior in an individual, and now we have the idea of the collective individual. Which is a valid thing: There is a collective group, there's a collective cluster of theorists, and there's a collective political party. Anyway, I throw this out: History is made. How was history made that was the most monumental thing that happened during our lifetime? What about the group? What about the leader? Could Hitler have been elected in England?

Mitzman: No, only if England was where Germany is now and had the history of Germany.

Rangell: Now, say more about the elements, the components that make for the receptive large group to take in the tentacles from the individual. Another interesting thing which was brought up was about his undescended testicle. We didn't react to that, and we shouldn't. It shows the pitfalls of psychobiography without data coming from the subject about whom you are writing a biography. Anyway, you touch on a very vital thing and I encourage you to discuss it further.

Mitzman: If you want to get into this kind of question of national psychology, which I suppose is vaguely related to questions of national identity, then you will go back to the work of Parsons and of Hans Ulrich Wehler, who both emphasize the extreme importance in German history of overlapping systems of hierarchy and authority. There are all of these social-historical frameworks that go way back and have a great deal to do with the development of the country in one direction or another. These overlapping patterns of authority in Germany, which made it very, very difficult for anybody to find any kind of breathing place independent of those structures, have a lot to do with the lack of resistance to authoritarianism and then to totalitarianism in Germany. These are all things which function totally independently of any kind of personal identity, but which shape such identity over the course of hundreds of years.

Rangell: Now, they're also a result of identity as well as shaping it.

Mitzman: No, no.

Rangell: Because there is the voter.

Mitzman: The voter is the end result of this process.

Rangell: He has an identity, too, the identity that evolves in that historical process. When one presses the lever down of his own free will privately, in a secret ballot, that's the iron test.

Mitzman: Help! What is free will?

Rangell: No, you then are exercising your final decision as to whether you identify with this kind of person or that, with the charmer, with the industrious person, with the corrupt person, with the hypocrite, with the loudmouth or with the softmouth, with the id, the ego, or the superego. And when they pull the lever down for a corrupt leader, there is an identification with the corrupt superego in order to lessen guilt, individual guilt. And the identity then, the sum of the identity at that particular historic, developmental—development assists here, too, the individual developmental level at that moment—is: "Oh, I have had enough of this goody-goody stuff; to hell with it, come on." And then the right-winger, the forceful—give them the pistols and let them shoot other men—will get more than 50%; that's all he needs, 50.1%.

Mitzman: Hitler never got that.

Rangell: No, he got 40%. My point holds there, too: When someone didn't vote for him, it was for a similar reason; they were on the side of reason. Well anyway, identity can not be eliminated, because the person has an identity, whether he exercises it to the right or to the left—it needs to be just on one side of the middle.

Mitzman: Yes, of course he does. But what you're talking about that can't be eliminated is personal responsibility, but that's in another framework. It's in a totally different context, this whole question of personal responsibility.

Rangell: Namely what framework?

Mitzman: Of ethics.

Rangell: What's ethics, what is the bottom of the iceberg that ethics rests upon? Ethics has got a frame, too; what is the frame that's different from human psychology?

Mitzman: Ethics are a matter of consensus. We don't do some things now that we did hundreds of years ago. We don't burn people alive because we disagree with them, but in practically every country in Europe at a certain point in time we did that.

Rangell: Where is the civil courage against the popular times, when the popular times or the majority, as Ibsen says, are wrong? The minority may be right sometimes.

Mitzman: Yes, but the thing that has to be explained is where that civil courage comes from. Because the thing that really requires explanation is going against the tide in your own time and country, not going with it, as the vast majority of people always do.

Rangell: Right. But what is the explanation? I agree that it needs an explanation, but the explanation is the unique identity of the courageous person. The individual who doesn't have it is more average, actually.

Mitzman: That is a description, rather than an explanation.

Rangell: Well, it's not one or the other. It's a description that is explained by the developmental history of the individual. Someone else might go further and say: One's history doesn't explain it either, his mid-brain explains it. I don't go that far. I say his life history explains it, and then, how he amalgamated his life history into an active ego. In view of everything that went into me, I will do this and not that. These factors are mostly unconscious. That's why an action is always unpredictable, because no matter how much you know about the person, he may surprise you. He may have unknown courage or unknown cowardice. During the McCarthy era in the United States, people who were introspective said: I can't fault him, who caved in, because I don't know what I would have done. And that's true. No one knows what they would have done. Why doesn't he know? Because what he would have done is dictated by his unconscious. And at the last moment he might surprise himself, being brave, braver than he thought. You know when you're brave, when you're saving your loved one, that's when the greatest bravery comes in. When you're saving a stranger, you have a little less civil courage. Erikson pointed to a ubiquitous, universal, never-absent phenomenon. But it isn't the whole explanation, because what caused the identity and explains it is how the mother treated him, and such things as whether he had two testicles or one, his biology, everything about it.

This discussion highlights the challenges of talking across disciplines about the same phenomenon. Is it possible to make biological, psychological, social, and historical perspectives compatible? The questions that emerge set the stage for the discussions that follow in this volume. Should one perspective simply be reduced to another? Are different views merely different, yet equally informative? Can the levels of analysis favored by different disciplines be layered in such a way that each perspective can enrich the others? Or must interdisciplinary discourse be consigned to the Tower of Babel, with representatives of each perspective destined to talk past one another? Although readers of this volume must make these judgments for themselves, we hope to show that a careful analysis within and across disciplines can yield a fuller and richer understanding of the two compelling concepts of identity and development.

PART I

Psychoanalysis

TOBI L. G. GRAAFSMA

Although the term *identity* is generally associated with the work of E. H. Erikson (e.g., 1950, 1956), psychiatry and psychoanalysis took interest in problems of identity long before that. As discussed in Chapter 1, identity disorders, subsumed by the concept of multiple personality disorder, were already being studied around 1900. In spelling out some basic motives of our mind's activity, Freud considered (the search for) identity to be one of these motives, exactly because such an identity guarantees safety and wish fulfillment (Freud, 1900). Freud (1926) later used the term in the sense that became well known through the work of Erikson, referring to the similarity and continuity he felt between his own "mental construction" and a certain (Jewish) sector of his environment. That stable similarity provided him with "a clear consciousness of inner identity, the safe privacy of a common mental construction" (Freud, 1926, p. 274).

In general, psychiatry and psychoanalysis use the term *identity* rather loosely, just as these disciplines do with such terms as *self* and *personality*. Sometimes the concept of identity serves as an explanation: Symptoms and behaviors are explained as being caused or motivated by a search for identity. This practice is especially commonplace in adolescent psychiatry. Erikson (1956) added to this situation, since he linked a syndrome called *identity diffusion* to adolescence. At the moment, this syndrome is seldom considered to be a separate entity.

Symptoms of identity diffusion are considered to be a part of the borderline syndrome (Kernberg, 1984). In the transition from version DSM-IIIR to DSM-IV of the well-known psychiatric classification manual, the so-called identity disorder, which had been considered a special disorder of adolescence, lost its status of disorder altogether.

In fact, this transition illustrates two central difficulties regarding the concept of identity. The first difficulty relates to the explanatory value of identity. No one doubts the descriptive and experiential value of the concept of identity. Indeed, a sense of identity, as the relatively enduring, but not necessarily stable experience of oneself as a unique and coherent entity over time, is very important in many ways. The same applies to the second aspect of a sense of identity: the experience of a persistent sharing of some kind of essential character with others. But one still has to explain why such an experience is needed, what causes its necessity. Rangell (Chapter 2) will argue that identity theory is more like an intermediate theory than a theory referring to a psychological endpoint. He even argues that identity theory shows features of so-called inexact interpretations, explanations that omit important aspects. Both Rangell and Graafsma (Chapter 3) consider identity to be one of the elements of the dynamics of the human mind, especially of the ego. Identity is integrated into the whole of psychoanalytic theory. From this perspective it should not stand as a theory of its own.

This discussion highlights the difference between many psychiatrists and psychoanalysts, and developmental psychologists conducting research on identity. Many of the latter, working along the lines developed by Marcia (Chapter 4) consider identity to be a positively valued end state of human development. They share with some psychoanalysts (e.g., Lichtenstein, and Kohut and Klein, when speaking about the self) the opinion that identity (or self) is an ultimate goal in itself.

Although identity researchers in developmental psychology base their work to various degrees on Erikson's writings, Erikson himself occasionally expressed his amazement that the concept of identity was embraced so warmly. His intention had been to add a psychosocial (or even a psychohistorical) view on development to the theoretical structure of psychoanalysis. He did consider the maintenance of a sense of identity a lifelong task, given the facts of maturation and development. Erikson was more interested in psychosocial development than in the separate phenomenon of identity. A psychosocial point of view on development, however, has never definitively been added to the well-known metapsychological points of view that constitute the theoretical structure of psychoanalysis, presumably because psychosocial theory has been subsumed by two later but more influential theoretical streams: object relations theory and the theory of narcissism (later called self-psychology). The more psychohistorical aspects of Erikson's psychosocial theory continue to remain more or less on the periphery of psychoanalysis.

A second difficulty regarding the concept of identity is its problematic definition. Identity is sometimes distinguished from a sense of identity. Often, identity is considered to be a social category; how one is identified. Sometimes identity is considered to refer to an inner, basic core, especially to character and the sexual core: gender identity. But terms like identity suffer from definitional fuzziness. This can be seen in developmental psychology (see also Van der Werff, 1985), but also is often true in psychiatry and psychoanalysis. The careful reader must determine exactly how the term is used in every case. The Glossary at the end of this book may be of help, as well as the following remarks from a psychoanalytic point of view.

Identity in general refers to an awareness or a perception of persistent sameness between two or more things or states. A sense of identity refers to the subjective experience of such sameness, both within one's own body and mind, and within an average expectable, recognizing and sharing environment where one feels in place. Such a sense of identity does not have to correspond exactly to reality; indeed, it often does not, as can be seen in Graafsma's contribution (Chapter 3). Fantasy plays an important role in the emergence of a sense of identity.

A sense of identity is considered to emerge very early in life, in the course of the first separation-individuation phase, between approximately 8 and 36 months of age. There, in respective steps, gender identity, self- and object-constancy, and identifications stabilize the child's affects, wishes, and behavior. Of course a child changes necessarily with maturation and development, but so slowly and in tune with environmental timetables that an awareness and experience of sameness can persist (although fantasy and negation of change and difference may play an important role here).

Naturally, identity is closely related to the constructs of self, character, and personality. Although these terms are sometimes used interchangeably, one should remember that identity refers to an aspect of mental organization and functioning. The term *self* generally refers to one's own person, body and mind together. Individuals base their conceptions about this self on experience, wishes, and the like, which result in one's self-concept: a composition of representations and images that one maintains about one's person. Some aspects of self-concept can be realistic, whereas others can be very unrealistic. Self-esteem is derived from an appraisal of the self.

Character, discussed extensively in psychoanalysis, refers to the habitual mode in which a person (more specifically, the person's ego) adjusts to internal and external demands and tasks. It is important how the person's ego reconciles intrapsychic and external conflicts, and it is because of this that character is often considered to be an unconscious but very stable compromise formation. Character pathology has been studied extensively in psychoanalysis, especially by the ego psychologists.

The term *personality* refers to the observable, typical, and usual traits and behaviors that characterize a person in day-to-day life under ordinary circumstances. This term is more commonly used in psychiatry than in psychoanalysis. In psychiatry, one speaks of a personality disorder when personality traits are inflexible or maladaptive and cause either significant functional impairment or subjective distress. Rigid personality traits may cover up severe identity problems (Kernberg, 1984).

When one surveys the literature on identity development, it must be admitted that the term *identity* is often used too loosely and too broadly. There is often much overlap with concepts like self, character, and personality. Without minimizing the importance of the concept of identity or the clinical relevance of problems of identity, the chapters that follow strongly suggest that the concept of identity be more sharply defined and theoretically better situated.

2

Identity and the Human Core

The View From Psychoanalytic Theory

LEO RANGELL

The two words *identity* and *development* are a felicitous choice for an interdisciplinary discussion: identity, how a thing, in this case a person, is known; development, how its course, the events and sequence of its life cycle, determine and affect that identity. Of the two concepts thus paired, composing an area of central relevance to the human condition, I will focus on identity. Here is where ambiguity, even theoretical obscurity, lies. Development is less of a puzzle or debate. It affects and shapes the identity, as it does all mental processes and functions. Its role is acknowledged and studied equally in all theoretical systems. My contribution will be from psychoanalysis, as this discipline views both the horizontal characteristics and the longitudinal, that is developmental, aspects of an individual's identity.

The linkage of the two nuclear words as the anchor of this discussion is also a fortuitous circumstance because it leads naturally to a mental domain that is the central concern of psychoanalysis. Both subjects are conceptual signposts that point to the role of unconscious factors. The acronym for this interdisciplinary discussion, moreover, brings home even more succinctly the appropriateness of this collaboration of psychoanalysis with the range of social scientists assembled here. "ID," as it appeared on the stationery inviting me to participate (the logo of the Identity and Development conference), by serendipity spells out the area of ingress of the first psychoanalyst into the mental realm, and was the original identity of psychoanalysis, connoting the mental domain that was its first discovery. This did not remain solitary and isolated, however, but went on to comprise a total and internally coherent theoretical system. Further development led to new trunks and branches, demonstrating, within the discipline from which I will approach our subject, the first example of the effects of development on identity.

The content of the interdisciplinary discussions and the nature of the participants bring to mind another fortuitous phase in my own development, a personal historical era having to do with attempts at a definition of my own professional identity in relation, as on this present occasion, to the wider family of social sciences. More than a quarter of a century ago, in 1962, I enjoyed a sabbatical year from my clinical practice as a Fellow at the Center for Advanced Study in the Behavioral Sciences at Stanford, California. There my colleagues consisted of the spectrum of behavioral scientists, all pursuing their individual research interests while interacting freely with each other. In a group of 50 representatives of the behavioral sciences, mostly humanistic disciplines from academic life, there were two clinical psychoanalysts. The one other besides myself, again by serendipity in relation to today's subject, was Erik Erikson, whose major contribution, developed shortly before that time and since associated with his name, was that of *ego identity.* He had come there from his first trip to India, where the plan for his book on Gandhi (Erikson, 1969) had just been born. Another Fellow during that year was Carl Rogers, whose widely supported concept of the person (Rogers, 1942) also has relevance to the subject of this discussion.

During my year of residence at the Center, asked to deliver the Franz Alexander lecture in Chicago, I chose for my topic: "Psychoanalysis, Affects, and the Human Core" (Rangell, 1967), with the subtitle, in view of my current association with the family of social sciences, and again by serendipity with respect to the topic of this volume: "The Relationship of Psychoanalysis to the Behavioral Sciences." My conclusion in this paper, delimiting the area of psychoanalysis from its contiguous disciplines, was that the central core of mental functioning that defined the concern of psychoanalysis had to do with the realm of "unconscious intrapsychic conflicts." Each word had a specific, substantive meaning and application: unconscious rather than conscious, intrapsychic as differentiated from interpersonal, conflictful rather than conflict-free functioning.

In a series of later writings over decades, I extended the central concept of the human core from the realm of unconscious intrapsychic conflicts to a more generalized "unconscious intrapsychic process" (Rangell, 1969), operative in the human unconscious both behind and preliminary to all overt action and external behavior. This was an expansion of Freud's concepts of signal anxiety and thought as (intrapsychic) experimental trial action. Following and extending a line of thought from Freud, through Hartmann and Rapaport, I tried to show that this intrapsychic process and unconscious cognitive-affective motivational stream of psychic activity, ongoing behind all human mentation preparatory to action, now comprised the conflict-free as well as the behavior resulting in and deriving from conflict. This line of thinking is consonant with the expansion of psychoanalysis from a psychology of conflict to a general psychology. The ego tests all intended and impending actions for their capacity to produce signal anxiety. Depending on the results of such internal and often unconscious trial actions, either conflict or conflict-free states may ensue.

A Definition and Location of the Concept of Identity

Within this ubiquitous unconscious mental process are embedded an individual's unconscious thoughts, emotions, fantasies, conflicts, defense mechanisms, the origins and dynamic background of all external behavior, including moods, conceptualized as "enduring low-key affective states" (Jacobson, 1957). Contained in and deriving from this unconscious dynamic sequence is a person's identity: his or her concept and evaluation of his or her characteristic behavior. Based largely on an aggregate of unconscious fantasies, this identity plays a prominent, although unconscious role in determining and shaping one's social behavior.

The identity of an object (thing or person), from taxonomic descriptions to subjective experience, is related to but is not necessarily confluent with what its essence is. Identity is a constellation by which a person—I will refer only to the human entity here—is known. What he or she actually is, is the self. Identity, not in a physical, chemical, or mathematical but in a psychological sense, is a person's sense of self. Identity, a conceptualization of the self, is a fantasy that is mostly unconscious, however close or distant from the reality of the total person.

With respect to identity and identification, a person's identification is how he is known to others. His identity is how he is known to himself (better said, psychoanalytically, what he thinks and feels about himself). Identification in another, metapsychological, sense is a mental mechanism, used both as defense and as a method of growth and development. Identity is the broader term; identity is built from multiple identifications. Both processes unfold primarily unconsciously. Identifications can be temporary, identity tends to be fixed; identifications partial, identity global; identifications more changeable, identity cumulative. One patient feels deeply that he or she can never be a success; this applies to every quest or endeavor, from trivial aims to long-range life goals. This chronic negative sense of identity, developmentally acquired, affects and determines the outcome of much of what he or she sets out to do.

To continue descriptive and definitional considerations with regard to identity and the self, as identity is made up at least partially of identifications, the same is true of the self in its mental aspects. The self, paradoxically never defined by Kohut but by Jacobson (1964), comprises the totality of the individual, somatic and psychic, body and mind. The self is what identifications lead to. Identity is what identifications cause one to believe about oneself. The self is actual, identity is a mental state.

While formed neuroses and the other final psychic products of behavior, as dreams, actions, affects, and even moods, took precedence historically and occupied the attention of the early clinicians and theoreticians, it was not until Erikson's concept of ego identity was put forth in a forceful and focused manner in the 1950s that this entity began to command wide interest, both within and outside psychoanalysis (Erikson, 1950, 1956, 1959). What followed was what has taken place repetitively with similar advances that introduce a global concept, relatively easy to absorb and accept, at the expense of interaction between internal parts. The new compelling concept captures the imagination of the scientific community, the lay public, and even the press, and typically undergoes a history of an initial steep rise in popularity, followed by a flattening out, then a decline.

The concept of the whole is eagerly accepted at the expense of a theory of component parts. I will not belabor here the reasons for this, except to summarize what such developments have in common. The suggestion of a specific internal structure, even if only a conceptual one, acting as agent, just as happened with the discovery of the unconscious, threatens the sense of mastery and control. Simultaneously, any theoretical dissection into internal components is reacted to subjectively as a fragmentation of the self. From the earliest objections of such initial separatists as Jung and Adler to libido and later drive theory; to such culturalists and environmentalists as Horney, Kardiner, and Rado of the 1930s and 1940s; to the interpersonal theory of Sullivan of the 1950s and 1960s and the current self-psychology and object-relations theories, all such developments have in common a preference for considering the person or self, at the cost of considering the ego as agent. It is preferred to view conflicts as occurring between people and not intrapsychically, within the individual.

Actually, Erikson's contributions bridged the two conceptual orientations. Although the new focus was widely embraced and reacted to as though it made unnecessary the consideration of internal conflicts, Erikson's specific phrase *ego identity* connoted the fact that an inner concept of the composition of the self existed within the ego. The power of the concept in fact emanated from just such a subjective feeling, or fantasy, or unconscious insight. Each individual has an internal concept of the impression he makes on others, an image that another part of him finds either satisfactory or disappointing.

Identity is incorporated into and integrated with total psychoanalytic theory and does not stand out as a theory of its own. In total psychoanalytic theory, identity is a summation of self-representations, much as de Levita (1965) described it. This aggregate representation exists and is utilized within the ego. A crucial internal relationship is how this composite self-representation is regarded by the superego in comparison with the ego ideal, another internalized element, part of ego and superego, by which the ego is guided. Too great a distance between the two is a frequent dynamic behind depression (Jacobson, 1953). In another gradient of self-appraisal functioning, the superego and the rational judging ego further assess how convincing or spurious the operation of the self-critical system is itself, how believable, how worthy of inner respect or support it is. An outcome of this universal ongoing unconscious process is the sense of true or false self that has been a hallmark of the contributions of Winnicott (e.g., 1965), whose work taps the same affective reaction on the current scene as Erikson aroused 35 years ago.

Erikson's ego identity, which initiated an interest in this direction, led to a major theoretical thrust. It was not, however, just the problems of identity Erikson introduced, such as identity crisis, identity diffusion, and so on, but specifically, as it was stated, an ego identity. Though this brings up questions of precision and of microscopic conceptualization,

I believe that Erikson himself did not have in mind such fine point differentiation. In spite of his inclusion of ego in the phrase, the so-called abstract theory (metapsychology) of psychoanalysis never was as deeply a part of Erikson's professional identity as psychoanalytic clinical theory. Although the phrase Erikson chose was a significant one, it was, in my opinion, a more definitive statement than he intended it to be.

The main point for Erikson was the problem and the challenge of the global self-concept, its pitfalls and vicissitudes in normal and pathological development. I believe, from personal experience, that Erikson was using ego loosely in this later-popularized phrase in the same sense as Freud had interchanged self and ego in the early phase of his writings. The ego's being inserted at this time came from Erikson's inclusion, at that historical period, in the small group of vigorous and important ego psychologists of the 1950s and early 1960s: Hartmann, and especially Rapaport, with whom Erikson was associated at the Menninger Clinic. All were following and building upon the work of Anna Freud on defense. As I said earlier, my impression is that Erikson himself had little concern or predilection for (abstract) metapsychology. That structural psychology was of little interest to him in comparison to clinical concepts and clinical language. The phrase probably became ego identity because of Erikson's association with and identification with these prominent ego psychologists of the period.

Erikson's clinical and phenomenologic preferences, however, did result in a specific and strong linkage between ego identity and psychological development, the two factors linked in this book. Basing his developmental progression upon the libidinal phases, of central interest to the psychoanalytic world until then, Erikson postulated ego developmental stages as well. He extended the progression of the developmental levels from infancy and childhood through maturity to old age, capturing the entire life cycle. This contribution proved in fact to be more enduring than the emphasis on identity and its problems.

The Development of Identity

Identity, a sense of unique individuality, can be said to start developmentally in its rudimentary form with separation-individuation: with the separation and individuation from the psychologically preexisting mother-child unit (see also Mahler, Pine, & Bergman, 1975). Yet the initial seed for development toward an identity for the new evolving individual precedes and has its origins well before that. The contributions of the parents whose genes fused to birth that person were not only genetic but have already been and will continue to be psychological and experiential as well. Each parent, and the pair as a unit, directs his/her mental attitudes toward the unborn baby from their first awareness of conception, even before that, at its anticipation. The given name is a symbol of unconscious fantasies and expectations. Even without this conscious and unconscious choice, the automatic surname that attaches to the infant carries with it a generational line of transmission of common traits in the identity of the lineage. Both the genetic and these unconscious psychological contributions of the parents assure and bring about generational continuity.

These early seeds are earmarked for use and influence at the appropriate time, particularly at the future unconscious level. All such early inputs, however, will be able to be used only later, after a self comes to exist and a sense of identity begins to form. For this, an ego is necessary to shape and develop an image of the whole. At the time of what Mahler called the "psychological birth of the human infant," the newly evolving mental apparatus is still without such a competent ego. The psychological birth of the human individual, at the time of self-object differentiation, is a more likely moment for an identity to begin taking form.

The characteristics of the genes from each side, and their unique oneness in the particular individual who combines them, are a rock-bottom base that should be neither underplayed nor overplayed, although it is subject to both excesses in "scientific" assessments. As a powerful beginning example of how the developmental progression and the problem of identity fuse, as well as the unity of the biological and the environmental, the newborn comes with constitutional givens and the already established nature of the parental inputs, which will constitute his or her most formative external psychological determinants. The constitution itself includes somatic and psychological factors, those factors already present and in evidence, and others which will determine the maturational sequence of progressive developmental unfolding. The newborn's gender, the order in the family, circumstances at the time of conception, parental conditions and relationships during the gestation period and through the birth process, all play their parts in shaping and molding the parental attitudes toward the new arrival and his or her future vicissitudes. At every subsequent moment and phase, present factors are grafted upon the past history, immediate and distant, which together make for the totality of the currently operative psychological field.

The global self-representation, an amalgam of a person's mental representations of his or her total being: body, facial expressions, posture, the swathe he or she cut in space, how this looks to him or herself and therefore, by projection, what he or she thinks is elicited from others, undergo the developmental vicissitudes of all the phases and experiences of life. Following the built-in ingredients already mentioned, "the gleam in the mother's eye" emphasized by Kohut (1971, 1977), or its absence—at times made too much of, in my opinion, by schools that emphasize preoedipal development and conflicts almost exclusively—the growing child undergoes the "wear and tear of everyday life" (Rangell, 1960, 1973). The multifaceted oedipal experience, which has become part of human knowledge, is followed by latency and prepuberty, by the surge of pubertal growth, by the spiky adolescent years, and by the entrance to adult life, at which stage this conference has mercifully stopped. There is little time in this discussion to linger over any phase. Just as Mahler has written of "the psychological birth of the human infant" (Mahler, Pine, & Bergman, 1975), not confluent with the act of physical birth, I have written of the age of 17 (Rangell, 1989) as the birth of the adult; by serendipity, the late adolescent transitional stage is the focal point of this discussion.

Identity: Intermediate or Endpoint?

There is no minimizing the importance of identity and its status in determining the subjective sense of well-being in its positive state and of ego alienicity during its disturbances in psychopathology. The goal "to be a whole person" can occupy a firm niche as a major principle in human functioning, in line, from another vantage point, with the integrative function of the ego. Problems of identity do have a strong and ubiquitous clinical relevance. "To know who I am" is a desideratum that can be acknowledged and accepted by any patient, or nonpatient, bending under the general ennui or alienation considered to be characteristic of and intrinsic to modern society.

Interpretations along these lines readily exert a resonance and are acceptable, even beguiling, to individuals and groups to whom such explanations are addressed. The same is true of the appeal of self-esteem, both as theoretical explanation and in its clinical adaptability. The ease with which these are accepted, in fact, suggests that such interpretation of pathology is generally safely above the level of resistances. In this respect, they share characteristics of the inexact interpretations in psychoanalytic treatment whose efficacy have been noted by Glover (1955). They are correct but incomplete and often themselves serve as a defense against deeper and more repressed etiologies. In one patient, such a defense was considered as a conscious possibility. His parents were about to visit him from their home in a foreign country. Having emoted against them long and violently in his analysis, the patient wondered how he would receive and greet them. "Should I tell them the truth, or should I just say: 'I am trying to find out who I am,' and shit like that?"

It is, however, necessary to distinguish as much as we can between global assessments and phraseology and more specific understanding of the psychology of unpleasure, toward which psychoanalytic theory and thinking have gone a long way. Just as I have pointed out (see Rangell, 1978, 1987) that the presenting affects of the patient, such as the initial complaints of "I feel terrible, I feel upset, I feel weird" are composite affective states. The analyst performs the function of dissecting them into their component affects of fear, depression, guilt, or shame. He explores the role of anxiety through many of these. Given the fact that a symptom as a compromise formation is an aggregate composed of impulse, defense, superego input, anxiety and its derivatives, other repressed affects, and more, it should be realized that so are subjective complaints about not feeling like a whole person similarly global and composed, this one suggested and given status however by group, social, and cultural repetition. What lies behind this generalized description of one's sense of failure or incompleteness is a convergence of various symptoms, conscious or unconscious repressed affects. In fact, a complex mixture of repressed unconscious ego-alien phenomenology is often condensed into this overall subjective sensation of unpleasure and ineffectiveness. Structurally, this articulated complaint connotes a subjective sense of inadequate control (of the ego) over the id, superego, and external objects, as well as of other parts and functions of the unconscious ego itself.

Though symptoms related to feelings about one's identity play a distinct role in clinical phenomenology (see also Graafsma, Chapter 3), these need to be seen in perspective to the entire etiologic sequence of psychopathology. On a par with other such global assessments or universally dystonic affects as feeling unloved, uncared-for, unadmired, or unwanted, the phrase or formula of "Who am I?" does indeed play a role, perhaps even a universal one, within the total array of subjective ego-alien symptomatology. However, its role has in my opinion been generally misapprehended, overplayed quantitatively, and largely misunderstood in a qualitative sense. As is common in the history of psychoanalytic thought, fashions in theory and practice can reach high degrees of popular acceptance without a concomitant expansion of insight into unconscious processes. Swept up by popular phrases, current patients are more apt to present an initial overall complaint along lines of identity problems than they were during the first half of the existence of psychoanalysis. In addition, and from the reverse direction, as often as not, concepts of identity confusion or diffusion may be, in my opinion, implanted into the patient by the analyst, if they do not already exist. In such cases, there is in this respect an unconscious collusion between patient and analyst. The patient's subjective cognitive-affective dilemmas and ambiguities appear understandable to the eager analyst who, also impressed at the moment by the latest popular wave of understanding, then informs his puzzled and conflict-laden patient with the explanation-interpretation: "You don't know, or you wonder, who you are," a formula that the patient has no reason to reject or oppose. It fits at some level, being felt to apply to the current state of perplexity and indecision, and to offer at least potentially some way station of support. On today's psychoanalytic scene, with the ascendance of self-psychology, this mutuality has perhaps been replaced, by both the analyst and the informed patient, by recourse to the complaint and feeling of a fragmented self.

As I have pointed out about unconscious fantasy (Rangell, 1988b), also sought for assiduously by many analysts as an endpoint in itself, the identity concept is an intermediate formation, rather than constituting a psychological endpoint. The empirical fact is that identity as an endpoint in psychoanalytic explanation, coming more as it does from the latest fashion or public interest than from incisive clinical data, does not serve to deepen the analytic process. Indeed, its function is often to block or even to terminate further psychoanalytic explanation. Like other unconscious fantasies or affects, however, it is composed of centripetal ingredients feeding into it, which determine its composition as well as serving to further direct centrifugal psychological pseudopodia toward the external world as components of external actions or behavior. Beyond defenses, what is it that the patient does not know of his or herself, by way, for example, of cognitive and affective aspects of traumata, which make for this not knowing of self? To Gitelson (1951), psychotherapy, as differentiated from psychoanalysis, reached plateaus of such intermediate levels of interpretation. Psychotherapy did not aim or go beyond these. Rather than utilizing it in a cliché formulation that throws off the psychoanalytic scent instead of serving to expose and deepen its roots, it would be well not to allow the concept of identity to produce a unidimensional effect, but to use it as a way station pointing to significant antecedents and subsequent psychological formations that more effectively expand the understanding of unconscious processes.

Contrary to common concerns, in the intrapsychic and tripartite (id, ego, and superego) structural point of view in psychoanalysis, the whole person is not neglected but preserved. The charge of the ego is no less than the total self, which, stated earlier as defined by Jacobson (1964), includes the biological and psychological, somatic and mental, body and mind. Nor does the role of the external object become of lesser interest. Just as the self does not lose importance because of a technical appreciation of the role of the ego, so are object relations not diminished as to their role in mental life. The self and the object are included in the intrapsychic process and its dynamic unfolding, both as memories of self-object relations and their consequences in the past, and as currently invested entities, whose fates and vicissitudes are the key elements in evaluating the expected results of intended acts. There is no detraction from the importance of social life, of the role of objects. These have been stressed and made the theoretical, motivational center in a succession of theories, from Sullivan's interpersonal psychology (Sullivan, 1953) to Fairbairn's object-relations theory (Fairbairn, 1954), or as seen from the vantage point of the self, as in currently in vogue self-psychology (Kohut, 1971, 1977). Both self and object are as crucial in total and inclusive psychoanalytic theory as in any of the externally or socially oriented theoretical systems, or as the "I" and "Thou" in the spiritual social philosophy of Martin Buber.

Low self-esteem, a common variant and accompaniment of the "Who am I?" syndrome, is as easily come to as an answer or explanation in a surface evaluation of one's feeling bad. Attributing such unpleasure to deficient or inadequate self-esteem, feelings about oneself of depreciation or unworthiness, surely can stand further probing and insight to achieve a deeper understanding of the meaning and causes of such dysharmony. As with dystonic affects related to problems of identity, only the full range of intrapsychic as well as inner-outer conflicts can deepen and expand the psychology of self-esteem by including its internal and internalized ingredients.

Identity spans from the molecular to the sociocultural. Identity is a function of what a person thinks and feels about what he or she is internally and who he or she is in space in interaction with fellow beings, from love objects to more distantly invested interpersonal relations. Positive self-estimation is an outcome of harmony and satisfaction in the gamut of these relationships. The identity molded at each evolving experience is both the result of and the cause of the choices made and directions taken by the ego for the self at that moment in life. During this life course the identity residing within the individual ego constitutes a firm yet bending armature, shifting with experiences from inner development and external history. A person adds to his or her identity in interpersonal and group relations from dyadic to the widest cultural influences. Freud, without using the term, expressed his identity as a Jew in Vienna. The conflict connoted by "a problem of identity" is operative and used from the individual to the widest group formations. The interpretation or diagnosis of identity disorder is actually more appropriate as an endpoint in groups than in individuals. The former Soviet Union was headlined as suffering an "identity crisis." In an individual it is possible and indicated to proceed from that level of pathology and explanation to its underlying inputs and causative conflicts.

At its peak, identity has been used to define an age, or a historical era. The "age of narcissism" is another such widely accepted explanation-interpretation that has resulted in deflection rather than penetration. This formulation, stressed sociologically by Lasch (1979), following Kernberg (1984), also is functioning as the inexact interpretation pointed to by Glover. It serves as defense more than as insight or content. The "age of anxiety" has not passed, nor has it been replaced by narcissism in its central role in pathogenesis. In fact, anxiety is not of an age, but is a permanent part of the armamentarium and the psychological equipment of humanity, protective in basic aspects and nodal in the causation of neuroses as well. Narcissism and anxiety, as well as the ongoing operation of an ego identity, are central nodes in mental life, contributing important motivational roles to the gamut of psychic outcomes, and behind all conscious and unconscious decision making. Self-preservation, the aim of narcissism and self-love, is as ubiquitous an unconscious regulatory principle as the guarding against danger in the living of one's life, the central function of anxiety as a signal. The same motivation fuels the support of an ego identity, which is to sustain individuality and maintain esteem for the self.

Identity and the Unconscious Decision-Making Process

With regard to the substructures underlying these more general presenting syndromes, there is a central issue embedded in psychoanalytic theory and methodology that needs confrontation and clarification to avoid a justified doubt about the science of psychoanalysis, a doubt that comes mainly from outside psychoanalysis. I personally find merit in the reservations of Sartre and the existential school that the psychoanalytic method, as developed and practiced, leads all too typically to indecision and inaction. Though it provides insight, the other side of the same coin is the abrogation of responsibility. "Tout explaner, tout excuser," goes the criticism. My clinical research over decades has been centered on countering this very point (Rangell, 1971). Missing or incomplete until now within the routine framework of psychoanalytic theory has been, in my opinion, the role of the active ego in resolving unconscious conflicts, and in effecting and directing outward behavior. In writings over many years, I have added and stressed decision making in the unconscious intrapsychic processes. I pointed to various active points of ego functioning during the process of trial action. To Camus, as to Sartre, life is the sum of the choices we make. I add (and highlight) within psychoanalysis, the unconscious ego will, the source of those choices. Unconscious choosing, the unconscious will, bypassed and singularly missing from the psychoanalytic theoretical framework, has too long been obscured. Actions do not come about passively, nor are they all consciously made and shaped. We have been in the habit, since the advent of psychoanalysis, of assigning to the unconscious the motivations for external acts but not their final choice among competing alternatives. From a lifetime of clinical experience and observational data, I have stated (Rangell, 1971) that there is as much active choice in the hidden unconscious aspects of the iceberg as there are motivations for the choices made. There is also as much motivation to keep the choices unconscious as there is to keep their motivations hidden. It is impressive how people attribute the course of their lives to others or to chance, not to their own choices, which, having been made largely unconsciously, they typically disavow. My own wonder is how this aspect of behavior has itself remained unconscious and escaped common psychoanalytic discourse for so many years.

The effect of admitting unconscious decision making into the armamentarium of ego fuctioning is to introduce a concept into psychoanalysis that is the reverse of a pervasive attitude usually assumed. Sartre's correct criticism of analysis as leading to indecision and the avoidance of responsibility is not intrinsic to psychoanalysis, but was an incompleteness of it, due to the stage of development of the science. Adding, or uncovering, this active node in unconscious mental functioning supplies the missing link. An additional fact adduced, or conclusion that can be come to from this insight, is that people are not less responsible than they think for what they do, but more responsible than they let themselves know. The complete state is that they are both less responsible and more responsible at the same time. Psychoanalysis has shown in other respects that, in the unconscious, contradictions exist side by side. Psychoanalytic treatment alters the balance between the two toward a more rational ratio, to separate what was done automatically, reflexively, following irresistible impulse, from that which was directed actively by the unconscious ego. Psychic determinism, introduced by psychoanalysis, is relative, not absolute, just as autonomy, introduced later, is also relative (Hartmann, 1939a, 1964; Rapaport, 1958). The analytic test, with respect to responsibility for one's actions, is to determine the proportions of each.

With these extensions of theory, I have also over the years spread my psychoanalytic concerns from anxiety, depression, trauma, and neurosis to a stratum of clinical phenomena that expands the interests and scope of psychoanalysis, questions of integrity, sincerity, responsibility, and accountability, phenomena that do not often come under the purview of the analytic quest. Character traits, more accurately ego styles, of charm for example or even of charisma, are drawn under scrutiny, any of which traits or characteristics can rest as much upon defensive elements as on positive and adaptive elements. How much of the patient's character is genuine (compare Winnicott's true self; Winnicott, 1965), versus insincere, hypocritical; how much consistency, loyalty, along with object constancy, versus opportunistic (differentiated from taking advantage of opportunities, which is a desirable trait and capacity); self-love versus smugness; arrogance, as distinguished from pride, or ambition; all of these separated from normal narcissism.

This range of problems is more ego-syntonic. That means they are not so much complained about and therefore they are less accessible to analysis. All are more difficult to treat as such, but they can be rendered ego-alien in analysis, within and outside the transference, and, within certain limitations and technical problems, can be subject to insight and change. These expansions of psychoanalytic interest and the psychoanalytic reach into more subtle ego-syntonic character traits continue the centrality of the issue of identity within the intrapsychic spectrum, with its own complex etiology and its further derivative outcomes. In a sense, my expanded interest, intensified over the past two decades, is a renewed continuation of Erikson's early contributions about integrity, trust, generativity, hope, and responsibility (Erikson, 1959, 1964); although my addition in the sphere of "the compromise of integrity" (see, e.g., Rangell, 1974, 1976, 1980) is with a different center and orientation than used and intended by Erikson.

Theory Refinements Are Not Always Theory Replacements

Grünbaum (1984), a philosopher who concerns himself with the methodology of psychoanalysis as well as its validity as a science, comes to conclusions with which I generally agree. I share with Grünbaum his disagreement with those analysts (Spence, Schafer, Klein, Holt, Gill) who, in stressing hermeneutics, reject the construction of a scientific theory of psychoanalysis. Psychoanalysis indeed bridges both. The hermeneutic and the natural science aspects of psychoanalysis coexist harmoniously (as held by Freud, Hartman, Rappaport, Anna Freud, Kris, Loewenstein, and so on). Meanings and mechanisms are both encompassed within the psychoanalytic view and understanding. Waelder (1962) has shown the nature of the relationship between the so-called clinical and abstract theories. Unlike Grünbaum, who is concerned with the lack of validation in the psychoanalytic method or process, I agree however with Hartmann (1964), who points out that the criteria for scientific validation are different in the soft than in the hard sciences, that is, in the social and behavioral sciences, including psychoanalysis, as compared to physics, chemistry, biology, and the like.

In a currently ongoing debate over "one theory or many," a multiplicity of theories of equal validity versus one overall psychoanalytic theory (see Wallerstein, 1988), I hold for one "total composite psychoanalytic theory" (Rangell, 1988a). Under one umbrella theory, which has grown by a cumulative rather than a replacement process, many modifications have been made and additions successfully adhered. As I have pointed out, self and object, and now identity, are well included and find comfortable places within such total psychoanalytic "theory by accretion." As Fenichel (1945) states: "There are many ways to treat neuroses, but there is only one way to understand them." Many theories that replace also eliminate vital and hard-won insights. Although self-psychology, for example, has contributed an overall pronouncement of "tragic man" (Kohut, 1977) as exemplifying humanity's fate, to me this should be added to, rather than being an alternative to, "guilty man," which it proposes to replace. Biological and psychological limitations, developmental crises and impasses, are added to the vicissitudes of the oedipal drama to make for one's existential fate from birth and creation to deterioration and death.

These differing theoretical orientations are neither academic nor an intellectual exercise, but have direct applications, not only in the main derivative arena of the clinical process but in applied analysis as well. In current works on psychobiography or psychohistory, primary examples of applied analysis and of central interest in the discussions of this volume, it matters much which theory is considered to represent psychoanalysis and is therefore utilized in these pursuits. A psychobiography written from the perspective of a psychology of the whole, that is, of self and object, without an awareness of or concern with component parts, can of necessity focus only upon interobject tasks and dangers, and internally on problems of cohesion versus fragmentation of the total self. Sacrificed are intrapsychic conflicts over sexuality and aggression, individualized developmental interstructural problems, pregenital perversions, the gamut and web of repressed sexuality. There have been in this vein voluminous but superficial "explanations" of monumental subjects, such as detailed yet glib accounts of the psychology of Hitler, an object-relations-centered biography of Mustapha, other biographies in terms of the vicissitudes of the self, or the true or false self. There have also been many psychobiographical studies, brief and extensive, which, within methodological restrictions, have nevertheless contributed significant psychoanalytic insights to historical, literary, and artistic figures (I think of Frederick the Great, Conrad, Huckleberry Finn, Houdini). Erikson's own studies of Luther (Erikson, 1958) and Gandhi (Erikson, 1969), virtually introducing a new literary genre, are far more than the analysis of identity crises. Although Erikson builds these psychobiographies fiercely around the respective identity crises of the two subjects in their mid-20s, these works would hardly have withstood the scrutiny of time were they not also based on broad psychoanalytic ground from childhood, even infantile, conflicts to the widest sociocultural inputs. Besides his contribution of an important node of mental functioning, both clinically and extending into his applied psychohistorical studies, Erikson remained a complete psychoanalyst of his times.

3

A Psychoanalytic Perspective on the Concept of Identity

TOBI L. G. GRAAFSMA

In this chapter I argue that developmental psychology generally uses the concept of identity very loosely and quasi-explanatorily. Identity is often considered to be the central achievement of adolescence, as some sort of optimal psychological state to be achieved at the end of the adolescent years. However, clinical psychoanalytic experience suggests that identity primarily refers to a more encompassing phenomenon: to the tendency of the individual ego to perceive or to deny identity between wishes, feeling states, and reality. I suggest using the concept of identity in two general ways: first, macroscopically, for referring to the dynamics of the integrative, attuning efforts of the ego; and second, microscopically, for referring to unconscious actions of the ego, in which identity between some feeling state and reality is either urgently pursued or disguised and rejected.

Introduction: Identity as a Special Perception

Generally, when one feels confronted with the necessity to reflect on one's functioning, aims, expectations, and self-image, one says: I reflect on my identity. Sometimes one even perceives passing through a crisis of identity. Such a crisis may occur especially in times of transition, whether intrapsychic or more psychosocial. Adolescence can be such a time of transition. Geographic and social migration are also often accompanied by conflicts and crises in the sphere of what one might denote as identity. To say one is going through an identity crisis sometimes implies a sort of explanation for why one feels undecided about where to go, is hesitant or unable to commit oneself in important areas of life. This is a strange state of affairs. Because, in fact, one states the same in somewhat more distant, abstract terms. Nevertheless, this explanation may bring some relief because one seems to know the reason for uncertainty. Sometimes adolescents in clinical treatment use the term identity in this way, as some kind of explanation for why they feel unable to continue developmental progression. But when questioned more closely, they often do not understand what in fact brought them into a deadlock. The dynamic backgrounds of their experiences often remain unknown and willfully so. Adolescents are often simply satisfied with calling their distress an identity crisis. They are not at all interested in knowing the exact meaning or reasons behind the crisis. This intellectualistic description, which psychoanalysts would assume might imply some sort of defense, should explain enough. All this is typical for adolescents: They prefer to look ahead and outward before they look behind and inward.

Logically, the concept of identity implies the assumption or the perception of some permanent correspondence, of sameness. Identity implies a continuing, persistent sameness between two entities or between two states of one entity (for example at two moments in time). Identity is the outcome, the conclusion of a perception (and here I use that term rather loosely) or even a feeling. Identity refers to an interior act of association and comparison, in which certain essential qualities remain constant, invariant, and identical in spite of a change in state or perhaps in spite of a change in other less essential qualities.

There can be little objection to this definition of psychological identity, that is, identity in the psychological realm. The concept may be applied to individuals, to the inner world of the self, or to the self and its object world, as psychoanalysts say when speaking about the relation between subjects and their human and nonhuman environment. The concepts of self- and object constancy for example refer to identity operations that are performed in early childhood. They have a decisive influence on a child's sense of well-being, even early in childhood. The concept of identity may be used for psychosocial phenomena and even for psychohistorical phenomena. This is what scientists indeed do (this volume is an example).

Scientific explorations of psychological identity meet some special problems. Psychological phenomena cannot be measured and compared repeatedly and exactly. Nor do they show perfect and persistent correspondence. They are too weak for that. So we generally adjust our demands and accept that we have to look for concordance and enduring harmony between psychological phenomena in some essential function.

In addition, the individual perception of some psychological identity is not necessarily conscious, as is the case with so many mental activities, although it can be. The basic assumption behind this statement is psychoanalytic. It concerns the ego, a psychic structure to which we ascribe the task of reality testing and the task of reflection. Most of the ego's registrations and activities happen outside conscious awareness. Often one notices its decisions and doings only through affects, one's feeling states. (Therefore, I added the word *feeling* to the statement that identity is primarily a perception.) We should recognize that moods and affects do have a very important signal, and thus potentially a communicative, function. Many of the reflections the ego performs also happen outside awareness. The ego operates for the most part in a dynamically unconscious manner. And so it may be, as I hope will become clear from this chapter, that we become aware of the outcome of silent (because unconscious) operations in the sphere of identity primarily in an indirect manner through affects: such as feeling at home, or crisis-like and through anxiety, such as feeling unhappy and alarmed.

Unlike many other authors, I do think that the experience of identity in some areas of one's life, whether intrapsychic or psychosocial, is not in itself a situation that is always wished for (with the exception of a sense of "I," a matter which, because of its scope, will mainly be left undiscussed here). This is not even the case during adolescence, a phase whose major developmental task, it is said, is identity formation. It may be so, but this depends on the qualities or situations being compared. Identity is a truly relative concept, and the personal evaluation of a correspondence felt somewhere may be favorable, but also very unfavorable. Clinicians know that feeling much concordance or harmony (eventually preconsciously experienced) may sometimes be frightening, or most welcome; little concordance may be frightening, but may also be comforting. One only has to look at adolescent behavior to understand this. Much concordance with the expectations and norms of adults may be frightening because one might still be considered a child. Identification with certain character traits of a parent may horrify adolescents. But much harmony with the expectations of peers may make one very popular. So one should be careful to keep in mind that identity is not always something that is desired. Adolescents, in their struggle for dis-identification (Greenson, 1954) often note (feel) too much similarity between themselves and their parents. Identity may be defended against in some specific area. (See Goffman, 1963, writing about stigma; and Lifton, 1968, writing about the unwanted but compelling identification of Hiroshima survivors with those who died, which lead to what Lifton called a "hibakusha identity.") It seems to me that it is wise to keep this situation in mind, because so often identity is simply taken to be a goal in itself as some sort of ideal norm.

The Concept of Identity Is Used in Very Different Contexts

Although he was not the first psychoanalyst to use the term *identity,* it was Erik Erikson (1950) in particular who explored the significance of the concept. In addition to the so-called metapsychological points of view in psychoanalysis, he developed a psychosocial point of view on development and behavior. Erikson's epigenetic chart of psychosocial development proved to be especially valuable and became an important addition to general psychoanalytical developmental theory. He followed Hartmann (1939a, 1939b) in his adaptive point of view and expanded it in at least two important ways. First, Erikson developed the epigenetic principle, which means that every stage in development adds something specific to all later ones and remolds all of the earlier ones; and second, Erikson, expanding on the fundamental work of Spitz (1945), focused on the continuous mutual attunement of the growing child and his society, referring to it as mutuality. This attunement, as we now know better (see, e.g., Brazelton, Tronick, Adamson, Als, & Wise, 1975; Stern, 1985), is essential to normal development in childhood and throughout all the stages of the life cycle. For Erikson, the concept of psychological identity fundamentally belongs to this realm; it refers to the vicissitudes of attunement processes and mutual regulation, both internal and interpersonal. It is most unfortunate that the concept of identity in most academic research has completely lost this dynamic context. A similar critique can be found in Côté and Levine (1988) and in Blasi (1988). But Blasi also loses sight of the function of the identity concept in Erikson's work and in psychoanalysis. With the concept of identity Erikson introduced concepts such as relativity and complementarity to psychoanalysis. He added to Hartmann's concept of preadaptedness, social modalities and modes, and especially to the concept of epigenesis. By no means does this concept refer to a mere succession of developmental stages. It essentially means that each stage has its specific time of ascendance and integration. Here Erikson uses an organismic point of view, borrowing, for example, from embryology (see Erikson, 1982, p. 27).

Erikson, however, did not get mired down in the concept of identity, but gradually focused on the interplay between individual life cycles and social forms of communality. As will be argued later, he used the concept of identity in a rather macroscopic way, trying to bridge and connect very personal phenomena with very social, even generational and historical, phenomena. The title of one of his books illustrates this: In 1978 he published *Life History and the Historical Moment* (a title, by the way, that corresponds to the raison d'être of this volume). In short, Erikson (1959, p. 102) stated that:

> [T]he term identity expresses a mutual relation in that it connotes both a persistent sameness within oneself (self-sameness) and a persistent sharing of some kind of essential character with others. . . . At one time it [identity] will appear to refer to a conscious sense of individual identity; at another, to an unconscious striving for a continuity of personal character; at a third, as a criterion of the silent doings of ego-synthesis; and finally, as a maintenance of inner solidarity with a group's ideals and identity.

So, under the heading of psychosocial identity, Erikson pointed out a personal and a social tendency (one might even say necessity) to mutual attunement and regulation, again expanding on Hartmann's (1939a, 1939b) concepts, especially on that of "fitting together." This concept was brought into psychoanalysis from biology. And although the concept of identity did not gain a central place in psychoanalytic theory, the two assumptions underlying Erikson's work, the epigenetic principle and the principle of mutual regulation, stood the test of time. The position of psychosocial theory as one of the metapsychological points of view in psychoanalysis, however, is still unclear. It may well be that the growing body of knowledge in the area of object relations makes the problem obsolete. Later on in this essay I will return to Erikson's views. At this point it is more important to keep in mind that the concept of identity was embraced warmly by some, and rejected as superfluous or too vague by others, both inside and outside psychoanalysis. But seldom was its essential context and Erikson's motive for using the term retained (for an exception, see Josselson, Chapter 5).

Some academic psychologists have considered the concept of identity to be a fruitful starting point for bridging the gap between the more experimental academic tradition and the clinical observations on which psychoanalytic psychopathology and psychoanalytic developmental psychology are based (e.g., Marcia, personal communication).

But such a bridge is difficult to build, certainly when such a controversial matter as identity is chosen for a starting point. For example, academic psychology does not make use of a concept such as overdetermination, which is of central importance to psychoanalysis. Overdetermination essentially states that all human behavior has multiple determinants, is multifaceted. Such a concept also applies to Erikson's epigenetic principle because it assumes overdetermination by definition. Psychoanalytic observations can still hardly be put to the rigors of experimental testing because no experimental design fits a concept like overdetermination. Cook & Campbell (1979, p. 64) call this "construct underrepresentation." But observations in and from the clinical psychoanalytic situation still defy reliable quantification, and replication outside that situation. This fact is often used as a major objection to psychoanalysis, Erikson's psychosocial theory of development included.[1] That is not fair, however, because quantification and replication of psychological phenomena are general problems in psychology. The problems are often hidden behind the general tendency to pay attention to all kinds of probable dimensions and relations of the phenomena described, or concealed behind a defensive tendency to refine methodology by cleaning the scientific glasses without looking through them. One only needs to consider all the years of academic identity research behind us (Bourne, 1978; Marcia, 1988) or academic self-concept psychology (Van der Werff, 1988, gave an overview) to see the modest results. Kaufmann (1980, p. 109-110) even states:

> No unpoetic psychologist [Freud is described as a "poetic," creative psychologist] has contributed half as much to human self-understanding as did Goethe, Nietzsche and Freud. Most of them, like most philosophers and academicians in other fields, are engaged in busy work that, whether "scientific" or not, contributes nothing much of enduring importance.

This is true, of course, and the fact that we still lack sufficient knowledge of the economy of the border area between the biochemistry of the brain and the workings of our mind affects psychoanalytic theory as much as psychology in general. It is interesting to note that on the mind-body problem there is one theory called identity theory. This theory basically assumes that correlated phenomenal and neurophysiological terms have the same denotation but widely differing connotations (see Feigl, 1958). The economic point of view in psychoanalysis works with quasi-quantitative concepts that cannot easily be translated into mathematical formulae. So, for the time being, we cannot do otherwise than pass on the mistakes we make here to every new formulation we develop, maybe until we find convenient measures for psychic energy—if we ever do find them.[2]

When the concept of identity is defined to include the notions of individuality or self, a large academic tradition comes into view. In this tradition the emergence of a sense of self, of individuality, and also conceptions of the characteristics of that self have been investigated (see Wylie, 1974, 1979, for an overview). Within psychoanalysis, it is the theory of narcissism that concerns itself with the vicissitudes of the libidinal and aggressive investments of the self. Theories about the development of the healthy self have emerged and, in conjunction, have led to theories on the psychopathology of narcissism and psychic pain. These last theories pay much attention to the stimulating, generating function of significant others.

The concept of identity occupies a central place (more closely resembling the exact meaning of the term) with regard to the well-known problem of self- and object constancy in so-called borderline conditions. This is so because the perception of the self and of objects as being similar and continuous in the course of time (especially the case for affective states) is unstable, as is the integrative function of the ego (a function we will explore later).

As stated earlier, much academic research on identity somewhat neglects the theoretical basis Erikson gave to the identity concept and operationalizes the concept by asking subjects to define, to characterize themselves, which is precisely what identity is not about. The well-known question: "Who am I?" seems to reflect the answer to the question of identity. Here in essence the term *identity* is used on a par with terms like *the self* or *individuality*. But when one tries to focus on the essence of the sense of identity by asking subjects to characterize (or to identify) themselves through answering the question "Who am I?", one is on the wrong track.[3] Identity is not encompassed by that question, if indeed one answer would ever be possible. The question

"Who am I?" leads to a characterization of aspects of the self as one distinctive, continuous, and whole entity. It does not invite subjects to compare, or to relate. It leads subjects to focus on the visible, outward side of what Fenichel (1946, p. 467) defined as the character of the self, and not on identity as defined here or for that matter by Erikson. Moreover, as may be expected, subjects who try to answer that question tend to hesitate, because the question may be understood as: "Be sincere and reveal your true, most authentic nature, the core of your self." That question is intriguing but no doubt difficult to answer, if one ever knows. Or maybe better: if one ever wants to know. For it seems that only when in psychological trouble does one consider exploring one's psychological depths. And, even then it's not done without much resistance: The truth about oneself is generally pretty painful.

The question "What am I?" approaches the question of identity because it is more of an invitation to reflect. But still it does not capture the essence of identity. That would be sharing a correspondent aspect between two substructures in the self (for example: ideals and morality), or between one's ideology and the community morals. Identity is not the same as the self or self-representation. It is not the same as the "I," a term that refers to that vital but troublesome phenomenon of consciousness and centralized awareness. Identity indicates a common quality in structures, while not being a structure itself. Identity refers to some common ground, and identity may be desired as a quality. Isn't this, for example, the basis of many identifications and imitations? It probably can be said that some (and one has to specify which and where) identity can be pursued, but as will be shown later, a perceived identity can also result in massive defensive activity.

Clinically, the concept of identity has been of some value in reference to special conflicts in adolescence. Erikson (1956) described a syndrome called identity diffusion, which was a part of the psychopathology of adolescence (see also de Levita, 1965). This syndrome arises when the normal confusion to be met in adolescence is aggravated by a pathological regression. The syndrome may resemble an irreversible psychotic process, but it differs because the integrative function of the ego remains intact. The diffused adolescent basically tries to restore some developmental dialogue. This sometimes occurs in a strange mixture of primitiveness and modernity, in search for solidarity and fidelity, in trying to combine proud partisanship and group acceptance, in searching for ideologies and a zeitgeist that fit with one's characteristic self.

I assume that Erikson tried to draw attention to the fact that much adolescent psychotic-like behavior may be less malignant than one might think. At present, however, a sense of identity confusion is considered to be a symptom belonging to adolescent and adult borderline conditions. Kernberg (1984) and many others show the specific ego weakness in the sphere of integration and development of mutuality that is characteristic of borderline patients. For example, see Rosenfeld and Sprince (1963) and De Blécourt (1980), who refer to the fact that borderline patients balance on the edge of (primary) identification and object cathexis, in which a sense of selfhood remains intact. According to them the integrative function of the ego is also seriously disturbed. The so-called insecurity about identity thus simply refers to the fundamental problem borderline patients experience in relating to themselves, to others, and to their past and future.[4] Basically, their individuality is constantly at stake. Here, the concept of identity has found a proper and dynamic place.

There are more clinical syndromes in which a serious disturbance of the sense of identity takes place. Consider the psychogenic fugue states, the multiple personality disorders, and the cases of psychogenic amnesia, in which patients speak about a certain loss of identity. These disorders are seldom studied by academic researchers of identity. It seems to me, however, that when we want to discover more about the psychological backgrounds of problems around identity, it will be profitable to study the reasons for the general ego weakness in borderline patients; and the sudden changes in identity reported in the multiple personality disorders, which more properly might be called severely dissociated personalities; or in cases of loss of some personal identity in psychogenic amnesia (first systematically described by Abeles & Schilder, 1935). Unconsciously, a wish seems to be acted out, and the loss of a sense of identity seems to be an indispensable part. Sometimes the patient is aware of the amnesia, but in general seems indifferent. When we want to discover why a sense of identity is sometimes so needed (Erikson even thinks that deprivation of identity can lead to murder), or why identity seems to be a hindrance and dispensable (and even sometimes consciously is lost), or even why some egos cannot perform identity operations successfully, it is clearly not very helpful to direct all our attention to the ways in which people characterize themselves.

It is also not helpful to consider identity as the central achievement of adolescence. Of course there are core processes through which adolescents proceed. The normal achievements in adolescence have been described extensively from several points of view. Blos (1979) and Laufer and Laufer (1984) describe the tasks from a psychoanalytic point of view, as did Havighurst and Taba (1949) from a more social-psychological point of view. With regard to the adolescent process, we should consider the fact that Erikson tried to complement, not discard, the existing psychoanalytic theory about psychosexual development. He did this by working toward an epigenetic chart that paid systematic attention to the ego's function in balancing the changing sense of individuality and communality. Erikson truly expanded on what Hartmann considered the ego to be: our psychic organ of equilibrium. (Another term for such an equilibrium is homeostasis, which comes from the Greek *homoios*: identity.) According to Erikson, a sense of identity may accompany (I think one may say reflects the subject's monitoring and contentment about) the process of intrapsychic and psychosocial differentiation and integration in adolescence. There is no doubt that this adaptive balancing partly determines the normality or pathology of psychological development in young adulthood. However, accepting the fact that such balancing is important does not imply that it is the most central achievement of adolescence. It is and remains important, vital, throughout human life.

Thus, when seen from a (psychoanalytic) dynamic point of view, gaining insight in how people maintain or even lose a sense of similarity and correspondence in some areas of their mind, relations, and behavior seems worthwhile in spite of differences and change. From a psychosocial point of view, it seems worthwhile to gain insight into how people manage to maintain a sense of connectedness and mutuality with significant developments in their environment while at the same time they may want to be unique. Wanting to be unique simply means wanting to be out of phase instead of feeling identical with one's (parents and younger peers?) environment. Although starting from different points of view, both approaches should keep in mind that the concept of identity essentially concerns matters of complementarity and relativity.

The Development of the Person as a Whole, the Position of the Ego, and Identity as an Ideal for the Ego

No behavior stands in isolation; all behavior is that of the integral and indivisible personality (Rapaport, 1960, p. 42). This organismic point of view has underlain psychoanalytic theory from the beginning. One of Freud's breakthroughs, however, was that he dissected the whole in parts, assigning a coherent function to each. Despite the organismic assumption of wholeness, reality shows, not just in psychopathology, that there are many instances in which the experience of a divided, unconnected, and uncommitted self prevails. One might say as Rangell (1982) did: The whole works together in various degrees of harmony or disequilibrium. Gradually it has become clear (Hartmann, 1964) that one of the central functions of the system ego is to bring cohesiveness and continuity to all behavior. The ego is conceived of as an organization (when seen from a structural, anatomical point of view) and as an organizer (when seen from a dynamic, physiological point of view). The ego is even given a certain character (Fenichel, 1946) when considering habitual ways in which the ego decides and responds. The fact that the ego has both a structural and dynamic character seems to be a neglected topic of consideration (see Graafsma, 1992). The ego guards the person's indivisibility by its abilities to reconcile the discontinuities and ambiguities that are inescapable in human life. The ego has many masters: the id, the ego ideal, the superego, the environment (from adolescence on, time included). One might say that the ego, when viewed as a whole, has a superordinate selecting and organizing function, taking care that one is neither thrown off balance by impulses and wishes nor overwhelmed or overtaken by the external world. All this occurs in the midst of maturation and all kinds of other conditions. All its masters want, so to say, is the self to be identical with them. And because development during adolescence has a rapid pace and is crucial for the psychological quality of adulthood (adolescents "know" this very well, and often feel as if they do not have enough developmental time, a situation Erikson pointed out when speaking about the adolescent need for a moratorium), the ego can be under great strain.

At first, Erikson called identity *ego identity,* arguing for a place for the concept within psychoanalytic ego psychology (Erikson, 1956). His summary (Erikson, 1974, pp. 92-93) of the integrative function of the ego is well worth quoting:

> In psychoanalysis . . . the ego is that balancing function in mental life which keeps things in perspective and in readiness for action. With the help of a sound nervous system, it mediates between outer events and inner responses, between past and future, and between the higher and lower selves. Above all, the ego works at all times on the maintenance of a sense that we (and that

> means each of us) are central in the flux of our experience, and not tossed around on some periphery; that we are original in our plans of action instead of being pushed around; and, finally, that we are active and, in fact, are activating (as well as being activated by) others instead of being made passive or being inactivated by exigencies. All this together makes the difference between feeling (and acting) whole—or fragmented. Obviously, to convince itself of such a position, each ego must maintain a certain sense of omnipotence as well as omniscience which, if not kept within the bounds of the shared omnipotencies and omnisciences of a joint world view will, in the long run, make us criminal or insane.

Erikson summarizes the formidable tasks of the ego very well. The ego is, to say it somewhat anthropomorphically, essentially a problem solver and a reconciler. Adaptation and development make this necessary.

But where does the concept of identity fit in? I think Erikson described some ideal norm for the ego as a whole. The term *ego identity,* in my opinion, reflects this ideal: Identity refers to and reflects synthesis at its best. It is an ideal for the ego. It seems to me that the experiential sense of identity Erikson depicted so well corresponds to the closeness between the ego and this ideal ego.[5]

Erikson (1968) distinguished between ego identity and self-identity. The former corresponds to what I stated earlier, probably with this difference: Erikson did not consider ego identity to be an ideal norm for the ego, but to be a reachable though necessarily changing (because of maturation and development) norm, such as described in the psychosocial strengths of his epigenetic scheme. Self-identity corresponds, so it seems, to what more adequately might be called self-constancy in its (late) adolescent form. However, that is basically the result of another important aspect of adolescence: the second separation-individuation process (see Blos, 1967). The term *self-identity* has gradually disappeared, probably because of the theoretical problems in differentiating the ego from the self. Erikson later used only the word *identity*.

The very fact that the mind is a divided entity, that it consists of parts, that it is not just a mass, makes it possible to study intrapsychic interactions and conflicts. This can occur within the ego itself, for example, but also between the subsystems one can discern in the mind. Psychoanalysis first of all studies (unconscious) psychic conflict and synthesis. Freud did this in *The Interpretation of Dreams*. I think that the phenomenon of dreamwork (which is about how the manifest content of a dream is made) essentially refers to the unconscious and preconscious synthetic activity of the ego. But we seldom pay attention to this phenomenon, just as we seldom pay systematic attention to how the ego reaches harmony and synthesis. An exception is Lichtenstein (see, e.g., Lichtenstein, 1977), who published a series of important papers on identity. In these, he leans heavily on ethology and suggests that before a child can discriminate between self and other, many "identity themes" are "imprinted " (transmitted).

Such synthetic activity is a sine qua non, however, for the continuity of functioning in every organism, humans included. Synthesis and adaptability must simply go hand in hand for the sake of self-preservation over time. Ego identity refers to optimal or ideal adaptability, which is internal and, when psychosocially viewed, also ecological. Such a situation, however, can only exist when the ego never becomes completely identical with one of its masters, but keeps (maybe silently) always in tune with the others. And it may be called to mind that without some dialectic tension between the synthetic function and process on one hand and conflicting parts on the other, there is nothing to prevent the mind from being completely homogenized. Friedman (1988) explained this extensively. Exclusive attention to the process aspect (synthesis included) and a relative neglect of the impact for development of the conflict aspect has the attraction of a seemingly humanistic approach to development. Identity would always be something striven for indeed. In fact such a vision is rather romantic, exactly because it neglects the fact that conflict and destructiveness are always present, and indeed are major incentives for adaptation and development. This applies to individuals, but also to societies at large; without the normal ritualized conflicts between the generations, societal institutions become dull and sterile and gradually die. I think that only when one neglects internal conflict and destructiveness in human behavior and in development can one indeed defend the notion that identity is something desirable in itself; for example, the central achievement of adolescence.

Synthesis still remains a major function of the ego. The tendency to synthesis is certainly not the only tendency within the mind. Of course the wish to avoid pain and unpleasure is unifying. Indeed, one might basically contend that the pleasure principle itself seeks some kind of identity: identity between wish and reality. This could be motivated by exactly the reason that such identity would mean wish fulfillment. But the ego as a system is also influenced and constrained by specific and incompatible interests. Erikson recognized this when he added to his description of the integrative function of the ego: "This organ of adaptation and of adjustment is also the seat of man's corruptibility" (Erikson, 1974, p. 93). This refers to conflicts between the ego and the superego, or between libidinal and aggressive wishes. Rangell (1976) wrote from a psychoanalytic point of view about the compromise of integrity. Rangell (1990, p. 241) also directs attention to the fact that the synthetic function of the ego may be disturbed by the unconscious oedipal wish to keep the parents apart, and, in connection, there may be an unconscious refusal to integrate identifications with both the parents. See also Rosen (1955), who described a case of dyslexia based on such a disturbance. Everyday life shows that the ego compromises. Some of these compromises are adaptively and developmentally better, others worse; and some of them are more creative than others.

Searching for Identity Is One of the Motives for the Ego in Action

Where do we stand at this point? I have considered identity to be part of an associative action of the ego, looking for some permanent correspondence. That correspondence may be located within the self and/or between the self and its environment. I stated that identity is a qualitative notion, and that its content, its essence, must always be specific. Initially, however, I evaded the question of what correspondence and what quality. I may even have given the impression that the nature of the quality does not matter. It does, because a closer look at the basis on which the notion of identity rests leads to interesting areas of investigation.[6] Additionally, the affective and moral evaluation of the noted common ground can widely differ.

Why would one search for identity? The first and most basic answer from psychoanalysis is because of wishful thinking. That means because of an attempt to find a correspondence between some inner wish or state and a perception or, gradually, between a wish and external reality, because that implies wish fulfillment and the absence of anxiety or psychic pain. In the context of cognitive psychology, the findings of Piaget and coworkers support Freud's clinical findings. Piaget, for example, reports that "It would seem, then, that the roots of identity are to be found in the complex involving 'own body × body of another × permanent object' . . . derived from the functional unity of the exchanges between the subject and his physical and interpersonal surroundings" (Piaget, 1968, p. 29). Of course these exchanges initially center around the baby's well-being.

Freud introduced the concept of identity into psychoanalysis. At an early point in time he assumed that, basically, any psychic activity aims at establishing identity between wish and perception because such identity guarantees wish fulfillment (Freud, 1900). Everyday experience and maturation (especially secondary process thinking) modify this activity, and instead of this *Wahrnehmungsidentität* (perceptual identity) a *Denkidentität* (thought identity) is the aim. Freud did not elaborate on this latter term as far as I know, but one may assume he had hallucinatory wish fulfillment in mind. Later, Lampl-de Groot (1962) showed that here we encounter a forerunner of the later ego ideal, which, as was earlier stated, is essentially an agent of wish fulfillment. It is basically anchored in this early stage of primary narcissism (shared with a caring mother), a stage in which there is no awareness yet of separation between self and objects, and no awareness of helplessness. All this means that the ego ideal is in part a reaction to and the result of the unpleasant but inescapable frustrations and pains life brings. It is a narcissistic agent, seeking (one might say rescuing) states of omnipotence and bliss and seeking distance from psychic pain. Consequently, in later stages of development one must theoretically assume that any psychic activity aimed at searching for identity between some inner and outer state unconsciously aims at the restoration of that early narcissistic state, to which one basically may feel entitled. In this I follow Freud's remark: Unconsciously one never gives up a pleasure once experienced. Scanning external reality for a place one feels at home in, as adolescents in a moratorium do, will have something to do with a disturbed narcissistic equilibrium. Clinical experience does amply support this statement (see, e.g., Jacobson, 1964). Psychoanalytic experience with children and adults also shows that disturbances of narcissism lead to intense envy and to large quantities of destructive rage. These are difficult to bear because they seem to destruct the feeling of "I" itself. Therefore, they generally are repressed and unconsciously projected. So it seems reasonable to assume that narcissistic vulnerability and disturbance may form an (unconscious) background to what is experientially felt as a problem of identity.

But Freud assumed still another motive for a search for identity: the repetition compulsion. Repetition, which of course implies recovering identity, can be very pleasurable, which is readily apparent in the pleasure of children who are fond of hearing exactly the same stories.

However, according to Freud (1920), the repetition compulsion exceeds the pleasure principle in its tendency to restore an earlier state of being. This assumption leads to a second motive for seeking identity. Compared to the first motive, its character is more regressive and developmentally destructive; it does not create moratoria or other transitional spheres.[7] In fact, it is assumed here that the ego may sometimes actually seek de-differentiation and try to loosen its ties to, for example, the superego. The ego does not want identity there because of the pleasure in letting itself go completely. Many adolescents, among others, try to establish environments and states of consciousness in which this is possible.

A third motive is the adaptive one discussed earlier. It was basically spelled out by Hartmann (1939a) and applied by Erikson to the position of the ego between inner and outer reality in the midst of maturation and development. As said earlier, here identity refers to synthesis at its best, to optimal adaptability, to the ideal ego. Erikson wrote about the culture of the ego related to the culture of society. He extensively discussed the synthetic, integrative methods individuals and societies develop to maintain identity in spite of change. He discussed play, ideologies, and ritualizations in this context, and he discussed the psychosocial strengths that (should) emerge from each stage. For example, one can imagine ritualizations and mental states functioning as some sort of adhesive (giving the subjective feeling of solidarity, connectedness, and influence) in the changing matrix of self and objects. But compared to the amount of attention given to the psychosocial stages and the importance of developmental dialogues for individual and social maturation, Erikson did not say much about other possible reasons behind the wish for identity. For that, a more microscopic view on identity (as advocated here) is needed, whereas Erikson uses the concept generally, loosely, and macroscopically.

Association and Dissociation: Silent Reflections on Identity

Without some associative and monitoring mental action from the side of the ego, identity is never established. Upon closer examination, this mental action can have a remarkable feature. Although I stated earlier that a search for identity may be based on the wish to recover a perception, that same search may run counter to other central functions of the ego: reality testing and maintaining full consciousness. Normally, reality testing and perception are closely related. But the wish to establish identity in some area is sometimes stronger than the wish to hold on to reality, especially when that reality is frightening.

A well-known phenomenon, in which the perception of identity plays a central role, is that of déjà vu. Here, the ego falsely notes an identity between an actual experience and an assumed earlier experience, although one does not know exactly where and when that must have been. It seems, so to speak, that one assures oneself: Don't worry, all this has happened earlier and you have gotten through it all right (see Arlow, 1959). In fact, the ego wishes to perceive identity in an effort to defend against anxiety, and therefore associates the correspondence. This anxiety may concern an emerging trauma or some (by the superego) forbidden sexual or aggressive wish. Psychoanalytic experience shows that the assumed earlier experience generally concerns a wish that has not been carried out and remains unconscious (until psychoanalytic treatment gradually reveals its existence). But there is some awareness of a feeling of familiarity, which is transferred to the new situation. The phenomenon of déjà vu is related to the degree of consciousness, and in line with that to the experience of a sense of "I" (Torch, 1981). It seems that one may say that the ego unconsciously manipulates the situation by splitting itself into what is sometimes called *co-conscious mentation*: two more or less separate streams of consciousness with different senses of familiarity and mentation.

In contrast to the déjà vu phenomenon, there may be situations affectively excluded from the ego although they are familiar. I refer to the depersonalizations, truly dissociative disturbances, which to mild degrees are frequent and normal in adolescence. Here some sense of identity is unwanted, and the ego makes a familiar experience unreal and strange. The ego's sense of reality is temporarily coagulated. Apparently, the "I" feels forced to recognize some aspect of the self and seems to say: "I am not the one who wants this: I am not my self." Here one may also speak of co-conscious mentation, because two "I"s seem to arise: one to which one keeps feeling familiar, which observes from a distance; the other experiencing and doing, but strange, unreal, and with a lower degree of consciousness. For some reason, the ego splits and does not want harmony and synthesis. Freud (1936) described an example of a depersonalization, which by now has become classic, in a letter to Romain Rolland. Standing on the Acropolis, Freud felt for a moment "so this exists really as we learned at school" and "what I see here is not real."

The symptom of depersonalization belongs to many syndromes (the borderline syndrome, psychogenic fugues and psychogenic amnesias, and many other dissociative disorders), and in mild, transient forms happens in normality very often, for example when one feels exhausted. The ego does not associate, as in the déjà vu phenomenon, but dissociates. But again, it does so because the ego defends itself against too much anxiety (would identity be perceived?), and therefore the ego unconsciously decides to split again, to give up some harmony. The "I" seems to say: I do not want to be the one I am or the one I ought to be. Depersonalization always refers to the problem of identity, precisely because it attempts to destroy identity that is nevertheless felt to some degree. Unconsciously, the usual sense of one's reality is temporarily abandoned, although a patient may feel that it got lost. Depersonalization comes into existence when the ego meets some inner, basic core it does not want to exist. Surface and core seem to meet in a frightening way. In theoretical terms, the rescue operation the ego performs is this: The ego regresses partly and withdraws its libidinal attachment to some thoughts and fantasies; in short, the ego dissociates. And to return to the example Freud described: While analyzing his thoughts on his moment of depersonalization, Freud discovered the repressed wish to surpass his father, a wish that was realized with the visit to that far country, Greece, and the Acropolis, a wish that still was forbidden.

The unconscious aim of depersonalization is to deny or bypass some psychic reality. The emerging correspondence between a wish and a perception gives too much anxiety and leads to a break in the synthetic function of the ego. The ego changes its own character. See also Deutsch (1942), who described personalities with an "as if" character. These persons overidentify with others, hiding their basic core behind defensive identifications. See also Greenson (1958), who described screen memories, screen affects, and screen identity as defenses against painful underlying memories and affects. In extreme instances the dissociation may proceed to the extent that a so-called multiple personality emerges.

The examples of déjà vu states and depersonalization indicate that the ego as a system may sometimes prefer to associate some identity, may sometimes prefer to deny some identity, and may sometimes prefer to pretend some identity when it feels endangered or on the edge of trauma. The ego can change its degree of consciousness (including a changing sense of "I"), it can bring about a split in its own system and partly regress, giving up its integration to some degree. One result may be a diminishing of anxiety; but another result may be a loss of an overall sense of familiarity with oneself, and of course a loss in the quality of ego identity.

Concluding Remarks

The ego unconsciously performs many operations in which the perception or the feeling of identity plays a central role. Identity between a wish, a feeling state, a norm or an ideal and reality is sometimes sought, sometimes unwanted, or even quite frightening. Identity does not explain anything in itself, nor is it a mental structure. Identity is a quality belonging to a mental activity of the ego, especially the integrative function. Identity refers to common ground; to levels of synthesis and integration; eventually, and here we enter pathology, to mental disharmony and its vicissitudes.

To consider the state of identity to be the central achievement of adolescence seems to be incorrect. This does not contradict the fact that adolescence is a developmental phase (with several important and very differentiated subphases) in which individual life history intersects social history, a sore trial for the integrative capacities of the ego.

A macroscopic view on the concept of identity may fruitfully use the concept when investigating the ego's performance in conflicts of mutual attunement between the essence of generational and historical development and some individual core. This applies not only when one is concerned with adolescence, but also in general: not only with regard to the main lines (or themes) along which the ego organizes, but also and with regard to questions of authenticity and sincerity, for example, which are important for many adolescents, but also for persons in other phases of life.

A more microscopic view on the concept of identity may fruitfully use the concept for exploration of the unconscious ego in action, looking for or precisely evading identity, both in normal and in pathological development. Here general developmental psychology can gain insight from psychopathology, because that which normally is silent and unnoticed can be seen and studied in pathology.

Notes

1. In an article in *The American Psychologist*, Hoshmand and Polkinghorne (1992), though wrongly opposing science and practice in the title of their article, invited academic psychologists to revise their view on the scientific value of clinical data. Although they do not mention clinical psychoanalytic observations, there seems to be no reason to exclude such data from their argument. The relationship between psychoanalysis and the universities, however, will probably remain complicated.

2. Rangell (1990, p. 770) writes that Marie Bonaparte once expressed the opinion to Freud that "those who thirst before everything for certitude do not really love the truth." That was true, Freud replied, and further, he envied the physicist and the mathematician who are better able to stand on firm ground. "I hover, so to speak, in the air," he said, "mental events seem to be immeasurable and probably always will be so."

3. For examples of conceptions of identity as theories about oneself, see Blasi (1988) or Berzonsky (1988). See Côté and Levine (1988) for a thorough critique on another approach to Erikson's concept of identity: in the use of commitment as a valid operationalization of the concept of identity. This critique is supported by the results of a study we undertook (Bosma, 1992; Graafsma & Bosma, 1991), in which 14 adolescents in psychoanalytic treatment were tested with the GIDS (Bosma, 1985). The GIDS also uses adolescents' commitments as measures of identity. However, the psychoanalytic profiles of the adolescents in the study showed that these commitments represented attitudes first, but second, sometimes reflected wishful thinking or some agenda for the future. Sometimes commitments were said to be present, though we could not confirm them from the psychoanalytic and factual data on the adolescent. This brings us back to the problem of what is to be understood precisely by referring to commitment. The more extensive the pathology, the more disturbed the pattern of exploration and commitment. It should be mentioned that Erikson (K. T. Erikson, 1973, p. 129) also objected to the use of the question "Who am I?" to represent the question of identity. It must be said, however, that he also used the question (see, e.g., Erikson, 1982, p. 72; Evans, 1969, p. 37) in connection with a sense of personal identity, thereby creating some confusion.

4. The *Diagnostic and Statistical Manual of Mental Disorders* (DSM-IIIR, 1987) uses the identity disorder as a disorder specific (because of its onset) for adolescence. The (assumed) inability to establish an independent identity (p. 89) is considered the essential feature of the disorder. That formulation, however, is a *contradictio in terminis*: Identity concerns both dependencies and independencies. Besides that, the statement that "frequently the disturbance is epitomized by the person's asking 'Who am I?' " (p. 89), as stated earlier, misses the essence of the problem of identity.

5. Considering identity to be an ideal for the ego, an ideal ego, may somewhat confuse the reader because there is a term *ego ideal* in psychoanalysis. This term is reserved for an intrapsychic agency that is primarily need satisfying. It also contains the narcissistic investments made by the parents and the ideals that are projected by the parents onto the child, and are normally unconsciously internalized. Its central aim is to restore the narcissistic balance, while the central aim of the ego lies more in the preservation of the self as a functioning, continuing unit, consciousness included. The confusion may stem in part from the fact that Freud did not systematically differentiate between the self and the ego; both were covered by the term *Ich*. Here I reserve the term *ego ideal* for agency, and the term *ideal ego* for ideal norm of the ego as a system in itself.

6. It leads to questions about the human core, about authenticity and essence (questions that are relatively recent historically), about the relationship (eventually the identity, or lack of identity) between surface and depth, private and public. The poet Matthew Arnold expressed it nicely (see Tinker & Lowry, 1950, used here with the permission of Oxford University Press):

Below the surface-stream, shallow and light,
Of what we say we feel—below the stream,
As light, of what we think we feel—there flows
With noiseless current strong, obscure and deep,
The central stream of what we feel indeed.

7. I have the impression that in adolescence the ego often makes use of this regressive tendency in a search for the shortest route to a reunion with the ego ideal, instead of gradually working its way through development, accepting dependency and normal feelings of weakness and anxiety. Adolescent identifications, for example, can tell much about the intricacies of adolescent conflicts with psychic reality. I remember an adolescent patient who came into treatment when he was 17 years old. He failed in school and retreated from social contacts, but he said he felt no worry about it, because he felt paranormally gifted. The only worry he felt, which shattered his self-confidence, was when he discovered a small scar on his nose. (I never saw it.) He did not know what he wanted to do, the only thing he knew was that his paranormal giftedness should be recognized. It took a long time before he truly entered treatment. Gradually, I was able to make it clear to him that he was trying to identify with everyone he admired because he was so envious of their qualities and positions. He then tried to convince himself that he could, for instance, influence the legs of a famous Dutch football player by thinking hard, and therefore be participating in the victories of the player. He even felt he wanted to steal the victory from the football player. The envious rage was very difficult to bear, and in this he hardly received any support from his family: There, envy was a central and fixated problem. The symptoms rapidly disappeared, but it took much time before he found satisfying ways to deal constructively with envy and jealousy. Ladame (1991) also described an example. For a discussion of the repetition compulsion, see also Brenner (1982). For another discussion on identity and the repetition compulsion, see Lichtenstein (1977, pp. 99-123).

PART II

Psychology

HAROLD D. GROTEVANT

The concepts of identity and development reflect longstanding interests of psychologists. The first concerns the person, the individual; the second adds a temporal dimension: How do individuals change over time? Since the domain of psychology has often been defined as the study of human behavior, and the study of human behavior has focused on the individual person, multiple constructs have been used to frame theoretical and empirical work: personality, self, ego, identity, and others. Likewise, studies of development have focused in different ways, sometimes looking for evidence of stability, at other times looking for evidence of transformation.

The chapters in this section address the roots of contemporary theorizing about identity and pay special attention to the seminal work of Erik Erikson. His extensive writings address the many faces of identity: identity as a structure, identity as a synthesizing process, but perhaps most significantly, identity as the intersection of the individual and society. Erikson's creative and almost poetic writing has stimulated almost three decades of empirical research as well. The most fruitful research program began with the dissertation research of James Marcia and has been continued by him, his students, and interested colleagues around the world. This empirical work on identity has had several salutary effects. It has provided ways to integrate psychodynamic theories such as Erikson's with differential approaches to personality, since the theory is grounded in psychoanalytic concepts but the measurement techniques have been developed to meet rigorous psychometric standards. It has stimulated a link to the literature on adult development, as identity researchers who initially were concerned with adolescence (such as Ruthellen Josselson and Jane Kroger) have now branched out to examine the transformations and continuities in identity across the life span. It has stimulated linkages between the psychodynamic identity literature and other literatures that have developed independently in the content domains of identity work, such as career development, political and religious development, relationship development, and the development of gender roles. Finally, it has played a role in the explosion of interest in adolescent development and has been a key concept in both theoretical and empirical work concerning that developmental period.

The three contributions in this section exemplify the ever-developing nature of the study of identity from a psychological perspective. James Marcia (Chapter 4) lays out his model, which depicts identity development at the intersection of two key processes: identity exploration and identity commitment. Exploration and commitment are jointly used to define four identity statuses, which have been the cornerstones of Marcia's research. He demonstrates how his empirical approach has grown from Erikson's theoretical statements and differentiates between the concept of identity and closely related constructs such as self and ego ideal. Marcia argues persuasively for both the clinical and the empirical usefulness of the identity status concepts.

Ruthellen Josselson's work on identity (Chapter 5) is grounded in the same Erikson-Marcia perspective but places greater emphasis on the relational aspects of identity. She asserts that identity is psychosocial, rising from the relationship between the individual and his or her social world. She presents a case study to illustrate eight dimensions of identity: holding, attachment, passionate experience, validation, identification, mutuality, embeddedness, and bonding. Although these dimensions have not yet been exposed to empirical testing, they have great potential for suggesting future research on the relational nexus of identity development. Josselson's clinical and empirical work have led her to conclude that the crucial identity events that people recount are relational in nature. Thus, she argues that identity emerges from "the continually redefined capacity to make use of it to respond to others."

The contribution of Guy Widdershoven (Chapter 6) reflects the current explosion of interest in the narrative perspective throughout the social sciences and humanities. He argues that the narrative approach moves away from the psychological view, in which identity is defined as individualistic and development is defined in terms of progress. Rather, a narrative perspective views identity as narrative unity, and development as change in the person's structure of meaning making. The narrative perspective is proposed as an alternative to the more traditional organismic and mechanistic models of human development, and Widdershoven develops the idea that narrative might serve as a bridge between contemporary philosophy and developmental psychology.

Thus, this section of the volume reflects the historical development of the psychological research literature on identity and attests to the heterogeneity of approaches used even within psychology itself. Perhaps it is fair to say that psychological approaches, compared to the other approaches represented in this volume, have strength in attending to individual development within the person's life span, but often neglect the larger historical context in which human development occurs.

4

The Empirical Study of Ego Identity

JAMES E. MARCIA

Theoretical Context

The empirical study of ego identity development by means of the identity status paradigm began more than 25 years ago. This model had its origin in Erik Erikson's (1959) ego psychoanalytic theory of psychosocial development. The identity status approach has been extraordinarily productive, yielding more than 300 studies (Marcia, Waterman, Matteson, Archer, & Orlofsky, 1993). In this chapter I shall describe our way of looking at identity, Erikson's theory from which it proceeded and to which it lends validity, and some of the results of the identity status research.

Erik Erikson, a psychoanalyst whose background in art and education makes him an especially relevant figure for discussion in this interdisciplinary book, has described a sequence of eight psychosocial developmental stages, which, at the early ages, parallel Freud's psychosexual stages but extend beyond them to encompass the whole life cycle (see Figure 4.1). Each stage consists of three components. The first is a physical developmental underpinning, which consists of the individual's needs and abilities, noted on the diagram as psychosexual zones and behavioral modes. The second aspect is those social contexts or institutions that have developed throughout a particular culture's history to be preadapted to individual needs and abilities, providing rewards and demands more or less relevant to them. The third component is the psychological meaning or sense of oneself the individual develops as a result of experience of himself or herself in his or her cultural context.

These eight psychosocial stages represent a sequence of ego growth occurring as the individual meets the challenges of different periods of life and resolves the conflicts that are inherent in those periods. For example, the task of infancy is the development of a balance between a sense of Basic Trust and its inevitably accompanying antithesis: Mistrust. A young adult is confronted with the necessity for coming to terms with Intimacy and its inescapable counterpart: Isolation. Middle-aged adults must deal with Generativity in the face of the alternatives of Self-Absorption and Stagnation. Older adults, approaching the certainty of death and the possibility of overwhelming Despair, have also the opportunity to attain a sense of Integrity.

From both the diagram and this brief delineation of four of the eight psychosocial crises, one may see that they are cast into the form of a dialectic, with a positive thesis, negative antithesis, and presumed resolution in the form of an individually fashioned synthesis whose content is partially determined by the relevant institutions comprised in the person's social context. (The accompanying diagram differs in form from those furnished by Erikson in that the "versus" between alternative stage resolutions [e.g., Intimacy versus Isolation] has been replaced by "and." I feel that this reflects better Erikson's intent, and our experience, that psychosocial stage resolution is not an either-or matter, but that, especially for stages beyond Industry, an individual constructs his or her own particular form of resolution incorporating both the positive and negative aspects of the stage. Also, related psychosexual zones and modes, as well as predominant object relational issues, are included along the far right-hand column.) The sequence of stages is assumed to be epigentically prefigured, and the more or less successful resolution of the crises is assumed to be within the capacity of each individual given "an average expectable environment."

Identity as understood within this context is a developmental achievement. It has developmental forerunners at previous psychosocial stages, and it reaches its time of ascendancy about middle to late adolescence. Although there are opportunities for its resolution later in life than adolescence, the pubertal and postpubertal period provides the optimal conditions for its initial resolution. Never again in the life cycle will there be the fortuitous confluence of individual physical, cognitive, and psychosexual changes with relevant social sanctions and expectations.

Identity issue at Integrity Stage ↓ (column 5)

CHRONOLOGICAL AGE		1	2	3	4	5	6	7	8
OLD AGE	VIII	T-M Intg.	A-S,D Intg.	I-G Intg.	Ind-I Intg.	Id-ID Intg.	Int-Is Intg.	G-S Intg.	**Integrity and Despair**
ADULTHOOD	VII	T-M G	A-S,D G	I-G G	Ind-I G	Id-ID G	Int-Is G	**Generativity and Stagnation Self-absorption**	Inty-D G
YOUNG ADULTHOOD	VI	T-M Int.	A-S,D Int.	I-G Int.	Ind-I Int.	Id-ID Int.	**Intimacy and Isolation**	G-S Int.	Inty-D Int.
ADOLESCENCE ○ Genital ◐ Mature intrusion-inclusion	V	T-M Id.	A-S,D Id.	I-G Id.	Ind-I Id.	**Identity and Identity Diffusion**	Int-Is Id.	G-S Id.	Inty-D Id.
SCHOOL AGE ○ Latent	IV	T-M Ind.	A-S,D Ind.	I-G Ind.	**Industry and Inferiority**	Id-ID Ind.	Int-Is Ind.	G-S Ind.	Inty-D Ind.
PLAY AGE ○ Phallic (oedipal) ◐ Intrusion-inclusion ● Individuation	III	T-M I	A-S,D I	**Initiative and Guilt**	Ind-I I	Id-ID I	Int-Is I	G-S I	Inty-D I
EARLY CHILDHOOD ○ Anal ◐ Eliminative-retentive ● Practising	II	T-M A	**Autonomy and Shame, Doubt**	I-G A	Ind-I A	Id-ID A	Int-Is A	G-S A	Inty-D A
INFANCY ○ Oral 1. ◐ Passive-active Incorporative 2. ● Attachment 3.	I	**Basic Trust and Basic Mistrust**	A-S,D T	I-G T	Ind-I T	Id-ID T	Int-Is T	G-S T	Inty-D T

↑ Precursor to Autonomy at Trust Stage (column 2)

○ *1. Psychosexual zone*
◐ *2. Related behavioral modality*
● *3. Object relational phase*

Figure 4.1. Psychosocial Stages
SOURCE: Marcia, Waterman, Matteson, Archer, and Orlofsky (1993, Figure 1)

In Western societies, we allow our adolescents (sometimes to their and our distress) a period of time-out so that they may leave the position of being cared for and orient themselves to the imminent roles of caretakers. In more traditional societies, we provide rites of passage to confirm in our adolescents their culturally sanctioned identity (sometimes to their and our psychological rigidity). Neither in liberal nor traditional contexts are we especially tolerant and supportive of identity crises in adulthood. Even the more psychologically sophisticated of us can refer to these somewhat pejoratively as midlife crises.

Let me discuss first this idea of precursors and successors. There are 64 squares in Erikson's diagram, not just 8. The heuristic significance of this is to illustrate that each stage occurs at every other stage. Hence, there is an Identity component in infancy, when the major issue is Trust-Mistrust, and in old age, when the major issue is Integrity-Despair. Identity development at adolescence, therefore, is the heir of the resolution not just of the preceding major stage-specific crises of Trust-Mistrust, Autonomy-Shame/Doubt, Initiative-Guilt, Industry-Inferiority, but also of the Identity components of the resolution of each of these issues. Specifically, with respect to Industry-Inferiority, the identity formed at late adolescence is dependent both upon one's sense that steady work at a project is worthwhile (the Industry component of Industry/Inferiority) and also upon one's sense of oneself as a competent worker (the Identity component of Industry/Inferiority) (Kowaz & Marcia, 1991). In terms of identity resolutions at successive life cycle stages, one can identify in his or her own experience the identity aspects involved in becoming a husband or wife in young adulthood, or in becoming a mother or father in later adulthood, or a grandparent in older age. Interestingly, in some work in progress on developing a measure of Integrity-Despair (Hearn, in progress) we have been able to isolate the Identity component of Integrity and establish its relationship to Integrity (Glenham & Strayer, in progress). It should be clear from the foregoing that in societies that permit some degree of freedom in identity formation, that is, where identities can be individually constructed rather than societally imposed, the identity formed at late adolescence is only the first identity; and it can be expected to change as successive life cycle issues make their claims for resolution.

The definition of identity that we identity status researchers have used springs directly from Erikson's theory. Identity refers to a coherent sense of one's meaning to oneself and to others within that social context. This sense of identity suggests an individual's continuity with the past, a personally meaningful present, and a direction for the future. Identity may also be spoken of in structural terms. That is, once a person forms his or her identity at late adolescence, how he or she views himself or herself in the world and how he or she behaves in that world are given shape by his or her identity. An identity may be expected to be disequilibrated and to undergo an accommodative process when it can no longer assimilate successfully new life experiences occurring later in the life cycle.

To summarize, within the Eriksonian framework, identity is the expectable outcome of a particular developmental period: adolescence. The reason that identity is not assumed to develop fully before middle to late adolescence is because the constituents to be integrated (one's gender, mature physical capacities, sexuality, abilities to reason beyond the concrete operational level, responses to social expectations to become more than a child) do not all exist together until that time. Furthermore, if the initial identity configuration attained at late adolescence is a self-constructed one, rather than one that has been conferred upon the individual, achieved rather than ascribed, successive identity reformulations can be expected throughout the life cycle as the individual meets and resolves the challenges involved in ego growth. Hence, the initial identity, if it is a self-constructed one, is not the last identity (Stephen, Fraser, & Marcia, 1992).

There are two concepts within psychodynamic theory that some may consider similar to identity and from which it should be discriminated. The first is the ego ideal. The ego ideal refers to that aspect of the superego that includes internalized goals and aspirations, as contrasted with the conscience aspect of the superego that embodies internalized prohibitions. It is the ego ideal, in particular, that undergoes significant modification during adolescence, as the individual exchanges parents for rock stars, and, eventually, it is to be hoped, integrates also the values of prized teachers and mentors. An identity, because it includes goals and values, is informed by ego ideal contents, but it goes beyond them to involve the individual's particular style or way of being in the world. Identity also refers to processes closer to the social interface of personality, where the pattern of the person's internal dynamics is expressed in interaction with the environment. Hence, while some ego ideal values are included in one's identity, the ego ideal has an earlier developmental history, lies somewhat deeper in the personality, and is less inclusive than identity.

The other concept to be discriminated is self. The theorists whom I see as having spoken the most clearly in developmental terms about the self are object relational theorists such as Mahler and Kohut (e.g., Kohut, 1971; Mahler et al., 1975). Combining these, perhaps somewhat simplistically, one might say that the self is the outcome of the separation-individuation and rapprochement process undergone by the toddler. This initial self must then be continually responded to and reinforced throughout the lifetime, although the quantity of support needed decreases and the figures qualified to provide it become more selected. Developmentally, the self precedes both the ego ideal and an identity and probably lies the deepest of the three within the personality. A solid sense of self is a necessary, but not a sufficient, condition for an identity.

Research in Identity: The Identity Statuses

Because, as psychologists, we have a commitment to go beyond the theoretical description of a construct and attempt to demonstrate its validity and usefulness in some empirical way, our initial task was to cast Erikson's artistically complex definition of identity into one that could provide a basis for measurement. In doing this, we came to realize, by means of observation, that the original dichotomy of Identity-Identity Diffusion (Confusion) did not capture adequately the variety of styles of identity resolution that our initial research participants described to us about themselves. Specifically, some arrived at an identity by means of an exploratory period; others just became more firmly entrenched in the identities bestowed upon them in childhood. Some seemed to have no firm identity resolution and were relatively unconcerned about this, while others, similarly unresolved, were very concerned and struggling to reach some closure on the issue. This observation of the differing modes with which late adolescents were facing identity formation led us to postulate four identity statuses. These identity statuses are four ways in which any late adolescent (approximately 18-22 years of age) may be expected to be resolving Identity-Identity Diffusion.

The identity statuses are determined by means of a semistructured interview and accompanying rating manual. The interviewer asks individuals about decisions that they may or may not have made, the process by which those decisions were arrived at, and the extent to which they are committed to the directions inherent in those decisions. The topics the interview covers vary from culture to culture and from time to time. However, the areas chosen must be ones that are personally important to the individuals being interviewed and must be ones in which people differ in the decisions that they make.

Almost all identity status interviews contain questions in the domains of occupational or vocational choice; ideology, consisting of religious and political beliefs; and interpersonal values such as sex role attitudes and sexuality. Additional interview domains, varying with specific times and populations, have been ethnicity (Phinney, 1989), hobbies (Bosma, 1985), role of spouse and career-marriage conflict (Waterman & Archer, 1993), and others.

Within a particular interview area, the two crucial processes we are looking for are exploration and commitment. Exploration refers to the extent to which an individual has genuinely looked at and experimented with alternative directions and beliefs. Usually, this involves questioning of childhood positions and some departure from them: ideally, in the form of a unique individual integration. Commitment refers to the choice of one among several alternative paths in the different interview domains. To be acknowledged as a genuine commitment, the choice made has to be one that the individual, at least at the time of the interview, would abandon only with great reluctance. To summarize, the identity status interview typically consists of questions about occupation, ideology, and interpersonal values. An individual is assessed according to the extent of exploration within these interview domains and subsequent commitment to some chosen alternatives.

Based upon the twin criteria of exploration and commitment, four identity statuses have been formulated. These are Identity Achievement, Moratorium, Foreclosure, and Identity Diffusion. Identity Achievement persons have undergone significant exploration and have made commitments in most interview areas. Moratorium individuals are currently in the exploratory period; hence, their commitments are not firm, but they are struggling actively to arrive at them. They may be said to be in an identity crisis. The third identity status is Foreclosure. These persons, while strongly committed, have not arrived at their commitments via the route of exploration; they have retained, virtually unquestioned, the values and occupational directions of their childhood. Hence, having interviewed a Foreclosure, one knows as much about the important figures in the Foreclosure's childhood as one does about the Foreclosure. Identity Diffusion comprises the final identity status. These individuals may have undergone some tentative explorations, but this has actually been more like wandering than exploring. The hallmark of the Diffusion identity status is a lack of commitment. There are subtypes of all of the identity statuses, especially Identity Diffusion (Archer & Waterman, 1990; Marcia, 1989). However, I shall present here only descriptions of the main types.

Foreclosure

This brief discussion begins with Foreclosure, that identity status characterized by commitment with an absence of exploration, because that is the most common identity status and also the one that is usually developmentally prior to the more advanced statuses of Moratorium and Identity Achievement. Foreclosures, in the interview, strike one as well organized, goal-directed, neat, clean, and well behaved. They usually appear well, although conventionally, dressed. Frequently, they live with or near their parents. Some of their experimentally determined characteristics are that they are authoritarian (they prefer to be told what to do by an acceptable authority rather than determining their own direction); set very high goals for themselves, which they maintain rigidly even in the face of failure; are somewhat inflexible in their thought processes; tend to espouse moral values at the level of law and order; report early memories at preoedipal levels of psychosexual development; are generally obedient and conforming; and deal with self-disconfirming information by means of either a facade of acceptance or active resistance. They report, and their families report, a great deal of closeness and warmth. Upon closer examination, this "family love affair" seems to be contingent upon the Foreclosures' continuing subscription to family values; remember, they are the identity status who does not explore. Their relationships with others, as assessed in interviews concerning Intimacy (the psychosocial stage following Identity), appear to be conventional and stereotypic. Because there is no exploration, and hence little attendant interpersonal conflict, their close relationships lack psychological depth. Also, because Foreclosures have little doubt about what is right, they tend to choose as friends and partners the right people, who are much like themselves. As long as a Foreclosure remains within the context foreclosed upon, this form of resolution of the identity issue is adaptive. It ceases to be adaptive when the context changes.

Moratorium

In describing the Moratorium status, we move from the Foreclosure position of no exploration to one of almost total exploration. The

Moratorium status is an in-process position; few persons remain there for a long period of time; most, but not all, move on into Identity Achievement. In the identity status interview, Moratoriums impress one as intense, sometimes active and lively—sometimes internally preoccupied, struggling, engaging, and occasionally exhausting. They tend to use the interview, and the interviewer, as an opportunity for expressing and working out their current dilemmas; hence, many Moratoriums' interviews will go on for as long as the interviewer permits. In studies, we have found them to be the most highly morally sensitive of the statuses as well as being the most anxious. In contrast to the Foreclosures, they are the least authoritarian of the statuses. They vacillate between rebellion and conformity. Frequently, on measures such as the ability to think clearly under stressful conditions, resistance to self-esteem manipulation, and developmental level of moral thought, they perform similarly to Identity Achievements. The family relationships of Moratoriums are marked by ambivalence. They, and their families, alternate between exasperation and appreciation. One has the feeling that both will sigh with relief when "all of this is over." Moratoriums' relationships with others are, as one would expect, intense and relatively brief; while they hold values consistent with Intimacy, they are in motion, and it is difficult for them to maintain a constant commitment to another person. Probably what makes Moratoriums the most engaging of the statuses is just that exploratory process that defines them. Since they are often dealing with fundamental questions to which there is really no one right answer, they arouse those same unanswered questions within ourselves and can set us, once again, to pondering significant issues.

Identity Achievement

Persons who are described as Identity Achievement are those who have undergone the exploratory process and made occupational and ideological commitments, are assumed to have resolved successfully the psychosocial task of Identity-Identity Diffusion. In interviews, they seem solid and settled, able to articulate reasons for their choices and able to describe how those choices were arrived at. They are not as engaging as the Moratoriums nor as certain of their beliefs as the Foreclosures. In the best of them, one senses that a process of identity formation will continue throughout their lives, and one would sometimes like to warn them that this is only the first time around. With others, there is a somewhat dull quality, and one fears that they may lapse into a kind of self-satisfied, quasi-Foreclosure position. On various experimental measures they perform well under stress, reason at high levels of moral development, are relatively resistant to self-esteem manipulation, and appear to have internalized self-regulatory processes. That is, although they are sensitive to external demands, they make their own decisions based upon internalized, self-constructed values. Identity Achievements seem to have made a kind of peace with their families, whereby differences among family members are acknowledged, accepted, and sometimes even appreciated, but they are not all necessarily reconciled. Identity Achievements seem to be the most developed in terms of the next psychosocial stage of Intimacy-Isolation, with a greater number of them than of the other statuses being on their way to establishing intimate relationships. I should like to make quite clear at this point that the initial identity configuration is expected to change at least with every succeeding psychosocial stage resolution, and perhaps even more frequently, as life crises arise. And such crises are more likely to arise for Identity Achievements than for the other statuses, because their greater ego strength permits them to see more alternatives and take more risks.

Identity Diffusion

Persons described as Identity Diffusion are those individuals who may have done some cursory exploring, but who remain uncommitted. Interviews with Identity Diffusions tend to be quite short. They have little to say about the topics in an identity status interview, although they may sometimes try to fill in the gaps with what amounts to chatter. There seem to be two kinds of Diffusion within a normal population: those who are apathetic and socially isolated and those who are like playboys or playgirls. The former try to avoid contact; the latter seek it out almost compulsively. Both are interpersonally shallow. On our experimental measures, Identity Diffusions have the most difficulty thinking under stress, conform the most to external demands, are the most susceptible to self-esteem manipulation, and have the lowest levels of development of moral thought. Their family relationships stand in greatest contrast to the Foreclosures'. Whereas the description of the Foreclosure family could provide material for a full-color government brochure on the happy, healthy family, the description of the Diffusion family is more dismal. Particularly striking is our finding that the adolescent feels that the same-sex parent can never be emulated, even though that parent may be highly admired. It is as if a blessing had been withheld and this is felt keenly by the young person. As one might expect, interpersonal relationships are either sparse or extraordinarily shallow for the Identity Diffusion.

While the foregoing may sound like narrative descriptions, it is important to emphasize, within the context of this book, that they are based upon numerous experiments involving researchers in North America, Europe, and New Zealand over the past 25 years. Scientific knowledge emerges slowly, the compensation being (it is hoped) its reliability. All of the research findings leading to the above descriptions of the statuses are reported in Marcia, Waterman, Matteson, Archer, and Orlofsky (1993).

Beyond confirming the validity of the identity statuses and telling us something about their antecedents and consequences, our research has also yielded some interesting information bearing on historical change. For example, when we began our research in 1965, it appeared that the identity statuses of Achievement and Moratorium were the most positive ones for men, while those of Achievement and Foreclosure were more positive for women. However, upon reviewing our accumulated findings in 1986, we discovered that this male-female disparity ended around 1976, and most studies after that time showed female patterns to be similar to males'. Our reasoning was that increased social support for women's financial and familial independence made the undergoing of a Moratorium a less threatening event for women, and decreased somewhat the social desirability of a Foreclosure resolution for them.

Another interesting finding has been a possible difference in the relationship between Identity and Intimacy for men and women. Men seem to follow the Eriksonian pattern of Identity being a necessary condition for optimal Intimacy resolution. However, women seem to be distributed among three patterns: the expectable one of Identity preceding Intimacy, more frequently that of Intimacy and Identity codeveloping, and in a few cases, of Intimacy resolution preceding Identity formation.

Finally, in the course of our years of research, we have found differing distributions of identity statuses according to different cultural conditions. For example, during the Vietnam period, we found a resolution pattern we called Alienated Achievement, a pattern not seen these days. However, we are currently finding, at least in our corner of Canada, a preponderance of Identity Diffusions, perhaps due to our recent financial and political situation. That the frequency of the identity statuses and their meaning, in at least narrowly adaptive terms, should change with cultural historical conditions is consistent with Erikson's general psychohistorical emphasis.

Intervention

Because I am a clinical psychologist and psychotherapist, the connection between the identity statuses and psychological intervention is important to me. Although I have spoken and written in other places about psychotherapeutic issues specific to the different identity statuses (e.g., Marcia, 1982, 1986), I think that the most important implications of our research for intervention have to do with addressing the two process variables of exploration and commitment. It may be the case that these two processes underlie all ego growth. At least they, or some form of them, seem appropriate for cognitive development and accompanying development of moral thought, and the attainment of a secure sense of self (Marcia, 1988).

One may consider intervention on societal, educational, and psychotherapeutic levels. If a society can sanction an exploratory period (Erikson's "psychosocial moratorium") and provide multiple valid niches for commitment, then it can contribute greatly to the ego development of its late adolescents. Educational institutions, within which late adolescents will develop a sense of identity, can refrain from requiring too hasty decision making about major areas of study and can support late adolescents in their occupational and ideological experimentation while, at the same time, they can facilitate and reward commitment when it emerges from the individual. One form this might take is allowing university students to switch major areas of study without serious penalty, offering some flexibility in curricular requirements, and providing counseling services geared specifically to identity crises. This would represent a move beyond mere training to true education of our young people. We psychotherapists can aid identity development by providing a safe context within which our patients can engage in exploration, both internally and externally, and provide some support and guidance as they begin to make commitments to new ways of being in the world. To take a specific example with the identity statuses: A safe context is not the same thing for a Foreclosure as it is for a Moratorium. To attack frontally a Foreclosure's rigid defenses and to successfully strip the person of internalized childhood ideals is to leave that person bereft of any internal guarantor of self-esteem and thence to risk an acute depressive episode. What must be done is to establish some connection based upon authentically shared values between therapist and client and then to slowly and gently disequilibrate the existing structure, providing plenty of time for the formation of new ego ideals. While a safe context for a Foreclosure is based upon some alliance with existing ideals, this is not necessarily the case for the Moratorium who is already in a disequilibrated state. What is required here is a validation of the process of struggle itself as an ingredient necessary for psychosocial growth. To make an alliance with either pole of the ambivalences with which the Moratorium is wrestling is to make oneself a participant in that struggle, and not a benevolent and dependable observer. The alliance to be made here is with the Moratorium process itself, and not with any one value.

Summary and Conclusions

I have kept the applied aspect of my description of the identity statuses quite brief because I have been asked to speak here more as a scientist than as a clinician. And as a scientist, I would like to state briefly what I think identity is and is not. Identity is a construct. It is not a thing, any more than an ego is a thing. As a psychological construct, identity is to be evaluated according to its usefulness in summarizing some behaviors and predicting others. The identity statuses are most accurately viewed as intersecting points along the two process dimensions of exploration and commitment. As psychological constructs, they may be expected to eventually become superseded by other constructs accounting for what the identity status constructs once did and entailing phenomena that they did not encompass. Such is the appropriate fate of scientific constructs when they are not kept alive by artificial means.

In closing, even though I have spoken here as to the results of the scientific study of identity, I am well aware that science is not the only validity game in town. There are other aspects to identity that have historical, literary, social, philosophical, and, above all, personal meaning for us that are not encompassed by empirical research. Regarding one author's view of psychological science—Canadian writer Robertson Davies, in his book, *What's Bred in the Bone* (1986)—we read this scathing indictment:

> Well, Science is the theology of our time, and like the old theology, it's a muddle of conflicting assertions. What gripes my guts is that it has such a miserable vocabulary and such a pallid pack of images to offer to us—to the humble laity. It's the most overweening, pompous priesthood mankind has ever endured . . . and its lack of symbol and metaphor and its zeal for abstraction drive mankind to a barren land of starved imagination. (p. 163)

Well, no one ever claimed science to be inspirational—only true to observations and self-correcting.

5

Identity and Relatedness in the Life Cycle

RUTHELLEN JOSSELSON

When I began doing identity research back in 1970, I opened my intensive interview with the question, "If there was someone who you wanted to really know you, what sorts of things would you tell them about yourself?" Very often the answer from the women I was interviewing was something like, "I'd tell them about my friends and my family" or "I'd tell them about the people I care about." I had thought, following Erikson, that I would hear about what my subjects did or what they believed in, what they aimed at or held dear and sacred. Instead, they told me about the people who populate their lives.

When we first meet people, we are apt to ask about their occupations. "What do you do?" seems to allow us to identify people, to place them in the world so that we can recognize them. Social convention does not permit us to ask the deeper question, "Who and how do you love?"—the question that would go to the heart of identity.

Identity as Psychosocial

Working and loving, being and doing, narcissism and object relations, agency and communion, outer and inner, these are the fundamental dualities with which both philosophers and psychologists have wrestled. In my view, Erikson's concept of identity (1968) was a way of integrating these tasks, of transcending Cartesian polarities. Identity is the overarching synthesis of these dualities, bringing the individual to the social world and the social world to the individual in an indivisible wholeness.

The French existential philosopher Gabriel Marcel (1962) made intersubjectivity central to his ideas about identity. Identity, in his view, is being with. And "withness" can only occur vis-à-vis other people who provide a consciousness with which one can be. In this view, the consciousness of existence itself is linked to the response of an other. Bion (1961), in his effort to understand the relation between the individual and the group, found them to be inextricably entwined. "Whenever I look for myself," Bion said, "I find the group; whenever I look for the group I find myself." This is a similar statement of fundamental identity, an intersubjective fitting together, at conscious and unconscious levels. The social constructionist movement in psychology is similarly advocating turning away from the fallacies of objectivist science. In their view, there is no independent self. Rather, the self arises out of and is created by relationship between the individual and the social world (Gergen, 1987; Markova, 1987). Identity, then, is not only an integration of ego functions; it is not solipsistic. From many directions comes the recognition that identity is at its core psychosocial: self and other; inner and outer; being and doing; expression of self for, with, against, or despite; but certainly in response to others. It is both those for whom one works and the work of loving.

Identity as Separation-Individuation and Connection

Until now, what we have learned about identity development focuses on the importance of separation-individuation processes, of becoming one's own self through precipitating out of the infantile familial nexus. Within this theory, the central issues are the reworking of childhood identifications, freeing from early punitive superego introjects, and the development and integration of ego functions independent of parental control (Blos, 1962; Josselson, 1980).

Researchers brought this theory to the study of adolescence, the period at which identity formation is most urgent and most visible a task. And they limited their study to male subjects. At first in the history of this research, adolescents, with their sometimes noisy affirmations of selfhood and tendencies to irritate their parents, confirmed the theory.

And men, in whom the experience of separateness and the consolidation of masculinity are linked in early childhood, readily spoke the language of separateness and individuality in describing their experiences. As a result, our identity theory tended to expand in the directions of doing, of agency, of self-assertion and self-awareness, of mastery, values, and abstract commitment. The integration of psycho and social that is self and other became muted.

More recent research has, however, begun to counterbalance these forces, to try to make our understanding of identity sit, however precariously, between these two streams. This research has shown that identity resides in connection to others as well as in separateness (Grotevant & Cooper, 1985; Hauser, 1991; Josselson, 1987).

Adolescents, to be sure, do undergo a separation-individuation process on the road to identity. But at the same time, they are not becoming "lone selves" needing no one, standing to face the forces of life alone. Rather, they are editing and modifying, enriching and extending their connections to others, becoming more fully themselves in relation. Individuation is reinvested in revised relatedness, and in these commitments lies the integration of identity.

The study of women has also led us inescapably in this direction. As Jean Baker Miller (1976) suggested years ago, women's sense of self is organized around the ability to make and maintain relationships. Years of research have made this conclusion incontrovertible. Adolescent girls, for example, who were subjects in a recent longitudinal study directed by Carol Gilligan, described themselves predominantly in terms of their interpersonal abilities (Gilligan, Lyons, & Hammer, 1990). Increased individual capabilities in these girls were not used to break away from others, but were funneled back into relationship. Thus, recent work has corroborated what I had found back in 1970 but then had no means to talk about. It seemed to me then that my subjects who wanted to tell a stranger about the people in their life were simply not talking about real identity. Now we can understand better the truths they were trying to tell. Perhaps relatedness is not central to identity in women only; perhaps these phenomena must also be addressed in the study of men.

Empiricism in this realm has, however, been hampered by the absence of a language in which to discuss relatedness. We simply lack the terms of discourse to conceptualize the myriad connections that people make with one another. We are therefore doomed to imprecision when we stray into the realm of communion. How can we be exact about something so nonverbal, so nonobservable, so affective, so, in Rangell's terms, core? In the absence of precise language, we are likely to speak globally of object relations to encompass a vast range of experience.

But we relate to others in various ways, classical psychoanalytic drive gratification being only one dimension of connection. As we grow, we become able to relate to others in more complex ways, which means that the influence of others on us—and our influence on them—becomes yet that much more multifaceted. And each of these streams of relational development, each of these dimensions of "being with," has its own course and its own implications for identity.

The Case of Eve

In the interest of hermeneutic understanding, I present a particular life history, a not atypical woman in contemporary America, a woman of 40, not a patient, a woman in the course of living her life.

There are a number of things to look out for here. One is that you may notice the way in which identity in women is relational. And second, if you try to conceptualize as the data unfold, you may experience the paucity of our capacity to name and understand the relational side of identity that sounds so clearly in this person's life.

I shall call my subject Eve. I had said that she was reasonably typical. But one thing that is atypical about Eve is that she had earned a Ph.D. in French literature from Stanford. But she wouldn't tell you that until you had known her a long time, if she'd tell you at all. She is more likely to tell you about the struggles she has figuring out the driving schedules to get all three of her children to their various activities, the time she spends working in the school library so that she can feel involved in their education, and the small writing business she runs out of her home to make extra money to fund her children's activities. Whenever she can find the time, she really enjoys playing tennis with Jeremy, her husband. She reads the newspaper but has never taken any political action, except to do some work for a good friend of hers who ran for the school board. In place of ideology, Erikson's crucible of identity, one finds in Eve's life interpersonal commitment.

In Marcia's terms, Eve is an Identity Achiever. She formulated her identity choices after a period of exploration and is living life on her own terms. But if we want to be able to define and use the identity concept to illuminate Eve's life, we must be able to place her within the relational context in which she embeds herself. Eve's identity choices are a product of a relational web in which her life is constructed, relational threads of different valence and quality that weave together to form the pattern of her identity.

Let us take a brief look at Eve's history, to see how she arrived at her present identity constellation:

Reflecting on her childhood, Eve remembered her grandmother as the most important person in her life. "She was wonderful to me, gave me unconditional love. She was stable and constant and I knew she loved me. My parents seemed like big children; the house was chaotic. My grandparents came each weekend and things were calm; they could be counted on to do things in a rational way. My grandmother was a source of physical affection. She lay down with me at night. She taught me a prayer I said every night of my life until my son nearly died: That's when I realized there was nothing for me to pray to. "

Throughout her childhood, Eve viewed her mother as someone whose approval she wanted and could not get. She described her mother as critical, unaffectionate, and without warmth. Eve remembers her father as shadowy and she does not remember any real involvement with him, except when he was drunk and he frightened her with his loud voice and occasional violence toward her mother.

Eve was jealous of her younger sister, whom her parents regarded as the cute and cuddly one. She often felt estranged and alone, and safe and wanted only with her grandparents.

By age 10, friends had become important to Eve. They offered her fun and respite, escape from the problems at home. She particularly enjoyed going to camp, a place where she could feel popular and have an existence away from her parents.

At age 15, Eve's world was much changed. Her grandmother had died, an enormous loss, and Eve withdrew into herself. Eve said, "I missed her and dreamt about her, dreamt she would come back to me. I had these dreams until the age of 35. I dreamed about her riding in a car, looking for me, sometimes driving right past me." Lacking the prized relationship with her grandmother, Eve became closer to her grandfather. "We would do things together now that he was living with my parents. He had collapsed, but we were renegades together. We would go down to the basement and smoke together. He took me to Europe when I was 16. He didn't talk much, but he was there for me: I knew I was his favorite and he loved me; I always felt he understood me without our saying anything."

Eve had no real friends at this age. No one really mattered to her; she spent much of her time writing out her sorrow, trying to create stories or perhaps a novel of great suffering. "My mother expected me to be a lovely, attractive, and popular girl, but I was dumpy and academic. I was fat, big, and my grades were uneven; I was incomprehensible to them. I missed my grandmother terribly."

Another crucial turning point of Eve's life occurred in college. She was admitted on a scholarship to UCLA, where met Arthur, her French professor, who was to influence the rest of her life. Here is how she described him: "I fell in love with him instantly when he walked into the classroom. He looked like a Greek god, had a great ass. I thought he was the most marvelous thing I ever saw. I had lost 35 pounds, I was feeling good about myself. I was madly, passionately in love with him; since the day I met him, not a day has gone by without my thinking of him. I wanted to win him, I was his star pupil. I made a dramatic suicide gesture when I finally had to realize he was gay."

Nevertheless, Arthur changed Eve's life inexorably. "We had a great friendship, and he was an ardent supporter. We had a lot of intellectual fun; he and his lover turned me on to literature. He was my champion and master. He psyched me to do a Ph.D. I was sick with love—he overshadowed everything."

Eve had a new best friend, Vicki, with whom she shared details of her growing passion for Arthur. "We were very close, going through the changes together, awakening intellectually, learning new things. Vicki and I lived together; we talked all the time. And she has stayed my best friend throughout my life. No matter what, I can always count on her to understand."

Because Arthur was not available to her as much as she wanted, Eve took Henry as a lover. They often made a threesome with Arthur. But even as Henry introduced her to the mysteries of sex, Eve's thoughts were mainly of Arthur.

When she was 21, Eve won a writing competition and was offered a contract for a novel from a major publisher. Arthur was proud about this; but her parents refused to support her spending a summer writing, and she never finished the novel.

The next year, Eve's grandfather died. He left her some money, which helped her to be independent of her parents and take a stand against their insistence that she be a teacher.

Following Arthur's advice and example, Eve went to Stanford to study for her Ph.D. She studied and did well, but wasn't really excited about what she was learning. She had a string of disappointing relationships with men. Then she met Jeremy. "I knew from the second time I'd met him that I would marry him. I knew he was special. He seemed competent and was kind, good to me, interested in me. I was never excited about him in an intense way, not like with Arthur. He was a wonderful lover and he was patient and giving. We married 8 months later." She still thought a lot about Arthur, although she saw him only occasionally.

After finishing her Ph.D., Eve decided that she didn't really like French literature, and began a career in business. Taking her first job at age 25, Eve found another central figure in Rita, her mentor at work. "She was my boss, taught me a lot and took care of me, and I in turn took care of her. We talked mainly about work-related issues. She was eager to develop my talents, and I was delighted to have a woman that age pay attention to me."

Eve's relationship with her parents remained troubled. "Once I got married, I again tried to establish a relationship. I thought I could have a family life, but this failed. They just wanted to make the decisions in our lives. They were critical; we didn't speak for several years." Eve was, however, developing a good relationship with her mother-in-law, who was good to them. By age 30, Eve's life course had turned again. The critical event here was the birth of her first child, a daughter. "I adored her, never put her down, loved nursing her, wanted a girl very badly, being a mother made me feel so good; I loved feeling all the feelings I [had] never really felt. I finally felt I had a family; I found her endlessly fascinating. When she was born, I knew I couldn't go back to work. I gave up the career I was building with no second thoughts. Jeremy didn't want to be sole support, so I started a freelance writing business at home."

Arthur remained important to her, although they had had no contact for 7 years. She was still fantasizing about him, telling him about her baby. In effect, she was making her experience more real to herself by sharing it with him in fantasy.

Eve realized that she was disappointing Rita by not going back to work. "I was no longer interested in the work issues she wanted to talk about, and she was not that interested in the baby." Eve found another friend, Meg, with whom she shared the experience of mothering. "We spent days together, we hung out as couples. She helped me get Jeremy to understand why I didn't want to go back to work."

Eve also became close to her neighbor, Janet, whose children were adolescents and could often help with babysitting when necessary. In

Janet she saw a perfect mother, supportive, available, and loving. Eve thought of her as the kind of mother she wished to be. She found herself watching Janet carefully, seeing what kinds of interaction she had with her children, noticing how she handled difficulties and tension without the violent tantrums that had characterized her own childhood.

At age 35, Eve was in a hard period. Two more children had been born and the youngest had a congenital disorder. "The baby almost died. The night of his surgery was the night I stopped saying that prayer that my grandmother taught me. There were problems in our marriage; sex was bad; Jeremy and I were in a rut of parenthood, had lost our independent relationship. I got depressed. With three children, I felt I was nothing other than a mother. I couldn't even speak to others. One thing that saved me was being in a mothers' group, a place where I could talk about things I was feeling—feeling crazy, fantasizing about men on the street, kids were smothering me—things I couldn't talk to Jeremy about.

"Leonard was a client of mine. We had a flirtation. He flattered me, offered me an escape. I had very erotic fantasies about him, but never acted on them. Arthur was still there in fantasy. There were also problems in my friendship with Meg. She wanted more intimacy than I could provide. I felt pressured by her: She wanted me to be intense and serious, and I felt invaded. I needed to get away from her. I was still really appreciating my mother-in-law for being so supportive and accepting."

Over the next few years, Eve was able to work her way out of the depression by reviewing and renewing her relationship with Jeremy. Now that she is 40, Eve's children are still the most important to her. But, being more independent, they also feel more separate. "Being a mother has given me the most satisfaction. By giving to them, I can give to myself all that I didn't have growing up."

Jeremy comes next in importance. "My relationship with him is stronger than ever: We're more separate, but I'm more excited by and attracted to him than ever before. We worked hard to reestablish our relationship as lovers and friends; we have a lot of interests in common and we pursue them. We started going out, talking to each other, playing tennis, relating as lovers." Eve continues to develop her business, to organize her children, and to read. And in times of distress, Arthur is still there.

The Relational Contexts of Identity

Eve challenges us with a complex identity that we cannot adequately describe without the capacity to articulate the multiple facets of the experience of *being with.* And indeed, some useful concepts are available within psychology, but they are scattered among various theorists who have tended to sound only single notes of relational themes.

In order to tell the story of identity fully, we would have to speak in stereo, one speaker voicing the themes of doing and self, the other carrying the counterpoint of connection. Although identity is in part distinct, differentiated selfhood, it is also an integration of relational contexts that profoundly shape, bound, and limit but also create opportunities for the emergent identity. Eve's identity embraces her struggles to be with Jeremy, Meg, her children, her mother, Arthur, and the others in her life.

Our theory of identity must include a vision of the individual developing more differentiated forms of connection with others while also cherishing movement toward self-realization. Individuation is toward greater belonging and sharing. We are most ourselves as we are meaningful for others. We are to others only in reference to how we experience ourselves. That is how the counterpoint would sound.

The question I pose is: What are these relational dimensions that underlie identity formation? How do people anchor themselves in "being with"? After a review of different theoretical analyses of relatedness and intensive interviews with people about their relational lives, I proposed that there are eight dimensions that define the relational space in which people live. (For a fuller discussion of these eight dimensions, see Josselson, 1992.) These are the anchor points we must consider in order to place identity in the matrix of relational development. These dimensions define the pathways along which people reach toward each other and define themselves in connection. The first four are primary, basic, largely internal in their influence, and often preverbal and unconscious. These are: holding, attachment, passionate experience (libidinal connection), and validation. The next four are developmentally later in appearance, demand cognition, and are, at least in certain aspects, conscious. These are: identification, mutuality, embeddedness, and tending (care).

Holding

The most basic relational dimension is holding, an aspect of relatedness much explored by Winnicott. The very earliest experience is that of feeling arms around one, supported. With development, a person who has been adequately held feels confident of survival, expects that basic needs will be met and that the world will not let one fall. But the need to be held, physically or symbolically, continues throughout life. We hear from Eve the fulfillment of her need for a holding environment, experienced with her grandmother and then internalized as her grandmother's prayer. We see her effort to construct a harmonious family life that will hold her and compensate for the chaos and disruption of her childhood. An important part of Eve's identity, then, is her effort to recreate a sense of being held.

A child who had been held well enough feels safe enough and protected enough to begin discovering aspects of himself or herself in the world. By adolescence, the young person has internalized a set of expectations about holding in a fundamental orientation of character. Like the securely held infant who, as a result of being securely held, is able to play and imagine, the adolescent who has been held well enough is able to venture forth into new experience, to risk separation and individuation, confident of a grounded world. Holding, then, becomes background to the more overt dramas of individuation. We ask, "Can this adolescent venture forth?" rather than "What supports this adolescent as he or she ventures forth?" The adolescent says, "I am president of the student government," and we may miss that he or she is also saying, "I am a member of a family that is sufficiently well-organized and reliable that I am able to have time and emotional energy free to pursue my own interests, but I also know that I have to spend some time and energy ensuring my membership in that family group so that they will go on holding me." Both are important aspects of this young person's identity.

Growth takes place only within the context of an adequate holding environment, which may be provided by an internalized representation of trustworthy others. But throughout life, people also need external holding environments that will contain and stay constant during periods of growth. Especially during the massive transformations of adolescence, schools and teams, teachers and other trusted adults are necessary to provide support: that is, to hold, to keep the growing person from falling. Often, heterosexual relationships in adolescence are first and foremost holding relationships, sexuality being relegated much to the background.

The presence and absence of holding internally and externally thus have powerful consequences for the formation of identity. The person who reaches adolescence with an uncertain inner sense of being held, who has difficulty trusting the security of the boundaries of the world, who fears falling into a groundless terror-ridden existence is likely to try to cling to whatever scrap of structure can be found in the external world. Substances like drugs or alcohol may seem like tempting holders. On the other hand, such adolescents might have a second chance if they are fortunate enough to discover an external holding environment in their teenage years that can support them, and encourage them, and restore their faith in living. This is sometimes what we try to provide, as therapists, should such a person come to us in the desperate hope that we can be containers. Other fortunate adolescents discover such holders in their ordinary world, can pull themselves toward growth because they feel some symbolic arms around them somewhere. Eve thus carried the holding function of her grandmother in the prayer she said each night.

We might also consider adolescents who've had good enough holding in early life and approach the adolescent passage with an expectation of safety and groundedness from the world, but do not find it in any external source. These are adolescents who are bright-eyed and hopeful, expecting the world to love them, respond to them, and take them in. Depending on their resources and the environment that they find themselves in, some adolescents are traumatically disappointed. They feel let down or crushed by experience, become distrustful of others, may stay close to home because that is the only safe place. If we listen carefully to adolescents, we will hear many stories of betrayal and disillusionment that may not have their roots in earlier experience. Perhaps the adolescent has been naive, too trusting, and has to undergo the pain of learning to cope with the inherent cruelty that exists in the world. It is hard to find a meaningful place in a world that is experienced as unreliable. It is this fear that underlies many of the phenomena of identity diffusion.

Attachment

Camus (1942) chose to begin his great novel of anomie and identity failure with the words, *"Aujourd'hui, Maman est morte. Ou peut-etre hier. Je ne sais pas."* What Camus tells us with these words is the depth of the disaffection of Meursault. He describes a sense of not belonging so great that even the death of Meursault's mother fails to stir response. Camus anticipated Bowlby by many years in noting instinctively the pivotal role of the attachment system in anchoring life.

This second dimension of relatedness, attachment, is necessary throughout life. Ethologically and biologically determined, attachment is a fundamental expression of being human (Bowlby, 1969). Attachment, unlike holding, requires an external object; one cannot be attached to someone who is not there. Here there has been a great deal of confusion in regard to adolescence. Because of the primacy of the separation-individuation concept, attachments, especially attachment to parents, have been regarded as failures of the separation-individuation process. In fact, however, attachment to parents persists throughout life. Separation-individuation revises attachment, but does not obliterate or supersede it, and the evidence is clear that the healthiest adolescents maintain strong attachments to their parents throughout adolescence and beyond, using their attachment as a secure base to which they return from exploration and, beyond this, enriching their lives through a persisting sense of affection and warmth (Grotevant & Cooper, 1985; Kobak & Sceery, 1988).

The complex interconnections between attachment and identity are just beginning to be explored. We know, for example, that securely attached late adolescents are most likely to explore and to feel confident of their identity. But even beyond adolescence, we know that attachments can covertly influence the aspects of self that can be expressed. We are all familiar with the person who loses a loved person and, after a period of grief, emerges as a "new person," dressing differently, trying things they would never before have considered, as though a new self has grown in the absence of the attachment figure.

On the other hand, there are people for whom the maintenance of attachment relationships becomes itself the nucleus of identity. Eve, for example, chose to make her attachments her work. For some people, attachment is identity, the sense of who one is for others only realized in the context of maintaining connection with those who are reliable and available. This is perhaps a part of what my subjects were trying to tell me many years ago: "The most important thing to know about me is the people with whom my life is intertwined."

Passionate Experience

Phenomena of attachment and their effects on identity are very different from libidinal connections, which form the essence of passionate experience, my third dimension. It is this realm that psychoanalytic theory, Freudian, neo-Freudian and post-Freudian, has explored in depth and in great detail. We know well the effects of idiosyncratic drive-related needs and the attendant defensive organization on identity. Particularly on matters related to sexual identity, unconscious management of internal conflict sets implacable limits on what it might be possible to become.

This libidinal dimension of relatedness gives rise to action in the service of passion, the search for union and particularity in love. The passions are foreground phenomena. Unlike the quiet security of attachment or the sense of solidity about being held, the passions take center stage; they are noisy and insistent. The passions constitute intense experience, aspects of experience that are affectively charged, that claim our attention.

In one form or another, people seek some kind of intense connection with others. Here the nature of the connection may be less important than its strength of emotional arousal. Fairbairn, who starts from the premise that libido is object-seeking rather than pleasure-seeking, demonstrates that both pleasure and pain are channels to the object. We can feel intensely connected to each other through hurt, anxiety, or hate as well as through pleasure. And some of our most intense relationships are marked by strong ambivalence, which is an alternation of these intense feeling states. The search for this intense connection, in whatever form psychodynamic patterning causes it to occur, is highly formative of identity. History and literature provide a wealth of testimony to this: The Trojan War, after all, was fought for a woman.

Beyond being driven to action by passion, falling in love may be a form of emergent motivation, an awakening of novel thoughts, feelings, and goals (Csikszentmihalyi, 1980). Thus, Eve's life was transformed by her passion for Arthur. It led her to follow him in whatever way she could, to seek to merge with him. As many poets have suggested, falling in love may be a key to new worlds, new organizations of experience. Merger with a passionately loved Other is a rich source of new interests and new aspects of self.

Eye to Eye Validation

In her classic novel of adolescent identity, *The Member of the Wedding*, Carson McCullers (1946) has her heroine Frankie survey her experience and conclude, "Of all these facts and feelings the strongest of all was the need to be known for her true self and recognized" (p. 74). The need to be known for one's true self and recognized is the essence of eye to eye validation, my fourth dimension. This core relational context of identity has, within psychoanalytic discourse, been explicated most fully by Kohut (1977). In this aspect of relatedness, one finds oneself mirrored in another's eyes. The developmental history of eye to eye contact is learning about how one is responded to by others, and how one's responses to others affect them.

Buber (1965) points out that it is a uniquely human need to require this kind of confirmation:

> An animal does not need to be confirmed, for it is what it is unquestionably. It is different with man: Sent forth from the natural domain of species into the hazard of the solitary category, surrounded by the air of a chaos which came into being with him, secretly and bashfully he watches for a Yes which allows him to be and which can come to him only from one human person to another. (p. 17)

It is through eye to eye contact that we discover our meaning to others and what we can come to believe about ourselves. By becoming real to another we become real to ourselves. Eye to eye contact reflects both a confidence in our own experience, which is what empathy serves, and an awareness of our own qualities, which is what validation is about. Identity must be affirmed.

But one can also be misapprehended, or one can see in others' eyes the wish for one to be other than one is. Through eye to eye contact also comes vulnerability to the emergence of what Winnicott called the false self, falseness residing in an identity that is not one's own. Eye to eye experiences form critical moments of identity growth.

The adolescent is preoccupied with how he or she is seen, discovering in others a mirror of the self. Exquisitely sensitive to his or her image, the adolescent self is always playing to an audience. The adolescent is a data collector of others' reactions, doing research on who he or she is for others. Instances of being criticized, of being rejected, of not being chosen, of being mocked, of not seeming important to others become the crucial episodes of this developmental stage. What is not responded to in the self by real external others may be lost forever. And a negative picture of the self held up to the adolescent may haunt him or her forever, regardless of the goodness of early experience, often regardless of later experience as well.

Eve discovered her writing talent through Arthur's recognition, but it was never realized because her parents could not see or value it. Thus her novel, born out of the loss of her grandmother, nurtured by Arthur's encouragement, died unfinished. In the absence of her parents' recognition, Eve could not take herself seriously as a writer. On the other hand, Arthur's validation of her scholarship helped orient her toward pursuit of a doctoral degree.

In this eye to eye dimension, one also experiences one's meaning to others, the degree to which one matters in the interpersonal world. Kohut speaks of the "gleam in the eye" as a measure of one's meaning for the Other (1966). Looks and gleams are far beyond words; eyes speak more profoundly than language the grammar of relatedness. They express surely and absolutely how much and in what way we matter to the Other. Thus Eve knew that she was her grandfather's favorite and that he loved her and was on her side, even though he rarely spoke.

What we read is a calibration of mattering to which we respond in a profound and authentic way. And this emotional responsiveness becomes a fuel of selfhood. The will to matter may be deeper and more basic than the will to power and may form the fundamental motivation for identity. Thus a late adolescent patient of mine thought of becoming a doctor not out of intellectual curiosity, humanitarian purpose, or even economic acquisitiveness, but because she noticed that doctoring was a way of really being somebody, of being the center of things, taken seriously by others.

The sense of mattering to another is an early form of locating the self. To the young child, the necessity of existence is necessity to one or both parents. Children respond to how much they feel wanted. "No one wants you," is what cruel children say to one another. "You don't even care if I exist," is often the depressed person's expression of despair that his or her existence is justified by his or her value to another. Our need for validation makes our identity always contextual and intersubjective. We are most firmly at home in our identities when we are most certain of what we mean, and that we mean, for others.

Idealization and Identification

A fifth dimension of relatedness is that of idealization and identification, another central aspect of identity development. The adolescent, on the brink of identity, looks to others to provide models for how and what to be. Idealizable objects delimit possibilities for growth, and there is no one more passionately devoted to a hero than the adolescent. Again, this seems not so much a result of ego impoverishment but of the need of the human being to reach toward a goal, most often a goal embodied in or realized by someone else. One young man in a recent study of mine, reflecting on his adolescence, told me that he had spent more time talking to D. H. Lawrence than anyone else. We pattern ourselves using templates derived from others. The capacity to imagine a possible self is in part a function of the capacity to invent those around us.

Failures and excesses of idealizing and identificatory processes can contribute to psychopathology of identity in adolescence. The adolescent who cannot admire, and cannot find a possible self in another, is often an adolescent caught in regressive struggles that leave him or her frightened of growth. At the same time, a too perfectionistic image of the other puts the self under unbearable pressure, and the adolescent feels that he or she can never reach the plane of experience of those he or she would most like to join.

It was one of Erikson's major contributions to point out that identification alone cannot organize human life. His need for the concept of identity was in part the need for a term that would signify the integration of modified and metabolized part-identifications. Identifications are only the building blocks, but they grow out of a relational context. As we attend to the phenomenology of identity in real people's lives, we are struck by the degree to which people move along in the world through relational connection. The development of interests, values, and even careers wends through a narrative of identification, with friends and strangers as well as with parents and teachers. Eve found the study of French literature because of Arthur. Later, she found her way to business through Rita. Still later, she looked to Janet for clues about how to be a mother. Identifications, then, are bootstraps as well as building blocks of identity. People pull themselves along through life in an often checkered fashion, based on identificatory ties to others.

Idealized others can also be an organizing context of identity. Kohut thought that idealizable self-objects, that is, people who embody ideals that we can internalize and reach toward, are necessary for primary narcissism to be transformed into goals and purpose. Idealizable others empower the self. Without heroes, life loses meaning. The incapacity to idealize leads to identity failure and ultimately to despair.

Mutuality and Resonance

The sixth dimension of relatedness, mutuality and resonance, involves needs for sharing of experience that neither shore up one's concept of self nor lead to growth-producing changes. In mutuality is the expression of identity, the putting of the self forward into the space between selves where it can intermingle with other selves and be itself.

Early in life, as the self matures and becomes more aware of others, the child will eventually discover the possibilities of engaging the self with others and will become able to experience companionship, which is a form of mutuality. In mutuality, we stand side by side with someone, moving in harmony, creating a bond that is the product of both people, an emergent "we" in the space between. In mutuality, we come together, not for merging but for connection.

Affective mutuality provides a necessary sense of vitality that mitigates existential aloneness. It is this sense of "us," a participation in the space between a "you" and a "me," that connects us in a deeper and richer sense of our existence. And this, of all the dimensions, is the hardest to talk about, partly because it exists so completely between selves.

Eve talks about her best friend, Vicki, who has always been there to talk to. She doesn't say that Vicki changed her in any way, just that knowing that her experience was shared by another, that it could resonate in another person, made Eve more able to be who she was. Similarly, later in her life, Eve found mutuality in a group of mothers with whom she had been meeting for some years. With them, she could talk about her feelings and her fantasies, and she could count on them to respond with their own painful or frightening experiences.

When we are most in touch with our experience of identity, we are most likely to want to resonate with others; this, Tolstoy taught, is the function of art.

Embeddedness

The seventh dimension of relatedness, embeddedness, is at the heart of the identity formation task of adolescence, and we owe much to

Erikson here. Embeddedness involves finding and taking a place with others; it encompasses belonging. This is one of the central questions posed by adolescents. What shall I stand for? How will I fit in? Where might there be a place for me?

Embeddedness, once achieved is, like holding and attachment, silent rather than active and eventful. It is the framework that gives shape to selfhood, the context in which we define ourselves, the togetherness in which we are alone. The issues of embeddedness are the issues of the individual in group life.

The relationships of embeddedness are the relationships of social existence that connect us to all the people whom we may not notice being there, but whose presence makes our existence possible. In defining the context of all relatedness, our embeddedness in a social context limits and gives meaning to all of our other relationships and endeavors. Embeddedness is the soil in which identity grows and is continually refined and redefined.

Erikson's concept of identity grapples with the individual joining society by making the self a part of the social world and, simultaneously, making the social world a part of the self. We are embedded in our culture, which is embedded in us, creating a sense of identity that, if firm and well integrated, organizes us to such an extent that we become unaware of it. We belong, we are connected, we are in the world that is in us. We have a socially based perch from which we will experience the world (with others).

Our language expresses our embeddedness in one nation or another; our accent within that language identifies our social class or place of origin; our choice of vocabulary links us to certain subgroups. We speak from our place within a society. No wonder, then, that adolescents, about to claim identity, are so sensitive to modes of speech—and may indeed, for a time, adopt a special subgroup language that helps to define their place.

To be embedded within a social network is to belong, to feel included, to share characteristics, to be the same as, to give up some individuality in the service of interconnection. To embed ourselves, we must learn social conventions beyond language: customs, mores, manners. We learn to conform our behavior to our group.

When one belongs, one merely fits in, undramatically, harmoniously. Identity is taken for granted. The moral of Hans Christian Anderson's story about the ugly duckling is that the conspicuous deviant is really just a swan and indeed has a context elsewhere, where it is unremarkable. In a group of ducks, the swan was vilified and rejected. With other swans, however, it would be simply taken for granted. Embeddedness, then, is the phenomenological sense of being just another swan among swans. The danger of not being embedded is to be isolated or ostracized, to be without a group.

The individual who wishes to belong but does not belong may have an intense sense of yearning, feeling left out of the ongoing process of human life. Again from *The Member of the Wedding,* Carson McCullers has her protagonist, Frankie, express this wish poignantly as a wish for "the we of me." Frankie's wish is to feel herself deeply a member, deeply connected. This is how McCullers expresses it:

> [S]he had only been Frankie. She was an "I" person who had to walk around and do things by herself. All other people had a "we" to claim, all others except her. When Berenice said "we," she meant Honey and Big Mama, her lodge or her church. The "we" of her father was the store. All members of clubs have a "we" to belong to and talk about. The soldiers in the army can say "we." And even the criminals on chain-gangs. But . . . Frankie had no "we" to claim.

This yearning to belong, then, is distinct from attachment or holding or validation or the other dimensions of relatedness. The "we of me" involves the linkage of the self to the larger social environment, the interdependence of the self on the social world for mutual definition. Here, one is oneself with others. Thus, we witness Eve joining a mothers' group, volunteering in the school library, attending PTA meetings, anchoring her motherhood in the broader social context. (We might also note that it is meaningful in terms of her identity that she does not belong to the Modern Languages Association.)

In less restrictive societies, people have more and more latitude about the forms of embeddedness open to them. People can be born poor and still aspire to join the exclusive country club or the prestigious professional society. In these more fluid societies, embeddedness becomes a form of identity formation: People come to be identified by society as being like those with whom they join. Adolescents are particularly sensitive to these processes, labeling and classifying each other like the most assiduous entomologist. This one is an athlete, that one a pothead, the other a brain or a geek or whatever category of adolescent language arises to fill the need.

Development in adult life often involves changing contexts of embeddedness. Midlife crises create disjunction with one's group, and an effort to search for another group whose rituals and symbolic life are more compatible with aspects of the self. The successful resolution of such a crisis of embeddedness is a deep sense of "Here, with this group of people, is where I belong." In such experiences, one feels profoundly at one with one's identity.

Tending (Care)

The eighth and final dimension of relatedness that I will discuss is that of tending and care. This is a dimension that is seldom talked about in relation to identity, especially to the extent that we regard identity as resting on the tracks of autonomy and individuality.

Although Erikson assigned tending its own developmental stage, under the name of Generativity, he also says that identity is synonymous with what one chooses to tend (1964). Our statement in declaring what we will stand for in life, our identity, in other words, is a statement about what we will look after. I would add to this that it is not just the *what* but the *who* that is central here. Because of our long tenure in childhood of being the object of care and solicitude, our longing is to grow into one who can be the source of what is so much valued. Erikson suggests that we create all-caring gods not only out of "persisting infantile need for being taken care of, but also [as] a projection onto a superhuman agency of an ego-ideal" (p. 131). We aspire, in this view, to the godliness of giving.

Carol Gilligan (1977, 1982) had enormous impact on the field of psychology by directing our attention to the ethic of care and responsibility as an organizer of experience. Taking issue with the exclusive focus on fairness and rights as central tenets of moral development, Gilligan showed how women's development often resides in the deepening of their understanding of care. Concern for and sensitivity to others, in conjunction with the responsibility for taking care, lead women to attend to voices other than their own in forming judgment. Moral awareness becomes an effort to orchestrate and be responsive to people's needs, rather than residing in allegiance to abstract principles. And this, Gilligan maintains, is where female identity so often diverges from male: Ethicality in women is fundamentally interpersonal, "defined in a context of relationship and judged by a standard of responsibility and care" (1982, p. 160).

Taking care can involve not only taking care of persons but also taking care of a relationship. Identity may reside in the effort to preserve and nurture relatedness, much as we see in the priorities of Eve. When asked about what is central in her life, after all, Eve relates the carpool schedules and her children's activities. The watershed experiences of her adult life were the birth of her first child and the illness of another. Despite her professional credentials and talents, her identity was rooted in her complex connections to others, and her efforts to sustain and enhance those relationships.

Conclusion

Viewed in the context of relatedness, identity emerges not from increasing separation and distinction from others but from the continually redefined capacity to make use of and to respond to others. People grow within relationships that change as a result of their growth, leading them to further differentiation that is observable as identity development. The crucial events that people recount in their odysseys of identity are usually fundamentally relational, rooted in ongoing efforts to affirm themselves in relationship, to express themselves with others while taking account of others' needs and interests, to recognize and resolve conflict, and to learn to live with unresolvable conflict while still sustaining connection. Identity is an integration of ways of "being with" others with ways of "being with" oneself.

Many aspects of relatedness sustain identity and provide a context for its growth and expression. Such an expansion of identity theory has been necessary to make sense of the experience of women and adolescents, but it may also enrich our understanding of male development as well. The relational, connected sense of identity is a higher order concept that subsumes and supplants the autonomous, separated self with which psychology has long lived. Needs for holding, attachment, and embeddedness provide the framework for identity, the outline and base within which people think about, feel about, and realize themselves. Eye to eye validation is the process by which people match their sense of themselves with recognition provided by others. Idealization and identification serve as the bootstraps for becoming, and the libidinal needs contained in passionate experience fuel self-expression. Finally, in mutuality and in tending is the expression of identity, being and sharing with others, investing the self in ever more complex interactions of extension and reception, engaging what feels most oneself in the relational world, in the space between.

Identity, then, is both cause and consequence of the relational world. The contexts of relatedness empower identity, which in turn finds expression only in some form of connection to others. Empirically, we must regard identity in its relational context; one finds, claims, and expresses one's place only in a web of relationships.

6

Identity and Development

A Narrative Perspective

GUY A. M. WIDDERSHOVEN

Identity and development are problematic concepts. The notion of the individual as a center of awareness and action, which was for a long time the core of the concept of identity, is questioned by present-day philosophers. The notion of progress, often associated with the concept of development, has recently been questioned. It may seem philosophers have undermined the foundations of a whole field of psychological research by questioning the concepts of identity and development. This conclusion is, however, premature. In fact, it may be argued that many areas of developmental psychology were already freeing themselves from individualism, and from a belief in universal progress, before philosophers became involved in the debate. Instead of marking the end of psychological theorizing on identity and development, recent trends in philosophy may aid existing discussions within psychology and place current research in a new light.

A concept that appears to be central in both present-day philosophy and in the human sciences is that of narrative. Philosophers present the notion of narrative as an alternative to individual consciousness (MacIntyre, 1981; Ricoeur, 1983). They stress that narratives are more than tales about human existence, because human life itself is narratively organized. Narratives do not reflect reality; human reality itself takes the form of a narrative. In psychology, the importance of narrative is stressed by

Bruner (1986). He distinguishes a narrative from a paradigmatic mode of thought. The paradigmatic mode of thinking tries to mirror reality, whereas the narrative mode of thinking is incorporated in the life it recounts. Psychologists have also used the concept of narrative to explain central aspects of human behavior (Sarbin, 1986). MacAdams (1985) defines identity as an internalized narrative integration of past, present, and future that provides life with a sense of unity.

The notion of narrative may serve as a link between present-day philosophy and developmental psychology in that it offers a nonindividualistic and nonprogressive image of human existence. This image may serve as a foundation for current psychological research. In the following I will first give a sketch of narrative in contemporary philosophy. Then I will turn to psychology and present a narrative model of development, comparing it to the mechanistic and the organismic models (see also Widdershoven, 1988, 1994). Next, I will describe three types of narrative identity, using illustrations from fiction. Finally, I will investigate some current approaches in life span developmental psychology and explain them in terms of narrative identity.

Narrative in Contemporary Philosophy

Modern philosophy, in contrast to premodern philosophy, places heavy emphasis on the role of consciousness. Kant examines consciousness in order to find the transcendental presuppositions of knowledge. According to Kant, the possibility of knowledge is grounded in the activity of consciousness. Our knowledge of the physical world does not stem directly from the world itself, it is structured by our concepts of time, space, and causality. We order and understand reality through consciousness.

Present-day philosophy is still a part of the Kantian legacy in that it is interested in the presuppositions of knowledge, and it acknowledges that (physical?) reality itself is not the base of knowledge. Contrary to Kant, however, emphasis is no longer placed on consciousness, but on language. The concepts that structure knowledge are not situated in individual consciousness, they are part of language and social life (see Widdershoven, 1991). The concepts of time, space, and causality are founded on our participation in a shared social world. It may seem as though the shift in emphasis from consciousness to language is simply a change from one principle to the other, in which both remain the same.

This, however, is not the case. The shift implies that consciousness itself has a linguistic structure, and that one experiences the world through language.

The shift from consciousness to language has generated specific attention to the concept of narrative in contemporary philosophy. Philosophers from various backgrounds stress the importance of narratives in human life. People interpret reality by telling stories, both in everyday life and in science and philosophy. Human knowledge is an interpretation of reality, it gives meaning to reality, it is a story about reality. This idea can be found in Anglo-Saxon philosophy (analytic philosophy and pragmatism) as well as in Continental philosophy (hermeneutics and deconstruction).

Although the importance of narratives, as ways of knowing the world, is acknowledged by many present-day philosophers, disagreement exists on the relationship between narratives and reality. This disagreement is very clearly illustrated in the philosophy of history. Some theorists argue for a sharp distinction between narrative and reality. They say that the historical past itself is just a series of events without an intelligible pattern, and that it is only through the narratives of the historian that the past becomes meaningful. This position, which is known as the *discontinuity thesis*, is defended by Mink, who says: "Stories are not lived, but told" (1987, p. 60). The discontinuity thesis is also supported by White (1981). Other theorists argue a continuity between the historical past and the narratives of the historian. According to Carr (1986), human life is already a meaningful unity before it is studied by the historian. He agrees with Barbara Hardy, who says in a famous dictum (which elicited Mink's statement, quoted above): "We dream in narrative, daydream in narrative, remember, anticipate, hope, despair, believe, doubt, plan, revise, criticize, construct, gossip, learn, hate and love by narrative" (Hardy, 1968, p. 5).

There surely is a difference between life as it is lived and life as presented in novels, history, or psychology. Still it seems that the defenders of the discontinuity thesis overlook the fact that living a human life always implies a certain ordering of reality, making sense of reality, giving meaning to it in socially organized practices. Every human activity is in a sense narrative in that it expresses a way of being, of experiencing the world as meaningful. This argument is developed by MacIntyre (1981), who states that human actions can be regarded as enacted narratives. A related, though somewhat different, position is taken by Ricoeur (1983). According to him human experience shows a primordial narrativity. It embodies a quest for meaning, which is made explicit in stories. In this regard Ricoeur introduces the notion of a prenarrative structure of experience. According to MacIntyre and Ricoeur, the relation between life and story is hermeneutic, in that the implicit meaning of life is made explicit through stories (see Widdershoven, 1992).

Both MacIntyre and Ricoeur discuss the consequences of a narrative view of human action for the concept of personal identity. Personal identity is a problematic concept, in that it shows aspects of strict identity on one hand (I am the same person, bearing the same name, during my whole life) and aspects of a changing identity on the other (I am not exactly the same person at age 20 and at age 50 when one considers my psychological characteristics). According to MacIntyre the notion of narrative makes it possible to combine these two aspects in a meaningful way. He says: "What is crucial to human beings as characters in enacted narratives is that, possessing only the resources of psychological continuity, we have to be able to respond to the imputations of strict identity" (MacIntyre, 1981, p. 202). Personal identity is the result of presenting one's actions as part of a meaningful totality and, consequently, presenting oneself to others as the subject of a personal history. In a discussion of MacIntyre's views, Ricoeur introduces the notion of a global plan of life, which structures separate practices and is modified by them. Contrary to MacIntyre, however, he stresses the difference between the (prenarrative) organization of life itself and the (narrative) structure of novels. He states that MacIntyre underestimates the importance of a refiguration of life in fiction, and says that a "detour through fiction" may help us understand the relations between action and person (Ricoeur, 1990, p. 187). Although Ricoeur disagrees with MacIntyre on the relevance of the distinction between literature and real life, they both agree that personal identity is related to the activity of structuring one's actions and presenting them as part of a lived narrative.

The upshot of this philosophical discussion on narrative and its place in human life is that narrative is fundamental to human existence in two ways. First, human existence is narratively structured in that it is an organized totality structured by a global plan of life. Human life presents itself as a lived story that can be understood. Second, this lived unity may be expressed in narratives, which make the implicit story of life explicit, and thus contribute to the organization of life. A narrative perspective on human life entails that life is a meaningful totality, which can be expressed in stories and is enriched as it is expressed in stories.

In the following I will investigate the fruitfulness of the comprehensive notion of narrative and narrative identity, as developed by MacIntyre and Ricoeur, for the psychological study of the development of identity. First I will introduce a narrative model of development as an alternative for the well-known mechanistic and organismic models (Overton & Reese, 1973). Later I will analyze several examples of a narrative approach in actual psychological research.

Models of Development

In their discussion of models of development, Overton and Reese (1973) focus on philosophical and methodological implications. I will follow the same line, elaborating upon the fundamental notions of each model, the corresponding type of explanation, and the possibility of making predictions.

Before presenting the three models of development, I will first specify the notion of development (see also Van Haaften & Korthals, forthcoming). Development is related to change. If something develops, it has to show change. Furthermore, development implies structural change. There has to be a qualitative change from one organizational structure (or stage) to the next. The notion of development does not necessarily include the notion of progress. A later stage may be preferable to a former one, but it may also show substantial losses compared to earlier stages. Finally, development is not necessarily brought about by internal processes; it may very well take place in interaction with an external context.

The Mechanistic Model

In the mechanistic model human beings are seen as mechanisms, behaving according to natural laws. It is characteristic for a mechanism that its parts can be separately described and explained. In an explanation of the behavior of elements of the mechanism, an event is causally related to prior events, which can be described without reference to the event to be explained. Genetic and environmental factors are seen as causes of moral development. It is presupposed that, under the same circumstances, equal causes have equal effects.

Central to the mechanistic model is the so-called deductive-nomological explanation. An event is considered to be explained if it can be deduced from other events with the help of a universal law. A universal law says that under specific conditions, certain events necessarily follow one another. The necessity in this case is physical: B necessarily follows A, given the structure of physical reality. The relationship between A and B is causal: A is the cause of B. The universality of the law enhances the possibility of counterfactual statements. Even if A and B do not occur, one may say: If A had occurred, B would have followed.

Deductive-nomological explanations afford exact predictions. If the relevant factors are known, the outcome can be exactly foretold. Although in the mechanistic model everything can in principle be totally predicted, a prediction doesn't always come true, because there may be some relevant factors that have been overlooked.

Within the mechanistic model development is the change from one state of affairs to another one, through internal and external causes. This means that one cannot distinguish qualitatively different stages in a proper way. The mechanistic model does not include the notion of qualitative change, because processes of nature are considered to be uniform and linear. One cannot distinguish a developmental pattern from a mechanistic point of view. This of course does not mean that such a pattern, once it is described, can in no way be explained in a deductive-nomological way. On the contrary, the proponent of the mechanistic model will hold that every change, including so-called stage transitions, can be explained causally.

The Organismic Model

In the organismic model human beings are regarded as biological organisms. An organism characteristically has a certain structure or organization. The organism is oriented toward a goal: maintenance and reproduction. All the different parts of the organism have a function in that they contribute to the attainment of this goal. Different parts of the organism cannot be described or explained apart from the whole. Processes that take place in parts of the organism can be explained in terms of their function in the survival of the entire organism.

In the organismic model of development, explanation is functional. One doesn't ask for the cause but for the purpose of the phenomenon to be explained. Phenomenon A is explained by showing that it is functional to phenomenon B. For instance, the emergence of lungs can be explained by noticing that lungs guarantee the intake of oxygen, which is essential to life and growth. Although it is assumed that A (the lungs) lead to B (the intake of oxygen), the point of the explanation is not that

B is the result of A, but that A has a specific role with regard to B and that B makes A intelligible.

In contrast to a deductive-nomological explanation, a functional explanation lacks total predictability. The intake of oxygen may be secured in different ways. Bertalanffy mentions in this regard the so-called principle of equifinality, which means that a goal may be reached along different lines (Bertalanffy, 1968, p.139).

Clearly there is room for a concept of development in terms of stage transitions in the organismic model. The organismic approach is interested in structural changes, and the notion of developmental pattern is central to the organismic model. The organismic model is, however, not the only model of development that makes use of the concepts of structural change. This also holds for our third model, to which we will now turn.

The Narrative Model

In the narrative model human beings are seen as persons who express themselves in terms of stories and whose actions can be regarded as elements of a story. A story is characteristically presented as a meaningful totality. Different passages make reference to one another, contribute to the meaning of the story, and derive their meaning from the whole. The organization of a story, its narrative structure, offers us a consistent and convincing history.

In the narrative model the story is not only a metaphor, but also part of the model, in that stories are eminent ways of self-representation. From a narrative perspective a person expresses himself or herself both in his or her actions and in the stories he or she tells about them. The narrative structure of life is made up of experiences as well as stories. Because stories articulate the implicit meaning of experiences, life and story are internally related (Widdershoven, 1993).

In the narrative model explanation takes the form of interpretation or hermeneutic understanding. An interpretative or hermeneutic explanation reveals the meaning of a phenomenon by showing the context in which it is to be understood. Thus an element of a story is related to the meaning of the story as a whole. The interpretation implies a hermeneutic circle in which part and whole clarify one another (cf. Gadamer, 1960, pp. 178, 250, 275). Every interpretation is also an application (Gadamer, 1960, p. 290). In interpreting a story we not only take into account what it signifies for our present situation, but are also oriented toward the truth it expresses. An interpretative explanation stresses the rationality of the interpretandum.

In the narrative model, meaning is dependent upon interpretation. The meaning of a story takes shape in a dialogue between the story and the interpreter. Each story is part of a history of interpretation, an ongoing effective history (*Wirkungsgeschichte*; see Gadamer, 1960, p. 284). In this history of interpretation the narrative structure of the story may change radically. A new interpretation may focus on elements neglected thus far and explicate relations between elements that were hitherto implicit. This may result in a new and richer narrative unity. In the history of interpretation the meaning of the story changes.

In the narrative model there is no room for exact predictions. Although we can explain certain expressions by showing that they make sense within a specific context (the narrative structure), we cannot predict their occurrence, because a context does not determine the figure that fits into it. Because the meaning of an element in a story can never be fully determined, its contribution to the creation of narrative unity cannot be established once and for all. An element that may seem unimportant at first may later appear to be crucial. As the meaning of the entire story is never totally given, the narrative structure may be rearranged in subsequent processes of interpretation. This unpredictability does not make the story purely contingent. The unity of a story is not just a matter of coincidence. It is the result of an ongoing process of presentation and interpretation.

Within the narrative model development is seen as a qualitative change in narrative structure. Human development thus implies a fundamental change in the pattern organizing a person's expressions. The story a person presents to others, both in performing actions and in accounting for them, is arranged in a new way. Both the new narrative pattern and the old one are seen as meaningful. Moreover, the change from the old pattern to the new one can also be regarded as meaningful, because the new pattern is supposed to create a richer unity. A change in narrative structure is not something that is simply there to be observed. It is created by the effective history of the story, which makes specific elements more visible. This means that development is not independent of its interpretation. Developmental steps are made explicit in interpretations and they cannot exist without them. From a narrative perspective, developmental theory is not a description of development, but it is an explication, which itself contributes to the phenomenon being investigated.

Three Types of Narrative Identity

The narrative model may not seem very common in actual research practice in psychology. It is, however, used more or less implicitly in many studies of developmental theory. This will be illustrated later on. First I will further specify the notion of narrative identity and distinguish several types.

From a narrative perspective personal identity is related to the activity of structuring one's actions and presenting them as part of a lived narrative. Thus, personal identity can be compared to the unity of a story. A story may, however, show various kinds of unity. The elements of a story may be integrated into a rigid pattern, or they may be bound together more loosely. At the end of the story all the pieces may fall into the right place, or a sense of ambiguity and uncertainty may remain. A story with a decisive conclusion does not necessarily show more unity than one that is open-ended. An open end may contribute to the meaning of some stories just as much as a clear conclusion does in the case of other stories. Stories show various kinds of narrative unity; consequently, one may distinguish various types of narrative identity, depending on the specific kind of unity they show.

One literary genre is especially suited as a model for identity, namely the detective novel. A detective novel describes a process of meaning making, a search for truth and coherence. I will illustrate various types of narrative identity with examples from detective literature.

The Closed Type

The first type of narrative identity may be defined as closed. It corresponds to a story that has a clear end in which all the threads are woven together. The unity of the story is achieved through a series of events contributing to the final outcome, the apotheosis. Each step in the story neatly fits into the total scheme. A closed identity is reached by a process of integration. Every action and every passion is part of the final arrangement. Life is seen as a coherent totality; there are no discontinuities and no deviations. What at first seemed to be an aberration turns out to be a necessary step in the end. The meaning of various elements in life may not be clear from the very beginning, but eventually they all come into perspective. The closed type of identity develops without deep crises; nothing is really new or surprising.

An example of the closed type of narrative can be found in Agatha Christie's detective novels. In a typical Christie case there is a master plan, which has to be discovered. Everything is part of the scheme; there is no detail that does not fit. In *And Then There Were None* (Christie, 1964), the murderer has planned all of the executions beforehand, leaving nothing to chance. In every Christie story there is only one solution to the riddle, although there may be several factors involved, as can be seen in *Murder on the Orient Express* (Christie, 1987), where it turns out that the victim is killed not by one but by all of the suspects. A Christie case always has a definite end. *Murder on the Orient Express* seems to be an exception, because Poirot offers two solutions. It is, however, clear that only one of them really matches the facts, whereas the other is just a nice construction. Poirot knows that the first solution is the right one, but advises the second one for reasons of convenience. A Christie case is always puzzling, but never really shocking. The world in which Poirot lives is well ordered. It takes only an intelligent mind to see through the apparent chaos.

The Open Type

The second type of narrative identity may be called open. It has the characteristics of an open story, which does not reach a final conclusion. Within an open story, several events are related in an intelligible way, but the unity thus created is only one of a variety of possible connections. The story shows a pattern, but the possibility that things might have happened differently is left open. There is no master plan in which all events are anticipated. Meaning is built up gradually. The story consists of a whole series of events that are individually insignificant but together result in an intelligible structure. An open identity is formed through various actions and passions, which are coherent because they all show one specific style. The development of an open identity has the character of a quest. It shows crucial changes, accompanied by crises.

Some good examples of the open type of narrative can be found in the work of Georges Simenon. In his Maigret novels, crimes are the result of trivial events in ordinary life, events that easily might have taken another direction. Still, they are not meaningless. Crimes are intelligible, not because they are the work of an ingenious mind, but because they follow from the situation. In the novels, the meaning of the crimes is gradually made explicit. In *Maigret et le Clochard* (Simenon, 1963),

Maigret tries to see life through the eyes of the clochard [tramp], who is brutally attacked, by playing with the marbles found in the victim's pocket. He spends the evening at the assailant's ship, attempting to understand the stifling climate. Finally he perceives a pattern: The clochard had by chance witnessed a crime on board the ship, and although he did not wish to denounce the crime, because he was no longer engaged in social life (for him life was just a game of marbles), he still was a potential danger to the shipper and thus had to be suppressed. Interestingly, the novel does not end at this point. Although Maigret has discovered the facts, he is not able to prove them, because the shipper keeps denying, and the clochard, who has regained consciousness, does not want to denounce the assailant. Thus the story has an open end. This is also the case in other Maigret novels. Even if the story ends with a confession, Simenon often alludes to the custody and the trial, during which the bond between Maigret and the criminal will be broken, and the crime will receive a new meaning. A Maigret novel usually shows critical turns. The investigation is characterized by changes in the attitude of Maigret and that of the criminal. They get involved with one another during the story. In trying to understand each other, each one puts his or her view of life at risk. For Maigret the meaning of life is not given, but created by his encounter with the criminal.

The Radically Open Type

The third type of narrative identity may be called radically open. It corresponds to postmodern narratives, in which the notion of a distinct story is fundamentally undermined, and replaced by an endless tale with innumerable variations. Within postmodern novels the elements may be related in various ways. There is no overall plan that determines the cause of events. There is not even a distinctive pattern that makes the story intelligible as a whole. Within a radically open identity there are no patterns of life that may connect various incidents. Life is contingent. There is not one logic that accounts for every event, and many aspects of the situation will remain unintelligible forever. Within such a life, there is no longer a distinction between important and unimportant events. In a way, everything is new and challenging. Consequently, there are numerous possible crises that may radically change life.

A good example of the radically open type of narrative unity can be found in the novel *The Name of the Rose,* by Umberto Eco (1983). The book starts with what seems to be a clear-cut event with a specific meaning. William of Baskerville, the detective figure in the novel, is able to infer that the monks he encounters are looking for a valuable horse. Later on, however, William explicitly states that his success was dependent on his ability to make the monks believe that he was clever and that he just as easily might have failed in doing so. In the monastery, William is confronted with a series of crimes. He tries to make sense of what happens by looking for a pattern that might explain every crime. In the end, however, he realizes that there was no pattern behind the various murders. The master plan that might explain all events was not there, or better: There was a person who had tried to make such a plan, but who was unable to keep things under control. William discovers the murderers, not by reconstructing their ingenious plans (they are either nonexistent or ineffective), nor by understanding their lives, but by following his own line of reasoning and by arguing with everybody who opposes his ideas. In the end it is hard to say whether he has succeeded or failed. He has succeeded insofar as the various murderers are discovered. He has failed, however, in that the monastery, whose good name he had to protect, becomes an object of scandal and is physically destroyed.

Three Approaches Within Life Span Developmental Psychology

In recent years the notion of narrative has become one of the central themes in life span developmental psychology. It is generally acknowledged that people have life stories and that developmental psychology must investigate how people organize their lives as narrative unities. Life span developmental psychology makes use of the notion of narrative, as proposed by philosophers like MacIntyre and Ricoeur. The narrative model of development is one in which development takes place as a qualitative change in narrative patterns. The notion of identity is also narrative in that the unity of life is seen as the result of structuring one's life as a meaningful totality. Within life span developmental psychology, however, the notion of narrative unity has various meanings. It may be interpreted as closed, open, or radically open. Consequently, various approaches within life span developmental theory may be distinguished according to the type of narrative identity they represent.

The Ageless Self

The closed type of narrative identity seems to be rare in life span developmental psychology, because the idea of an overall scheme integrating various life events into a rigid system has been widely discredited. Still there are authors who use the notion of a closed identity more or less explicitly. An example is Kaufman, who wrote a book titled *The Ageless Self* (1986). The title is significant: According to Kaufman, identities of persons are not based on notions of age but on perceptions of continuity in identity through life. She focuses on values that are held for a lifetime, despite the changes that occur in one's physical or social condition. She analyzes several life stories, recorded through semistructured interviews, and concludes: "The themes that emerge from these stories illustrate the individual's ability to reformulate lifelong values so that they (1) take on new meaning in old age, (2) promote a sense of continuity of self, and (3) contribute to an integrated and salient account of the life story" (Kaufman, 1986, p. 148). According to Kaufman, people integrate everything they encounter in their life within a unified system that consists of a few basic values. Her theory of identity in late life shows all the characteristics of the closed type of narrative identity.

The Identity Status Approach

A different notion of identity is presented in the well-known work of Erikson and in its continuation by Marcia. According to Erikson (1959), various stages in identity development are characterized by various choices. Thus the values around which a person's life is organized are not stable, but are subject to fundamental change. Adolescence is the only period during which individuals are exposed to a tension between identity achievement and identity diffusion. In this period of life ego identity emerges. Other phases of life are centered around other oppositions, such as Trust versus Mistrust, Initiative versus Guilt, or Integrity versus Despair. For Erikson, each individual is confronted with various fundamental problems, which can only be solved through crises. Marcia (1966) has elaborated upon the crisis of adolescence. He distinguishes four ego identity statuses, or styles used in dealing with the identity crisis. The statuses are described in terms of crisis and commitment. The Identity Achievement status is defined by clear commitments following a period of crisis. The Moratorium is a period of crisis with only vague commitments. Foreclosure is characterized by commitment without previous crisis. Identity Diffusion shows a lack of commitment without actual crisis. Both Erikson and Marcia describe identity as a narrative unity. Their descriptions fit into the open type of narrative identity. Development of identity is a quest, which brings one through severe crises. It may take different paths, depending on social circumstances and individual experiences. The choices made during earlier phases of development make those in later phases intelligible without determining them. Later phases are congruent with earlier ones without totally integrating them. The use of the notion of style by Marcia is also in line with the open type of narrative identity. A style expresses a unity that is neither preconceived nor contingent. Even if the style itself is rigid (as it is in the identity status of Foreclosure), it is never totally binding and immutable. Thus the notion of identity as used by Marcia can be qualified as open, even if some of the stages he describes are more or less closed.

Stress and Coping

Recently, stress psychology has made its way into life span developmental psychology. Stress psychologists exemplify yet another type of narrative identity. They start from the idea that changes are a potential threat to physical and psychological well-being. Individuals must acquire strategies, called coping skills, for dealing with such changes. For a long time the attention of stress psychologists was directed toward so-called important life events. These events, which include marriage, birth of children, death of relatives, retirement, and death of the partner, were seen as possible causes of stress. Gradually, the list of potentially stressful events became longer and longer. It now includes ordinary events, such as going to the dentist or losing a game (Reese & Smyer, 1983). Consequently, life is a continuous process of meaning making that is highly variable. Lazarus, the most important author on stress and coping, sketches an image of life that is characterized by individual variation (Lazarus & DeLongis, 1983). He emphasizes that people tend to get more upset by "daily hassles" than by dramatic events. According to him life is a "continuous story line," which shows large variations in personal agendas and conditions of life. The image of life fostered by stress psychologists corresponds to the radically open type of narrative identity. It consists of numerous crises without scheme or pattern. A person's life story is a continuous tale of larger or smaller successes and failures without an end or even a tentative conclusion.

Conclusion

Far from being obsolete, the notions of identity and development fit well into the narrative turn that is characteristic of present-day philosophy. Various theories within life span developmental psychology make use of the narrative model of development, according to which development may be described as a change in structures of meaning making and identity as narrative unity. Within developmental psychology we may, however, distinguish different kinds of narrative approaches, depending on the type of narrative identity in view. These types can be described as closed, open, or radically open. These different narrative approaches can be regarded as expressions of modern life in very much the same way as various detective novels give an image of modern social relations. Theories based on the closed type of identity reflect a clear social order, which corresponds to the picture of life in Agatha Christie's novels. In such a social order every person has a strict role. Theories that exhibit an open type of identity are in accordance with a social order that is more intricate, but still intelligible. This kind of order presupposes that individuals make their own choices more or less deliberately, such as described in the novels of Simenon. Theories that present a radically open type of identity are expressions of social relations that are radically contingent. These kinds of social relations are characteristic of a highly individualized society. They are illustrated in the work of Eco. As reflections of modern life, developmental theories do not describe universal, ahistorical developmental stages. On the contrary, they show us various tendencies in our time and make us aware of the various problems individuals have to solve within our society.

PART III

History and Literature

HAROLD D. GROTEVANT
HARKE A. BOSMA

From the point of view of a historian, the entire contemporary discourse on identity occurs at a specific moment in Western history and under very specific conditions. In many ways the discourse on identity follows the evolution of social, political, and economic structures. The fact that the conference from which this volume was derived was conducted in English says something about both the concept of identity and the cultural politics in Europe. The discourse on identity since the Second World War has been dominated by American traditions, exemplified by such a key figure as Erik Erikson. The historical disintegration of many traditional structures has raised questions about personal identity that psychologists and psychiatrists are attempting to resolve.

Historians try to understand and write about the past. In doing this the concept of identity is sometimes used for questions of collective identity, the emergence of a specific ethnic, religious, local group, or national identity in a specific place at a specific time. An important

---

AUTHORS' NOTE: Some of the text of this introduction relies heavily on the comments made by Professors Neubauer and Mitzman during the conference. The editors thank them both for reviewing this section for its accuracy, as the fields of historical analysis and literary criticism are outside those represented by the team of coeditors. Although the input of Neubauer and Mitzman was highly valuable, the editors must assume responsibility for any errors in interpretation.

aspect of collective identity is the way in which certain groups are viewed by certain other groups. For example, how are lower-class groups viewed by upper-class groups, and what effect has this on their awareness of their own identity? This example can easily be extended, in space and time, to a broad gamut of different questions of collective identity, such as regional, peripheral identities versus central, national identities. Examples of such peripheral identities are the Provençal and Celtic identities. In general there is the assumption that in these local, decentralized, popular (in contrast to elite, dominant), cultures, there is a certain immobility or static quality. Time does not actually make any kind of major change, whereas the elite culture changes paradigms at least once every generation. For historians this question of popular and elite culture is important: What is the identity of the popular culture of a particular place? Thus, studies of 17th-century villages make the argument that their mentalities can be perfectly well understood by going to a comparable deliterate of that village today and finding the archaic elements. This is all about collective identity.

Questions raised in this part of the book seek to explore how human existence is shaped either by impersonal historical forces or by the exertion of individual control. The sociological approach, asking to what degree an identity is stamped upon the individual, has dominated this tradition. However, Neubauer's contribution (Chapter 7) is an excellent example of an analysis that focuses on the interaction between the external, historical-cultural conditions and the internal, psychological changes of individual characters. The author claims that preoccupation with adolescence was a hallmark of turn-of-the-century culture, and he asks, as a literary critic, by what artistic, and specifically narrative, means writers have portrayed crises of identity during adolescence.

Such historical issues acquire a new meaning within the context of contemporary, postmodern developments in philosophy and literature, which question the traditional notions of the subject, its development and identity. If the modernists portrayed adolescence as a crisis within a succession of relatively stable forms of identity, postmodernists no longer perceive identity as a norm, or standard against which crises could be defined. The diffusion and splitting of identity now become the norm, and the various phases and transitions can no longer be described in terms of a development. As a consequence, postmodern fiction questions and often denies the possibility of storytelling altogether.

In his chapter, "Problems of Identity in Modernist Fiction," Neubauer uses the novel, *Silbermann,* by Lacretelle (1983), to illustrate how the identity crisis began being depicted as a defining feature of adolescence in turn-of-the-century Europe. His contribution to this volume explores the role of peer relations in shaping the personal identity of the novel's protagonist, but also examines the simultaneous contributions of ethnic and cultural identity. The chapter then moves to another level, analyzing the text from the perspective of the identity between the author and the narrator of the story. Neubauer notes that, prior to the second half of the 19th century, the literary device of the omniscient narrator was typically used, emphasizing the correspondence between the knowledge held by the author and that held by the narrator. Toward the end of the 19th century, these perspectives were more often differentiated. Another way in which the perspective of historical time is discussed concerns the trend toward creating temporal distance between the experience of the protagonist and the writing of the story. Devices such as these and their changing uses over time are shown to contribute to the interpretation of literature. Thus, the uses of identity and development are considered at several levels, providing a rich context for the exploration of these concepts.

Mitzman's contribution (Chapter 8) focuses on issues of individual identity and the place of the individual in history. First he discusses the evolution of the interest of historians in the individual. A distinction is made between psychohistorians, who study individual personalities from a psychoanalytic perspective, and social historians, who study how structures and mentalities shape individuals at the collective level. The evolution of both schools is described. The peril critics of the psychohistorical approach see is a certain withdrawal from the larger social historical networks of history and the danger of returning to "the great man theory of history" (e.g., the history of Europe in the 20th century was determined either by Hitler's missing testicle or by his terrible relationship with his mother). According to Mitzman this danger can be avoided by focusing on cultural history, in which an individual from the elite culture can be viewed as a reflection of the mentality within that elite, and by applying some of the general criteria of identity. These criteria can be used to look at major turning points in the life of an individual and then key them to turning points in the mental climate of the period. Mitzman gives an example of this approach in his chapter, and he also argues that "a proper inquiry into the identity and motives of individuals in history must take into account the historically shaped identity and values of the scholar himself."

Considered from the vantage point of all perspectives represented in this volume, those of historical and literary scholarship lie in juxtaposition to those found in psychology or psychoanalysis. Historians contribute the view that both identity and development must be considered within their historical contexts, and literary scholars go even farther in their interest of deconstructing these concepts. With respect to the concept of identity, both Neubauer and Mitzman have demonstrated their usefulness in multiple ways: Neubauer through his interest in adolescence as a period of identity crisis and also through consideration of the identity of author and narrator; Mitzman through his interest in the role of individual in history, as one both shaping and shaped by historical forces. Development has been considered through the impact of historical change, reflected in characters, authors, and even the historian or critic himself.

7

Problems of Identity in Modernist Fiction

JOHN NEUBAUER

Is Adolescence a Modern Phenomenon?

My topic is a twofold examination of identity crises in adolescence. First, I wish to show how adolescence became identified around 1900 as an age category and as a social phenomenon of identity crisis. Second, I wish to talk about the artistic means whereby early 20th-century literature attempted to portray adolescent identity crises. Since my questions are historically specific, I shall not attempt to define what identity and development are, but will, instead, attempt to portray how these terms gained new significance in an age preoccupied with adolescence.

Do teenage identity crises exist in all cultures and historical epochs? The question has been a matter of debate ever since the appearance of G. S. Hall's first great study of adolescence (1904) and Margaret Mead's subsequent claim that female adolescence in the native culture of Samoa was less stressful than in America (1928). The reopening of that case in 1983, through Derek Freeman's attack on Mead's conclusions, parallels the emergence of a debate among historians in the 1970s and 1980s, as to whether adolescence as a social phenomenon was a product of the 19th century or to be found in earlier Western civilization. The latter position has been adopted by Natalie Zemon Davis (1975), Lawrence Stone (1981a), and others in answer to Philippe Ariès

(1962), John and Virginia Demos (1969), John R. Gillis (1974), Joseph Kett (1977), and J. O. Springhall (1986), who argue that adolescence is a specific phenomenon of modern industrial societies.

In my recent book, *The Fin-de-Siècle Culture of Adolescence* (1992), I cautiously join this second group by marshaling a large body of cultural artifacts and social phenomena in support of the thesis that preoccupation with adolescence was a central feature of turn-of-the-century European culture. This evidence, I claim, allows us to pinpoint an emergence of adolescence in these decades.

A closer look at this process of emergence reveals a slow and silent shift (a development) in social structures throughout the 19th century, and a loud break, an outburst of artistic and cultural articulation of that change, at the end of it. In my opinion, this articulation constituted the actual birth of adolescence or, to put it in other terms, its "discovery," even "invention."

The silent shift was part of the European industrialization and accumulation of wealth, which led to an expansion of private and public secondary schooling during the 19th century. Ever larger numbers of middle- and upper-class children remained in school during their teenage years and enjoyed what Erikson (1968) calls a Moratorium. The growth in the number of pupils allowed age-grading in classes, and hence the formation of a tighter peer group.

The delayed, but sudden and sweeping cultural responses to these gradual changes covered all cultural fields and all of Europe's advanced industrialized societies, though they depended in each country on the specific institutional structures. The differences among the English public schools, the German gymnasiums, and the French lycées account for many of the differences in cultural articulation. The new discourses on adolescence involve a very large body of literature in virtually all languages; artwork by the artists of the Brücke group, Kokoschka and Schiele; some of Freud's important essays and case studies; psychological studies of G. S. Hall (1904), Mendousse (1909), Charlotte Bühler (1921), and Spranger (1924); the pedagogical reform movements; the conceptualization and institutionalization of juvenile delinquency; and, last but not least, the various youth movements, including the Boy Scouts and the German *Jugendbewegung*.

In all these studies and representations adolescence manifests itself as an identity crisis. Childhood identity, inherited from the parents, becomes diffuse, uncertain, and finally breaks down, due to sexual awakening and socialization within the peer group. The transition from childhood to adolescence was not perceived as a gradual development, but rather as a rupture. After the crumbling of old values, a phase of split and multiple identities follows. The first psychologists and artists of adolescence portray repeated role playing, constant mutations in voice and social behavior due to inner uncertainties. The primary context of the identity crises depicted was not the oedipal or generational conflict, but first and foremost a conflict within the newly formed peer group. Indeed, the adult preoccupation with adolescence was not merely a response to a rebellious new generation; the concern with adolescent identity crises was motivated to a considerable extent by a profound general cultural malaise, a crisis of identity in Western culture. As Hall's (1904) introduction to his great study best demonstrates, for many artists and scholars around 1900 the identity crisis of the age group became a kind of focusing mirror, through which the age as a whole could investigate its own problems of identity. When Kirchner, Heckel, and other artists of the Brücke group portray adolescent girls with techniques adopted from African and Oceanian native art, the product reflects both the identity crisis of the depicted and the artists' break with the paternal matrix of Western civilization.

Literature and Adolescence

Language use conditions identity crises and their resolution. This is why adolescents so often develop a sudden interest in writing, and why problems of identity are so often thematized by professional writers, who usually find themselves in a prolonged and even permanent identity crisis.

What role did literature play then in the cultural-historical invention of adolescence? How did it respond to the identity crisis of the fin-de-siècle? Did literature merely thematize adolescence and its identity crisis?

To begin with, we note that many of the canonized works of turn-of-the-century fiction are treatments of adolescence. They include, to name only a few, Frank Wedekind's *Spring Awakening* (1969), Thomas Mann's *Tonio Kröger* (1981), Robert Musil's *Young Törless* (1966), Hermann Hesse's *Demian* (1970), Alain Fournier's *Le Grand Meaulnes* (1966), André Gide's *The Counterfeiters* (1973), Rudyard Kipling's *Stalky & Co.* (1982) and *Kim* (1987), and James Joyce's *A Portrait of the Artist as a Young Man* (1977). But this is only the tip of an iceberg that stretches under the water far beyond the generally recognized boundaries of literature. The full mass includes not only lesser-known works about adolescence but also popular books and magazines published for adolescents, and an unknown quantity of diaries, letters, and other personal documents written by adolescents, of which Charlotte Bühler made pioneering collections and studies (e.g., 1925). Furthermore, stories about adolescents, fictional as well as true ones, had formative roles in all of the nonliterary discourses at the turn of the century, including psychoanalysis, psychology, law, and the youth movements. The narrative dimensions of Freudian psychoanalysis are, of course, well known. In the concluding chapter of my book I show that such fictional works as Thomas Malory's *The Book of King Arthur* (1906), Conan Doyle's Sherlock Holmes stories (1894), Kipling's *Kim* (1987), and Karl May's Winnetou stories (1893) served as models for the ideology and the institutional structures of the youth organizations. Finally, the literary contribution to the discourses on adolescence includes various forms of literary devices and structures, most notably metaphors and metonyms.

In this chapter, I must stay with the tip of the iceberg and concentrate on a single example of fiction about adolescence, Jacques de Lacretelle's *Silbermann* (1983). It will be necessary, however, to place it in the larger context of modernist fiction.

We think of adolescent self-expressions as immediate and spontaneous imprints of a self. But the great bulk of adolescent literature available to us is written by adults who recollect or imagine that state of mind. Hence representations of adolescence are almost always mediated.

If we take an overview of the turn-of-the-century literature on adolescence, we can observe a further aspect of this mediation: In contrast to what we may expect, very little of that literature pretends to be confessional, that is, a spontaneous outpouring of emotions and ideas. If we seek an explanation, it will not suffice to point to the mediated nature of most adolescent literature. To be sure, most fiction about adolescence is written retrospectively by postadolescents, often by young writers in their twenties. But given the professional uncertainties of the modern artist, these writers were often caught in a prolonged adolescent crisis that minimized the distance between their present and former selves. They could have chosen first-person narrative forms, and a narrative style suited to convey immediacy. Such a mode was common in 18th-century epistolary novels, for instance in Richardson's *Clarissa* (1962) and Goethe's *The Sorrows of Young Werther* (1949).

Around 1900, no such epistolary novels were written; fictional diaries and first-person narratives were rare. Why? The answer may be sought in the general cultural doubts concerning identity, which were first expressed by Nietzsche and became a central concern of the whole modernist movement. I must limit myself to a few remarks relating to literature.

In previous ages, literature was usually understood, and occasionally written, as the author's personal expression. Narrators provided generous commentary on the characters and events of the story, involving general religious, moral, and political judgments, and readers understood these as the author's commentaries and judgments. Of course, there were novels, especially first-person ones, where the narrator was obviously not the author, but these were exceptions to the rule.

This moralizing posture of the narrator-author was usually linked to a second narrative feature, the narrator's ability to read the mind of the characters. This judging and knowing narrator, often called omniscient, came under increasing scrutiny in the second half of the 19th century and thereafter; and the modernist authors of the early 20th century came to question the earlier narrative convention. On epistemological grounds they distrusted author-narrators who played God by constantly pontificating and by knowing so well the minds and hearts of their fictional characters. The modernists suggested that narrators ought to be "peeled off" of their authors; but at the same time, their exclusive, unified, and insightful vision of the fictional world was to be replaced by constantly shifting perspectives that could no longer claim to be absolute. In many modernist novels and in virtually all books about adolescence, the narrators surrender their traditional privilege of reading the minds of all fictional characters. Most characters are now seen from the outside only, even if a third-person narrative form is chosen. In Valery Larbaud's *Fermina Márquez* (1979) and some other stories about adolescence, only the adult minds become hermetically sealed; in most stories, as in the case of *A Portrait* and *Tonio Kröger*, the narrator can read only the mind of his protagonist. The technique is carried to its most consistent extreme by Kafka, who allows us to see the fictional world only through the mind of his uncertain heroes, creating thereby a sense of claustrophobia. As in modern physics, the position and character of the observer and speaker can no longer be ignored.

These changes in narrative conventions allowed for new modes of representing problems of identity in literature. In the earlier convention, identity was essentially fixed: The identity of the narrator was coupled with that of the author, and this author-narrator figure delineated itself in terms of the authorial opinions expressed. Furthermore, as Patricia

Meyer Spacks (1981) suggests, the identity of the fictional characters was also fixed. Whatever changes the fictional characters in the 18th century underwent had to be understood in terms of some essential quality and character trait in them. Tom Jones may make terrible blunders during his maturation, but we all know that he is fundamentally good (Spacks, 1981).

In the modernist narrative convention, identities became diffuse. Narrators could no longer be identified with their authors, the texture of fiction became saturated with interior monologues and dialogues. The former is typical of Joyce, the latter is the dominant form in James's *The Awkward Age* (1966), which is, not accidentally, a novel about adolescence. The most typical modernist stylistic device is the "free indirect discourse," (also called "narrated monologue," "style indirect libre," or "erlebte Rede"), which has an identity problem of its own since it is suspended between two speakers. Take, for instance, the symbolic initiation of the adolescent Stephen Dedalus as a writer, in the central scene of Joyce's *A Portrait of the Artist as a Young Man*: "A girl stood before him in midstream, alone and still, gazing out to sea. She seemed like one whom magic had changed into the likeness of a strange and beautiful seabird" (Joyce, 1977, p. 171). The literal speaker is the narrator, for he refers to Stephen in the "he" form; yet it is to Stephen, and not to his narrator, that the girl appears as a "beautiful seabird," for inventing the metaphor constitutes his initiation as a writer. Hovering between narrator and protagonist, the passage reveals a diffuse identity.

Although virtually all modernist narratives employ the free indirect discourse, they use different types of narrators. In Joyce's *A Portrait* and in Kafka's novels, the narrator virtually ceases to make judgments, and his vision is largely limited to that of the protagonist (we get no insight into the minds of the other characters). Conversely, in Thomas Mann's *Tonio Kröger* and Robert Musil's *Young Törless* the narrators remain very much present and engage in a dynamic interaction with their protagonists. This new, fluid relationship between narrator and protagonist is an important part of that perspectivism in the modernist novel that informs the representation of diffuse identity.

The Peer-Group Narrator and His Friend

The text I have chosen, Lacretelle's *Silbermann* (1983), employs a narrative convention introduced by modernists that foregrounds the interaction between narrator and protagonist and thematizes the identity of both. Unlike *A Portrait, Tonio Kröger* and *Young Törless, Silbermann* is a first-person narration, one in which the narrator is a participant in the fictional world. Such narration had existed, of course, throughout the ages. But, like Hesse's *Demian* and Alain Fournier's *Le Grand Meaulnes*, *Silbermann* modifies this tradition to allow for the foregrounding of diffuse identities. Traditional first-person narratives are ego-centered, for they are told both by and about the narrator-protagonist. In contrast, the mentioned novels are off-centered, for they are focused on the figures mentioned in the titles, Max Demian, Augustin Meaulnes, and David Silbermann, and their friendship with the narrator. If the fictional world of the traditional first-person narrative is a circle viewed from its center, that of the new ones is an ellipse in which the narrator and the protagonist constitute a double focalization. On one level, the story is about the adolescent identity crisis of the protagonist named in the title; on another, it is the story of an adolescent friendship, where the identity crisis of the narrator is conditioned through his friendship with the admired, superior, and enigmatic protagonist friend. The writing is part of the coping with the experience. The very structure of the new peer-group narrative convention reflects what I have suggested, namely that the primary context of turn-of-the-century identity crises is the peer group. The generation conflict plays only a secondary role.

Peer-group narration is a decidedly perspectival and relativistic mode of representation. Its very mode of portraying things and reading minds diffuses the traditional unity of vision, hence also what one might call the traditional narrative identity. In *Demian, Le Grand Meaulnes,* and *Silbermann,* the narrator's inability to read and display the minds of his characters becomes a crucial limitation, because we are denied access to the mind of the protagonist. It remains a closed book to us, available to us only by means of the narrator's reports and interpretations. The narrative strategy enhances the aura around the protagonist; or to put it another way, the protagonist's identity remains obscure, known only through those of its external manifestations that are perceived by his rather limited and emotionally engaged narrator-friend.

The reliability of the protagonist's image is further weakened by the retrospective mode of the narration. Neither of these stories pretends to be written during adolescence or immediately after the encounter with the friend. The temporal distance between experiencing and writing, adolescence and adulthood, allows for tensions and irony. Together with the external portrayal, this temporal distance makes confessional and immediate portrayals impossible. But, as Gide wrote in his notebooks accompanying *The Counterfeiters*: "Intimacy, insight, psychological investigation can in certain respects be carried even further in the 'novel' than in 'confessions' " (Gide, 1973, p. 415). Gide's point is nowhere better illustrated than in the novelistic technique adopted by the peer-group narratives, which are exceptionally well suited to the representation of diffuse identities and adolescent crises.

David Silbermann

The story of David Silbermann, as told by his unnamed narrator-friend, takes place around 1900. Like Meaulnes and Demian, Silbermann enters the life of his narrator by exerting an irresistible charm on him and opening his senses to hitherto unknown beauties in familiar things. Meaulnes discovers firecrackers in the attic, Demian reinterprets the biblical story of Cain and Abel, Silbermann brings Racine's *Iphigénie* to life:

> I listened spellbound, struck by a sudden discovery. These assembled words, which I recognized for having seen them printed and having stored them mechanically from beginning to end in my memory—these words formed for the first time an image in my mind. . . . I did not believe until then that a classical tragedy could be so vividly and sensitively rendered . . . his yellow complexion and the black bonnet of his curled hair made me dream of a magician in some oriental story who keeps the key to all marvels. (Lacretelle, 1983, pp. 21-23. All the translations from this book are mine, J.N.)

When Silbermann leaves later, this magic disappears and life seems dismal and worthless to the narrator.

One of Lacretelle's great merits is to embed the dynamics of this friendship in the social and historical environment of fin-de-siècle France. Indeed, the encounter between Silbermann and his narrator is prepared by the opening pages of the book, which portray the sociological problems of another friendship. The narrator, son of a puritanical Protestant judge, recalls how, at the end of a summer, he anticipated returning to school and renewing his friendship with Philippe Robin, son of an important Catholic lawyer. The reunion disappoints the narrator, but his mother wants him to cultivate the friendship for it may further his father's career.

To the disappointment of his mother, the narrator turns from the desirable Catholic Philippe to the undesirable Jewish Silbermann, who is a newcomer to the school. At first, Silbermann makes a negative impression: "He was short and of puny appearance. His face . . . was very well shaped but very ugly, with protruding cheekbones and a pointed chin. . . . All this suggested the idea of a strange precocity; it made me think of child prodigies that make rounds in circuses" (Lacretelle, pp. 11-12). Silbermann's intelligence and poetic sensitivity neutralize this initial impression, but the budding friendship gradually isolates the narrator. Some schoolmates envy Silbermann's superior intellect; Philippe avoids contact with him because he is under influence of his anti-Semitic uncle; and the narrator's parents are taken aback by Silbermann's precocious table talk. Silbermann is fond of his family, but has little in common with his father, who deals in art for pecuniary reasons. The opulent home of the Silbermanns overwhelms the frugally raised narrator.

When Silbermann becomes the target of anti-Semitic attacks, the narrator enthusiastically swears to stand by him, and he takes this oath of loyalty with all the puritanical severity of his upbringing. Confronted with Philippe's demand to choose between Silbermann and himself, he is tempted by the expected "gentle and controlled feeling, the unproblematic and permitted pleasures" in Philippe's friendship, but he is swayed by the "arduous task" of taking Silbermann's side: "I foresaw a painful destiny, and, exalted at the perspective of sacrifice, I responded by exclaiming irresistibly: Him" (Lacretelle, p. 48).

Loyalty to Silbermann becomes the narrator's mission. Although he does not intervene when his friend is beaten, he comforts him at the price of being ostracized. Their friendship becomes impossible, however, when Silbermann's father is accused of fraud by the right-wing press, and the narrator's father is charged with the investigation. Upon Silbermann's desperate request, the narrator attempts to sway his father, but is severely rebuked, suspected of an "abnormal attachment," and told to drop the friendship. He disobeys, but his parents persuade the school to remove the "divisive" Silbermann, who departs for America to enter his uncle's diamond business.

Like *Le Grand Meaulnes* and *Demian*, *Silbermann* is the story of the narrator's adolescent friendship with an outsider. But whereas Meaulnes and Demian become alienated because of their personal qualities, Jewishness is the decisive determinant of both Silbermann's identity and his exclusion.

It is particularly fitting that Silbermann should be seen only through the narrator, for his identity is also forced upon him from outside: He is not free to choose his identity, but is assigned a role in the social configuration of his world. Indeed, Silbermann arrives with a weak Jewish identity and a great desire to assimilate: He is neither religious nor respectful of his father's commercial success, and his dream is to make a glorious contribution to French literary life. But the attacks by his classmates stamp him a Jew, identify him with his father, and destroy his dream. By entering his uncle's diamond business, he assumes an identity that befits his upbringing and conforms to the image of Jews. Having previously been addressed by his friend only as Silbermann, he assumes his full name in a bitter farewell: "I have left my dreams behind. In America, I am going to make money. Having the name I do, I was predestined for it. Eh? . . . David Silbermann is more fitting for the sign of a diamond merchant than the cover of a book!" (Lacretelle, p. 109).

The Narrator's Identity

The powerful force of stereotypes in adolescent identity forming is equally evident in the narrator's own identity crisis and its resolution. Although he usually treats his friend as an individual, stereotyping is not alien to him. When Silbermann reacts mockingly to the injury he suffers from his classmates, the narrator labels him a "typical Jew": "That clowning displeased me. Words of the Bible occurred to me: 'Disbelieving and perverse race' . . . Be quiet I said to him impatiently. That was the first time that I treated him brusquely" (Lacretelle, p. 64).

Indeed, the narrator's identity formation is largely an acceptance of stereotypical roles. The self-image he adopts for himself is the role of a prodigal son: when Silbermann departs, the narrator returns to the bosom of his family. To be sure, the returning son finds the nest no longer as cozy and clean as earlier, and he is eager to show the reader that he can forget neither Silbermann's fate nor his father's refusal to be lenient with the antiquarian. That refusal is revealed as hypocritical when the judge later does become lenient with Silbermann's father to please a powerful deputy. The narrator's discourse skillfully blends self-criticism with self-promotion to demonstrate that returning to the father's world does not imply endorsing hypocritical puritan morality. He joins the celebration of his father's promotion (which was furthered by his leniency) by showing forgiveness and understanding of human fallibility: "Recognizing the fragile matter of that pure face [of my mother] I understood that however virtuous a soul may be and however it may aspire for sainthood, it cannot elevate itself above human imperfection." (Lacretelle, p. 119). The image of the tainted parents is meant to excuse the narrator's own taint.

This, at any rate, is how the narrator, full of self-chastisement, justifies his reconciliation with his family. But the concluding scene, which depicts his reconciliation with Philippe, belies these humane motives:

> [Philippe's] face was gay and serene. He seemed to pursue a much simpler path, one that was provided with easy sideways and advantageous safeguards, skirting chasms without ever straying into them.
>
> I felt that my future happiness depended on the choice I was to make between the two paths I was facing. I hesitated. . . . But suddenly the landscape on Philippe's side seemed so attractive that I relaxed and let a faint smile escape. (Lacretelle, p. 124)

The reconciliation occurs in front of a crude and faded caricature of Silbermann on the wall and implies an acceptance of the racial stereotype: "I turned to Silbermann's caricature and after some effort I said in a slightly mocking tone, whose perfect ease internally disconcerted me: 'This is very true to life' " (Lacretelle, p. 124).

The remark betrays Silbermann and marks a shift from sincere to hypocritical puritan ethics. Until now, the narrator assumed his defense of Silbermann as a puritanical mission of self-sacrifice: "I savored a delicious feeling. 'I offer everything to him' I said to myself, 'the affection of my friends, the will of my parents, and even my honor' " (Lacretelle, p. 91). When Silbermann leaves, the narrator falls into a "profound desperation" that has little to do with Silbermann himself: "Neither his person nor the end of our friendship were the reason for it. I suffered from no longer feeling upon awakening each morning, with the first ray of the day, the inspiration of that glorious task" (Lacretelle, p. 111). Now that Silbermann has left, the narrator's Calvinist sacrificial service for the persecuted Jew comes to an end. By choosing the "attractive" landscape on Philippe's side and accepting the stereotypical caricature as truthful, he adopts an attitude of expediency and social conformity.

The two identity changes move in opposite directions. Silbermann starts with a diffuse identity, but is compelled by external pressure to assume a "hard" one. The narrator begins with clearly affirmed beliefs and values, which crumble in the exposure to Silbermann and the subsequent reconciliation with the surrounding world. Since the old values are not replaced by new ones, the final identity merely extends the parental one and does not constitute a creative resolution of adolescence. The closing scene with Philippe reverses the earlier choice between the hard and easy paths, and marks the birth of a false consciousness.

Tentative Conclusions

By choosing an internal narrator, Lacretelle avoids giving the impression of objectivism: Our judgment of Silbermann will depend on our judgment of the narrator, his reliability, honesty, and prejudices. Such ambiguities are typical not only of modernist fiction but also of the social perception of adolescence at the end of the 19th and the beginning of the 20th century. The discovery of adolescence constituted first and foremost a plea to recognize the special problems and interests of the age group. Adolescence, it was claimed, could not be judged by adult standards or by norms derived from the treatment of children. More concretely, the psychological, pedagogical, judicial, and other discourses on adolescence pleaded to let adolescents experiment. A sound identity could be established only if adolescents had time and leisure to search and were not forced to become precocious adults. Precocity is perhaps the main target of Hall's study of adolescence.

Yet, we should not be swept away by the liberal rhetoric of these discourses, for the special adolescent formations that came about were inevitably harnessed by the power interests of the existing social institutions. The societies that pleaded for a kind of "adolescence for adolescents' sake" finally sent their youths into the trenches of World War I; and, just like Lacretelle's narrator, a majority of adolescents accepted the national and racial stereotypes they were offered. Here, perhaps, lies a major difference with the sudden resurfacing of the adolescent identity as a social and political issue in the late 1960s and early 1970s.

8

Historical Identity and Identity of the Historian

ARTHUR MITZMAN

Only connect.
E. M. Forster

Historians more frequently study the concept of identity at the collective than at the individual level: Questions of national, cultural, ethnic, religious, or class identity become, for particular groups at a certain point in time, important determinants of social or political behavior; individuals within such groups puzzle over their values and identity; and theorists discuss the ways of approaching this collective identity (see, e.g., Lorenz, 1987, pp. 255-262). Latent feelings of solidarity, among individuals who had hitherto only passively or objectively belonged to certain groups, have often been triggered into militant consciousness by new social or political circumstances in the group's environment. Thus in the cases of Jewish, black, and working-class consciousness in this century, and national consciousness in the period since the French Revolution, new group self-awareness has occurred

AUTHOR'S NOTE: This chapter was originally published in German as "Historische Identität und die Identität des Historikers" in 1992 in the journal *Psyche* and reprinted in 1993 in the book *Biographie als Geschichte* (Ed. Hedwig Röckelein) published by Edition Diskord, Tübingen. It is reprinted here with permission from both *Psyche* and Edition Diskord.

when altered cirumstances made the group's aspirations a reasonable screen for projecting problems of personal identity, and afforded a reasonable prospect of resolving material and psychological problems—"reasonable" used here not in any formal sense, but in the ideologically relative Weberian sense of "material rationality," which designates the system of values that any society or organized group of people uses to rationalize its actions. These and many other examples are very broad areas within which historians have worked out elaborate theoretical and practical subdivisions. One of the most interesting analyses of how changed circumstances produce radical changes in group and individual consciousness is the psychohistorical study of Weinstein and Platt (1969).

The question I will address here is not this large and important question of collective identity in history, but rather the related, if more intimate and subtle, matter of personal identity, which is inseparable from the historiographically central matter of the place of the individual in history. After reviewing the main lines of the discussion on this subject, I shall argue for an approach that mediates between the history of mentalities and psychoanalytic history writing. Furthermore, using an example from my own recent research, I will show that a proper inquiry into the identity and motives of individuals in history must take into account the historically shaped identity and values of the scholar himself.

The Individual and History

The interest of historians in the individual and in the related question of personal identity has had a paradoxical evolution in recent years. In the decade of the 1960s there emerged, as regards the individual, a tacit division of labor between two new departures in historical research; psychohistorians would study individual personalities with an instrumentarium derived from psychoanalytic theory; social historians would study the long-term evolutions of populations, kinship structures, and mentalities that shaped these individuals at the collective level. Psychohistorians did little with the social history of humankind; their inquiries claimed to shed light principally on major issues of political history, through the scrutiny of historical villains like Hitler and Stalin, secondarily on matters of intellectual history, as in Binion's (1968) analysis of Lou Andreas-Salomé or Mazlish's (1975) of James and John Stuart

Mill; social historians eschewed the individual as the locus of insignificant events, focusing on longer-term questions. The paradox lies in the fact that, whereas the psychohistorical faction seems to whither of late in sectarian isolation, the history of mentalities has reversed its long-standing resistance to the study of individuals and, in works like Natalie Zemon Davis's (1983) *The Return of Martin Guerre* and Carlo Ginzburg's (1980) study of a heretical Friulian miller in *The Cheese and the Worms* and in programmatic statements like that which appeared in the *Annales* in 1988 ("Histoire et sciences sociales: Un tournant critique?," 1988), has vigorously taken up the challenge of integrating the individual into history.[1] And at the same time, the major enterprise in psychoanalytic history writing, Peter Gay's multivolume study of the 19th-century bourgeoisie (1984, 1986) has focused not on the individual but on an age and its values. A brief look at the place that studies of individual personalities have had in the development of the historical discipline may explain this paradox.

Since the beginning of the modern discipline in the 19th century, there has always been a concern for the political and cultural contribution of important individuals to history, and this concern has been strongly encouraged by the inclination of the public to incarnate complex historical events in the famous individuals associated with them. The result has been a large number of "life and work" studies, with a fluctuating interest in the details of personal existence. In the course of the professionalization of the discipline, however, such studies have been consistently relativized or subordinated to more sophisticated views of historical process, usually fueled by concepts derived from the emerging social sciences. Awareness of the increasing grip of the ideological isms on the nation states and social classes of the modern world showed the relevance for historical inquiry of political science; the discovery of overriding material interests was justified by Marxist assumptions; and 20th-century concepts of sociology and anthropology inspired our colleagues to conceptualize the slowly evolving structures and mentalities built around kinship, religious beliefs, and traditional social organization, and to see in these structures and mentalities the real motors impelling the course of history. In most branches of the discipline, the overriding trend has been away from rational individual purpose to nonrational collective forces as the motor of history.

The ideational background of this trend, as we know, is profoundly rooted in the Copernican and Darwinian deconstruction of the traditional anthropocentric view of the universe, and Freudian psychoanalysis constitutes a crucial 20th-century addition to this cosmic deconstructionism. Indeed, it is psychoanalysis itself that, by its dethroning of the concept of the autonomous personality, has made the concept of identity so problematic. One might expect, then, that historians would have greeted the psychohistorical subdiscipline with the warmth they have accorded to local importers of sociological and anthropological wisdom, but for a variety of reasons, this warmth has been largely absent. When the psychohistorians were most active around 1970, they were in a small professional ghetto. In the two decades since then, their number has dwindled while their isolation has increased.

In retrospect, this is not surprising. The psychohistorical venture embraced individual destiny as a key to history in a way that was indifferent to and incompatible with the more sophisticated methods of scrutinizing collective behavior. Despite the radicality of its hermeneutic, psychohistory rarely broke out of the traditional confines of political and intellectual history, both of which share outdated assumptions about great individuals. Moreover, since many psychohistorians tended to accept uncritically a rather conservative version of the Freudian gospel, the attractiveness of the new method for potentially sympathetic outsiders was undermined by apprehensions of a new cult and a new dogma. Imposition of psychohistorical method without the necessary rounded knowledge of the individual subject, of his or her social and professional place and concrete historical setting, was a recurring point of criticism, as were the ahistorical assumptions of the universality of the Oedipus complex and the reductionism of relating all adult behavior to childhood traumas. Interestingly, the most telling criticism along these lines came from friendly, psychoanalytically schooled historians, Thomas Kohut and Joseph Woods. Kohut argued that good analysts approach their analysands not with theory, as practitioners of psychohistory frequently did their subjects, but with a sympathetic interest in their persons. And Woods pointed out that many psychohistorians failed to realize that recent emphasis on the preoedipal mother-child relation had relativized the significance of the Oedipus complex, and that object-relations theory permitted a nonreductionist approach to adult personality (see Kohut, 1986; Woods, 1987). Thus, despite the support for the use of psychoanalytic theory in history by some of the most important political and intellectual historians of the past 35 years—William Langer, H. Stuart Hughes, Carl Schorske, and more recently, Peter Gay—the psychohistorical subdiscipline seems to have shrunk to a dubious interdisciplinary sect, sharing the journal founded by Lloyd Demause, the *Journal of Psychohistory,* with unqualified amateurs from the disciplines of psychiatry and political science.

If the social-historical wing of the discipline had maintained the allergy for individual personality it had long displayed before 1980, the isolation of the psychohistorians would be understandable and perhaps inevitable. In fact, it is highly paradoxical since, as I have indicated, many of the practitioners of the new sociocultural history and history of mentalities in the United States and in France are becoming increasingly interested in individual life histories, and even in a psychoanalytic point of view, though without enthusiasm for the specifically psychohistorical approach.

This has been particularly noticeable in the group of social historians associated with the authoritative French quarterly *Annales E.S.C.* The Annales school, which had launched the history of mentalities as the long-term view of human emotions and values, has in the past few years modified its long-standing involvement with collective, quantitatively measurable, slow-moving processes of change, to concern itself with the smallest unit of history, the individual, and its relation to the other levels of historical scrutiny (see "Histoire et Sciences Sociales," 1988). Though the shifting focus of the Annales links up far more with prosopographical and linguistic concerns than with psychoanalytic ones, several of the French historians of mentalities of the seventies and eighties—for example, Le Goff, Ozouf, Le Roy Ladurie, Corbin, Burgière, and Muchembled—occasionally used psychoanalytic constructs in their work, and the disappearance of the two Freudian historians *pur sang* in France—Alain Besançon, by renunciation, and Michel de Certeau, by death—may create room for less ponderous ventures. Characteristic for the new interest in the individual is the fourth volume in the *Histoire de la Vie Privée* series, edited by Michelle Perrot. The principal contributions by Perrot and Alain Corbin are both important studies of the formative influences on 19th-century (French) personality: The chapters by Perrot emphasize the family as a historically grown institution, whereas Corbin's section tends to stress the influence of social, religious, and technological forces on individual identity. In the United States, too, the decline of psychohistory, accelerated by the sharp criticism of friends as well as enemies, has occurred in a period when social and cultural historians are becoming highly interested, from the standpoint of long-term social processes, in questions of individual psychology and identity.

An Integration of Social-Historical and Psychoanalytic Approaches

Since future interest of historians in questions of individual identity in history is likely to come principally from this new alliance of social and cultural historians, it may be useful to indicate some of the theoretical possibilities and models that I have found particularly useful in my own efforts to integrate social-historical and psychoanalytic approaches to character formation and personal identity.

First of all, I have benefited from the post-Freudian emphasis on the significance for character formation of the preoedipal ties to the mother, an emphasis that has relativized the importance of oedipal conflict. The balanced and lucid study of Gérard Mendel (1968), *La Révolte contre le Père,* has been particularly useful in putting such approaches—those of Melanie Klein and Margaret Mahler, for example—in a broader cultural and historical context.

Second, my work has relied on the social variants of the psychoanalytic instrumentarium, those that emphasize historically relative object relations and ego ideals rather than universal drive impulses, rigid superegos, and oedipal inevitabilities. It is striking that, despite widespread antipathy to psychohistory among American historians, these aspects have generally made a psychoanalytic approach more accessible to historians in the United States than in France. Indeed, the theory that was broadly influential in the human sciences in North America, that of Erikson, has been inherently much more congenial to a socially relativizing, historical approach than the equivalent theory in France, that of Lacan. This probably is the explanation for the tendency of French historians writing on the relation between historiography and psychoanalytic theory—De Certeau and Vovelle, among others—to emphasize the theoretical differences between the two approaches, whereas Americans such as Loewenberg and Gay stress the similarities (see de Certeau, 1978, 1986; Duby & Lardreau, 1980, pp. 104-106; Gay, 1985, pp.xii, xiv; Loewenberg, 1983, pp. 3-4; Vovelle, 1982, p. 94). Alain Besançon, analyst and historian, spent a major part of his professional career attempting to reconcile what he perceived as major differences between history and psychoanalysis and finally decided to stop trying. His two careers are now totally separate.

Thus even a social historian distant from the psychohistorical current like Natalie Zemon Davis has shown interest in Freudian perspectives in her work on the self-fashioning of individual identity, as has the

German social historian Andreas Gestrich. The latter works with the concept of *Selbstentwürfen* (self-fashioning) in the 19th century and combines a critical use of Freudian and Eriksonian perspectives with the symbolic interactionism of Erving Goffman (see Davis, 1988, pp. 601-602; Gestrich, 1988, pp. 14-18, 21). And Laurence Stone, whose overt anti-Freudianism has delivered him to the wrath of Peter Gay, the principal representative of the Freudian approach in contemporary historiography, fully acknowledges the importance of Erikson's work for the psychological interpretation of adult behavior (see Stone, 1981b, p. 218; and for a reply to his over-hasty critique, Gay, 1985, pp. 22-30), an appreciation he shares with Gay himself, as well as with the psychohistorian Bruce Mazlish (see Gay, 1985, p. 183; Mazlish, 1971, p. 19).

The principal contemporary justification for placing the individual at the core of historical inquiry comes, however, neither from a psychoanalytic historian nor from a social historian influenced by Erikson, but from the Italian historian Carlo Ginzburg, whose intellectual affinities are to Marc Bloch and the Warburg tradition of art criticism. In an essay exploring historical semiotics, Ginzburg distinguishes two epistemological traditions in Western thought (see Ginzburg, 1980). One, that of Galileo, is based on abstraction from individual perception, quantification, generalization, and the establishment of law-like scientific truths. The other, much older, seeks truth through sense perception and the intuitive comprehension of individual phenomena. Hunting, medicine, Morelli's method of establishing art forgeries, the detective work of a Sherlock Holmes, and Freud's psychoanalysis are Ginzburg's disparate examples of this epistemology, as is the discipline of history.[2]

If Erikson is relevant in making a Freudian approach viable for the study of adult personality, and Ginzburg for putting the individual at the center of historiographical concern, two theorists from outside both the psychoanalytic and the historical tradition have been of considerable importance in establishing the social parameters of individual identity, for myself as well as for French and American cultural historians in general: Norbert Elias and Mikhail Bakhtin. Elias's theory postulated a millennial civilizing process that began in the royal courts of Europe. Impelled by their need for a monopoly on the legitimate use of force, monarchs increasingly demanded nonviolent and decorous social behavior of the crude and bellicose aristocrats who populated their courts. Gradually, the rejection of interpersonal aggression was internalized outside court circles as well, together with refined table manners and more general inhibitions of physical impulse, a pattern of repression that responded well both to the Church's abhorrence of the body and to the needs of the emerging bourgeoisie for rational control over behavior. Historians since Elias have shown how this civilizing process filtered down from the aristocracy to the third estate and the popular masses. Since the 17th century, some have argued, the cultivated Western elite has seen its pedagogic task among its social and moral inferiors—women, peasants, artisans, proletarians and lumpenproletarians, ethnic cultures on the peripheries of major state centers,[3] and more recently, impoverished racial minorities—in the inculcation of these values, a stance that has been called a "civilising offensive" (see particularly Muchembled, 1978, 1988).[4] It is not far-fetched to argue that this aggressively virtuous solicitousness of those on top for the moral welfare of the less-endowed citizenry, by infusing successive layers of society with the values of work, sobriety, decorum, and deference to central authority, has had a powerful effect on personal experiences of identity.

There have, of course, been many other social determinants of personal identity. Estate, class, professional, guild, family structure and models, peer group, regional culture, religious conviction, and language have also significantly conditioned personal character. It is doubtful, however, if any of these has been as persistent and profound in its influence on individual character as the package of repressions and commandments inculcated by the civilizing offensive, which has operated in Western culture at a long-term level of mentalities and values.

Norbert Elias, though his metahistorical perspective derived from German sociology, in particular from the Weberian perspective of an increasing rationalization of human existence, clearly modeled his notions of repression and internalization on Freud. The same cannot be said of the Russian linguist, Mikhail Bakhtin (1895-1975), who is often favored by the same early modern social historians who value Elias. Bakhtin explicitly polemicized against Freud. Properly understood, however, his historical and literary concepts of *carnivalization,* and the *dialogic imagination* add significantly to the psychoanalytic understanding of human culture and personal identity.

Bakhtin's notion of carnivalization, worked out in his book on Rabelais, assumes an archaic level of consciousness and identity in the common people, which they have traditionally expressed during popular festivities. Contrary to the mandates of everyday existence—toil, scarcity, deference to social superiors and the rules of the social order, repression of sexual and aggressive impulses—the carnivalesque spirit temporarily suspends toil, ignores scarcity, turns deference and the social order into mockery and anarchy, and replaces repression by an exaggerated expression of the organs of the lower body. In a sense, it is the temporary deliverance of ego from superego controls and its subjugation to id impulses, and the social historian Peter Burke has not hesitated to describe the carnivalesque "rituals of reversal" of the old popular culture in these terms (see Burke, 1978, p. 190). It is the prototypical world-turned-upside-down, and if Bakhtin localized it in the European peasant culture of the late medieval period and honored Rabelais as its last great spokesman, scholars of the past two decades have seen multiple refractions of it in Western culture since the Renaissance, in both its elite and popular variants. (Historians who have used Bakhtin's notion of the carnivalesque and grotesque humor include Natalie Zemon Davis, Robert Darnton, Robert Muchembled, Vincent La Capra, Sidney Monas, and Peter Jelavitch.)

Indeed numerous examples from the social history of plebeian rebellion and the cultural history of antiestablishment literature attest to these refractions. One of the clearest literary instances is the passage in Victor Hugo's *Les Misérables,* where he cites the response of Cambronne, the French officer commanding the last handful of French soldiers still fighting at Waterloo, to the respectful summons of an English general to surrender: "Merde!" Hugo's comment could not be more explicit:

> From respect for the decencies of language this word, perhaps the greatest ever uttered by a Frenchman, is not repeated in the history books; the sublime is banned from the record. At our risk and peril we have defied the ban. Amid the giants of that day there was one greater than all the others, and it was Cambronne. . . . To meet disaster in this fashion, challenging Fate itself . . . to incarnate irony at the mouth of the grave, staying erect when prostrate; to demolish the European coalition with a word, fling in the face of kings the cloaca known to the Caesars, make the crudest of words into the greatest by investing it with the splendour of France, insolently conclude Waterloo with mardi-gras, complete Leonidas with Rabelais, compress this victory in a single word that may not be spoken, losing the field but gaining history and at the end of carnage winning to one's side the hosts of laughter—this is sublime. (Hugo, 1862)

Hugo's Cambronne is an especially interesting example, since it unites the carnivalesque to a moment in the evolution of French national identity. Interestingly, the long novel that follows on Hugo's celebration of victory-in-defeat at Waterloo also combines motifs of the grotesque and the elaboration of identity in the personal case of its main protagonist, but in a radically different way. The ex-convict Jean Valjean, symbol of the defeated French nation after Waterloo, struggles heroically throughout the novel to achieve a moral identity his circumstances threaten to thwart or undermine. At one point he does so by wading through the literal cloaca [sewers] of Paris, bearing the wounded, unconscious body of an escaped revolutionary whose survival meant the loss by marriage of the only person Valjean loved, his adopted daughter. Thus, if Hugo was willing to celebrate carnivalesque scatological humor at a level of political transcendence, when it came to personal identity, the lower impulses and their products were obstacles to be overcome by the new moral person of the 19th century, shining example of the success of the civilizing offensive in taming base instinct.[5]

In fact, the immanent, carnivalesque plebeian of Bakhtin and the transcendent, rationally controlled ideal of Elias's civilizing process are antipodes between which the identity of modern man is in continuous movement. (For a most interesting investigation of the connection between modernist theater and carnivalesque popular culture in 20th-century Germany, see Jelavitch, 1982. For a similar approach connecting Bakhtin's concept with the work of James Joyce, see Monas, 1983.)

Bakhtin's importance for the historical understanding of identity, however, goes beyond the concept of the carnivalesque to include that of the dialogic imagination, the notion that prose writing, like speech, always assumes an interlocutor with whom the subject is in continual interaction and that it is this interaction which is crucial for human identity (for this more general aspect of Bakhtin's theory, see Kinser, 1984). In elaborating this social aspect of literature, Bakhtin seems to have broached a developmental psychology that was explicitly anti-Freudian. Clark and Holquist, Bakhtin's biographers, describe this dismissal of Freud in Bakhtin's theory as follows:

> An utterance is always between a self and an other and constitutes the primal workings of self-identification. Like Freud, on whom he was working at the . . . time, Bakhtin has a specific conception of identity formation. But there the similarity ends, for Bakhtin's model is the polar opposite of that on which classical psychoanalysis is based. In Freud, the movement is from the infant's complete ego, through increasing repression, to the socialized self of adults who can delay ego gratification. In Bakhtin, on the contrary, the movement is from a nonself, through the acquisition of different "languages" to a self that is the sum of its discursive practices. In *Freudianism* he argues

> that "any instance of self-awareness (for self-awareness is always verbal, always a matter of finding some specifically suitable verbal complex) is an act of gauging oneself against some social norm. Social evaluation is, so to speak, the socialization of oneself and one's behavior. In becoming aware of myself, I attempt to look at myself, as it were, through the eyes of another person." In Freud, self is suppressed in the service of the social; in Bakhtin, self is precisely a function of the social. In Freud, the more of the other, the less of the self; in Bakhtin, the more of the other, the more of the self. (Clark & Holquist, 1984)

I will leave it to the experts to argue for or against the accuracy of Bakhtin's view of Freud and classical psychoanalysis. As luck would have it, however, shortly before stumbling on this passage in Clark and Holquist's work, I read the excellent brief statement of Nancy Chodorow (1986) in *Reconstructing Individualism, Autonomy, Individuality, and the Self in Western Thought,* where she elaborates on the object-relational, nonclassical variant of psychoanalytic theory (this volume also contains excellent essays by Stephen Greenblatt and Natalie Zemon Davis). Chodorow distinguishes two theoretical lines of development issuing from Freud's ideas. One, more traditional, emphasizes drive theory and the internal conflicts of personality, particularly the Oedipus conflict. The second, the object-relations school, emphasizes the evolution of personality from the narcissistic tie to the mother through the field of object relations, and understands identity primarily in terms of the interaction with the social world, the internalization and assimilation of the Other. Evidently, this object-relational variety of psychoanalysis comes quite close to Bakhtin's dialogic notion of culture and identity. Insofar as it puts a premium on the social components of identity, it is also far more usable by social and cultural historians than the classical drive model of analytic theory. In a recent article in *Annales E.S.C.,* Giovanni Levi recognizes this utility of the dialogic element in the shaping of identity: "La connaissance n'est pas le résultat d'une simple description objective, mais celui d'un procès de communication entre deux personnes et deux cultures"; he applies the dialogic principle particularly to the 18th-century autobiographic novels of Sterne and Diderot. He does not, however, acknowledge the work of either Bakhtin or the object-relations theorists (see Levi, 1989).

Both Bakhtin and Chodorow point the historian of identity to a crucial aspect of his inquiry: the implicit dialogue, the interaction between his or her own identity and values and that of the subject. That is, the extent to which one's own identity and values aid or hinder one's view of the subject: in analytic terms, the question of countertransference. In the remainder of this chapter, I wish to discuss an example of this problematic relationship from my own research.

Historical Identity: A Case Study

For some years, I have been working through the correspondence of Jules Michelet's son-in-law with a close friend of his youth. The correspondence is valuable in several respects: Alfred Dumesnil, the son-in-law, was, at the time he met Michelet's daughter, a young law student attending, with his mother, Michelet's lectures at the Collège de France. Michelet, a widower, and the youth's mother fell in love in 1840; when the lady died of cancer 2 years later, Michelet adopted her son, an only child, and made him his secretary. (In 1849, Michelet remarried, over the protests of his daughter and son-in-law; and the joint household, as well as Dumesnil's secretarial activities, ended.) Dumesnil's letters, though wordy and lacking brilliance, do provide unique testimony as to his father-in-law's ideas, states of mind, lectures, and other activities from 1841 to 1849. His friend, Eugène Noel, also an only child, lived with his parents in a village some 25 kilometers from Rouen, where the father, a former artisan, had a small dyer's plant. His education and his wit made Noel an interesting sounding board for the ideas and problems of midcentury France. Moreover, because of his plebeian situation, Noel's letters are full of insightful observations about the social conditions of the age. The two young men shared a number of friends in the Rouen area, several of them former schoolmates of Dumesnil; but it is clear from the quality as well as the quantity of their letters—thousands over a half century—that Dumesnil and Noel, both without siblings and with similar values and a strong bent for literature, had an uncommonly close relationship.

Their statuses were unequal. Dumesnil's father, separated from the mother for several years before her short-lived affair with Michelet, was a wealthy banker in Rouen; and Dumesnil, by virtue of his adoption, ascended immediately to the highest rank of the professional bourgeoisie. Through his father-in-law, he became familiar with leading intellectual figures of the day, such as Lamennais, Quinet, and Lamartine.

Struggling against depression and insecurity after his mother's death in 1842, he was encouraged by Michelet to finish his law study and to become a writer as well as the historian's assistant. Contrariwise, Noel's parents were one small step above the impoverished peasant farmers and artisans of the region. Although he attended the same elite secondary school as Dumesnil, he abandoned his law studies after a year, for unstated reasons. The fact that he was the only surviving child of seven births had created a very strong tie to his mother, often evident in his letters, and this, combined with the dreary dullness of law studies for literary spirits at the time, probably induced in him such profound misery that he collapsed and could not go on, much as it did a few years later in Gustave Flaubert, tormented by a similarly desolate student existence. Noel returned home and remained there until he was past 40.

Noel's correspondence shows him to be a highly gifted writer, a talent recognized early by Michelet, who met him on his rare visits to Dumesnil in Paris, read many of his letters to "Cher Alfred," and corresponded with him personally.

In fact, Noel ended up publishing some 20-odd books: biographies of Rabelais, Molière, Voltaire, and Michelet himself; essays, both autobiographical and parodistic; and many volumes about his native region around Rouen. Yet his material chances, except for that of being supported at home by his father's paltry enterprise, were nil. He never obtained the law degree necessary for advancement into the professional bourgeoisie, and he was only able to move from his parents' village in 1860, married and with a 5-year-old son. His first regular job followed some 5 years later, when he was appointed to the editorial staff of the *Journal de Rouen*. He was by then the author of several books and had for many years been writing for the periodical press. What was perhaps worst of all was that between the ages 20 and 30, he had, for lack of income or family fortune, been repeatedly forced to surrender women with whom he was in love to competitors who were financially better endowed. When he finally married, it was with the family housekeeper, a situation comprehensible to Michelet, since he had married the housekeeper in the house where he lived with his widowed father in 1824. In fact, Michelet could comprehend a great deal about the young Noel, and at times seemed to prefer him, as a kindred spirit, to his adopted son and son-in-law Dumesnil.

A Historian's Identity

As I examined the extensive correspondence of Noel and Dumesnil in the decade of the 1840s, saw how often Noel referred to Michelet and wrote passages about the ideas and social conditions of the age that Dumesnil showed his father-in-law, and read of Michelet's lavish praise for Noel, I could not help wondering if, behind the friendship of the two young men, there was not an unstated rivalry for Michelet's favor, indeed if Dumesnil might not sometimes have been jealous of Noel's literary verve and acuity, resentful of Michelet's praise, and fearful that Noel, if he every came to Paris, might take his place in Michelet's affection.

In an exchange less than a year before the Revolution of February 1848, I thought I had stumbled on the proof of my suspicions and had found the explanation of why Noel remained for so long in his native village. It seemed to me as though Noel, who, with parental support, was on the point of moving to Paris to become a writer, was stopped under hypocritical pretext by his insecure, jealous friend. In his letter of May 5, 1847, Noel wrote:

> Here is the situation, my dear Alfred, think about it seriously, talk about it with your wife, with monsieur Michelet but with no-one else and write me everything you think.
>
> Mama, yesterday, seeing me wandering like a soul in torment along our hedges (for I had been miserably sad for two days) came to me in great agitation and said: you are bored here, Eugène, that is obvious. How could it be otherwise? All your friends are married, are happy. Moreover, your father has for some time been getting too old to remain at the head of a firm. He would soon see the disappearance of what remains to him. Since I can see clearly that you do not want to take his place, that your tastes are elsewhere, would it not be preferable to rent out the mill than to continue to undermine yourself in all sorts of ways? We would return, your father and me, to live tranquilly in Rouen, but then what will become of you, since you cannot, my poor Eugène, I can well understand (and tears came to her eyes) lock yourself up with us in one room. So! If you think you can do something, do as you like, be free, for before I die I want to see you happy. Do you need to go to Paris? Then go. I will be sad, she added, but I would be much more so if I knew that you will miss your career because of me. It's not me that you should look at, I will be finished tomorrow; think of the future.
>
> Your father, moreover, is tiring and is saddened to feel himself so little assisted in his profession by you, who are always dreaming of other things;

we have to let him leave it, look for someone to rent it in 6 months or a year, when the occasion arrives, and then we can leave here.

At the end of this conversation, I felt so tumultuously moved by every feeling at once, my dear Alfred, that I could only kiss effusively my poor mother and tell her that I would ask the advice of monsieur Michelet. So here we are, my friend, before answering me on all this, think about it for some time. We have said nothing about this conversation to my father and I will only speak to him of it when I have received your advice. [*Vos conseils*—Noel is clearly more interested in Michelet's opinion than in Dumesnil's.]

Whatever comes of this discussion, at least it will have done me some good for a few moments. Don't rush to answer me, dear friends, I will willingly wait a few days.

Dumesnil did not wait a few days; although his letter is dated May 7, in fact internal evidence makes it a certainty that he wrote it on May 6, the day after the date on Noel's letter. He wrote back in a matter of hours that it was Noel's *devoir sacré* [his sacred duty] to remain with mama:

Dear Eugène
To the admirable remarks that emerged from the heart of your mother, one can only respond with a few words of common sense and all your friends would agree, would be as one person to utter them:

It is that you ought not to separate yourself from your mother, you ought to spend the greatest part of your time near her, it is with her that you [between the lines: always] should have your residence. Apart from all the reasons of an affection which deepens every day, it is a sacred duty for you. It is not at the moment that she will need your care that you will go to live elsewhere.

But since Mme Noel senses so well your need to make a career, you ought not to worry nor to go further to choose, cherish the life that you've been leading since we know one another, work vigorously, continue to prepare yourself for the difficult times ahead when there will be a need for real men [*oú il faudra des hommes*]. You will become the person I have always felt and loved in you: you have been endowed with life and with the power to communicate it to others. I do not know exactly what you will do, it would be necessary to know the future, nor how you will do such useful and beneficent great things, but you will do them if you want to, for you have the heart and the spirit for them.

But to act as you should, you ought neither to languish nor to dawdle, time is too precious. Consider, every day, that you are responsible for souls, that thousands await a voice that they will perhaps find in you alone. And when an idea comes to you or if you need books or research or conversations, come to Paris, if your mother's health permits, remain there for a few days, work

> in the libraries, listen to M. Michelet's lecture, visit the museums, are you not more than my brother, are you not the son of M. Michelet?

The letter continues like this for another page. It must have seemed an eternity to Noel, who was seeing his only hope of emerging from his "hole," as he often called it, buried under a muddy avalanche of hypocritical praise and sanctimonious moralizing. When I first read it a few years ago, it was difficult to keep from crying out in the sedate reading room of the Bibliothèque Historique: Salaud! It seemed so perfectly clear to me: dull, repressed, excessively voluble Dumesnil, incapable of writing a line without a platitude, banality personified, how you must have trembled at the thought of clever little Noel moving to Paris and edging you out of papa Michelet's affection.

There probably was something of that in Dumesnil's stiff-arming of his friend's desire to escape a life sentence with mama and the cows. Yet, in the past few years, I've had second thoughts, both about the values of my strange pair of friends and about my own. To begin with, my own. In my flash reaction to Dumesnil's sanctimoniousness, how could I have neglected my own motivations? Like so many Jewish sons, I fought a 30-year war against my mother before I could recover some of the love and respect I had felt for her as a child. Nothing unusual in that; it's normal for young men in this century to struggle against the bonds of parental control and attachment. And to view any injunction never to leave mama, such as Dumesnil's, with angry cynicism, at best a reflection of his guilt-ridden ties to his own dead mother. But is this not precisely the countertransference we have to watch out for in historical research? (See Erikson, 1971; Lacapra, 1984.)

Dumesnil wrote a second letter to Noel the following day, in which he presented Michelet as being of precisely the same opinion as himself:

> Here are the very words he said to me after reading your letter: there's no need for him to leave his mother but let him come to see us more often, let him work a little in Paris if he is spending almost the entire year in the countryside.

Noel's reaction to the two letters was brief: "Your idea, my friend, is absolutely my own and just what I had told mama: no separation, this is impossible, but only a trip from time to time." And he went on to describe the perilous position of his father, whose business partner had just swindled him and run away. For some time after this exchange, Noel's letters show him to be, understandably, depressed.

Yet one looks in vain in those subsequent letters for signs of tension between the friends, which one would expect if Noel suspected Dumesnil of sabotaging his Paris prospects to protect his exclusive position next to their common father-figure. And Noel was anything but unperceptive. Of course, one might argue that Noel was holding down his bitterness for fear that, if he expressed it, he would be in danger of losing his one regular source of intellectual support and his pipeline to Michelet and Michelet's Paris circuit. But in light of all the other evidence, that sort of argument would be akin to the adjustments in the Ptolemaic system to hold off the Copernican bad news about the geocentric theory of the universe. Other evidence about family mentalities and generational ties in Orleanist France is there in abundance.

There is evidence of great conservatism, probably based on the slow rate of social and economic modernization in 19th-century France. Although there are important demographic shifts from rural to urban, and economic ones from traditional craft to a modern industrial society, at no time before the Second World War was the rate of change comparable to that in England between 1780 and 1840, or in Germany and the United States between 1860 and 1920. Indeed, it was only in the interbellum that the percentage of Frenchmen living in urban circumstances exceeded that of the rural population. In the late 19th century the majority of the work force remained concentrated in traditional trades, and even in the 1930s, the average number of Frenchmen per industrial establishment was about one-fifth of the English or American average, and one-tenth of the German (Mitzman, 1990a, pp. 3-8).

Under such social conditions, the traditional French family structures and mentalities remained intact and largely unquestioned.[6] Sartre (1971/1972) noted in *L'idiot de la Famille* that when the youths of Flaubert's generation revolted against school discipline and clerical control, they did so not with the consciousness of generational rebels but rather out of a sense of solidarity with their parents' anticlericalism. True enough, horizontal peer relations were a powerful alternative to the vertical influences of fathers and mothers, but even here a broader perspective belies the assumption, based for example on youth bonding in the German youth movement in this century, that peer relations necessarily pitted the generations against one another. Despite their festive, erotic, and aggressive aspects, the traditional rural youth peer groups, in France the *bachelleries* or *abbayes de jeunesse,* were the major socializing frameworks for village youths in the traditional patriarchal morality. (See Gillis, 1974. Gillis draws most of his material from English and German history, but his findings are also relevant for France.) Among the progeny of the urban bourgeoisie, the loose group of friends around Dumesnil and Noel, and the better-known youth friendships of Flaubert, Hugo, and Vallès, echo at an informal level such rural youth peer groups. These bourgeois youth ties, though often in the service of the political or cultural avant-garde, had comparably conservative social functions for the family morality.

Except for Baudelaire's bloodthirsty outcry against his military stepfather during the heady days of February 1848, and Stendhal's retrospective death wish, in his autobiography, against papa Beyle, it is difficult to find direct expressions of generational hatred in 19th-century France; I know of none against the sacrosanct mothers of the time. (There was of course an abstract fear of "bad mothers" [*marâtres*], epitomized in the young Michelet's mother's identification of the material fatality of nature in India with the suffocating *marâtre,* quite possibly based on anxiety for his own dominant mother. But this rhetoric never shaped his conscious attitude toward her, which was always reverential. See Mitzman, 1990a). The radical rhetoric of Michelet's revolutionary patriotism was replete with worshipful references to the "fathers" of the Enlightenment, and Noel and Dumesnil applied this reverence to Michelet and others. The behavioral patterns do not belie this rhetoric. One did not, in fact, leave one's parents, except perhaps for university study or marriage. In Michelet's case, for neither. His mother died when he was still in secondary school. He remained with his artisan father throughout his university training and, from age 26, his marriage. In fact, he not only shared his house with his father, but his bedroom as well. Pauline, his wife, slept elsewhere. The case of Flaubert, who after dropping out of his Parisian law studies returned for life to his mother's side in Croisset, is well known. Dumesnil's relation to his parents, who separated when he was 15, reflected the same family mentality. His mother took him to Paris in 1837, where he completed secondary school and began his law studies. As we have noted, the mother attended his lectures with him, thereby meeting Michelet, and it was partly her attachment and love for her sickly son that inflamed the widower Michelet's amorous imagination. There are no signs that anyone interpreted that love as suffocating or debilitating, though it may well have been so. After the death of his mother, an enormous trauma for both the 20-year-old Alfred and her historian friend, Alfred proposed to Michelet that they bring his retired, elderly father, to whom he had earlier written complaining about the father's lack of support for his wayward wife, to live with them all in Paris. Michelet, who apparently distinguished between his obligations to his own father and to that of his son-in-law, found the suggestion excessive. But the fact remains that there was no one in Noel's immediate circle of friends who could view his desire to leave his parents to avoid a life of rural isolation and boredom, even with their consent and urging, as anything but rank abandonment. And Noel, swallowing his bitterness, was forced to agree.

Forced? Not really. Considering how strong his mother's position was in her family and how powerful his own ties to her were, he must have been highly ambivalent on the matter. For one thing, the father seems to have recognized the primacy of the mother's position, since the basis for his move to the Norman countryside in 1841 was the fact that her family came from there. For another, there was a powerful, unbroken symbiotic tie between mother and son. Invitations to visit Paris or to go on joint vacations with Dumesnil involved Noel, a man around 30, in what he once referred to as Talleyrand-like negotiations with his mother. It was a standing joke among his friends that his mother became ill every time he was on the point of leaving: One of them suggested to him that he stop negotiating and simply announce a day in advance that he was leaving. In fact, his mother had good reason to be anxious about losing him. Not only was he the only survivor of seven births, but he was also so sickly as a child that, until he reached the age of 20, his parents had frequently given up hope that he would survive. There was a positive side to this anxious closeness. He refers several times to a playful relationship with his mother—snowball fights and less aggressive games—as well as to an excellent relationship with his father.

In this case, then, guilt about leaving mama was complicated by genuine affection; and even when a move to Paris seemed to make perfect sense and she herself supported the idea, the voice of social conscience, the Greek chorus of Dumesnil and Michelet reminding Noel of his filial obligations, merged with his own reservations and dissuaded him.

History and Object Relations

In February 1848, 8 months after his abortive effort to leave his parents, revolution broke out in Paris, ushering in the French Second Republic. The classic literary portrayal of the inner failure of that revolution is in Part III of Flaubert's (1870) *L'Education Sentimentale,* in which the hopeless quest of the hero for a maternal older woman stands in an obscure symbolic relationship to the broader political fiasco of the period. Dolf Oehler, in a remarkable Sartrean analysis of Flaubert's novel, has argued that Frédéric's love for Madame Arnoux reflects a more general problem of the young men of his generation, their domination by and fixation on their mothers, and that it was the confusion between their political and their erotic ideals that doomed the revolution to failure. He wrote:

> Frédéric Moreau is the true hero of an "enthusiastic bourgeois youth" . . . which in the Revolution or in the Republic went in quest of its Madame Arnoux, a mother/Maria/lover of which it expected the most contradictory things: great freedom, infinite sensual pleasure, profound security, gentle indulgence, in short, the terrestrial paradise. Implicitly Flaubert interprets the desire for freedom of these so progressive sons of the bourgeoisie as an expression of regressive fantasies stemming from an unconscious fixation on a maternal image. This incestuous fixation makes comprehensible both the quasi-religious fervor of their love and its profound impotence: one can, in this frivolous Paris, no more seduce Marie-Angèle Arnoux than one can the sublime Republic. As for a direct confrontation with the father, Frédéric is as incapable of it as he is of separation from the mother; he dreams of deceiving him, of killing him; but he needs him both to sustain the fantasy that he will one day possess Madame Arnoux and at the same time to prevent the realization of this fantasy. (Oehler, 1980)

Noel and Dumesnil, though they had been talking apocalyptically about the coming revolution for years, though they were swollen with enthusiasm by the February days and had, with Michelet's support, both advanced their candidacy for the assembly in the first elections of the Republic, were as ineffective and disappointed by the harsh realities of 1848 as Flaubert's hero. Could Oehler's postulate of a connection between the mother fixations of Flaubert's antiheroes and their political impotence hold true for Michelet's two adopted sons? Here I have, of course, entered a highly speculative area. It would be rash to attempt to apply hidden messages in the *Education Sentimentale* to real persons who have never been mentioned as related to its characters. But even in this no-man's-land between fiction and reality, a few historical facts are ascertainable about the novelist's knowledge of the circle around Michelet. Apart from the friendship between Michelet and Flaubert in the 1860s, there is the fact that Flaubert, like Noel and Dumesnil, studied history at the Lycée Royale in Rouen under Michelet's disciple Chéruel, who in 1840 recommended Dumesnil as well as Flaubert to his *maître*.

Dumesnil and Flaubert, though there is no record of their contact in secondary school, would have received their *baccalaureate* in the same year if Dumesnil had not moved with his mother to Paris and Flaubert had not been expelled for insubordination in 1839. Moreover, they were both friendly with Louis Boivin, the literarily inclined son of a magistrate. Boivin's youthful letters to Dumesnil are part of the collection in the Bibliothèque Historique, and his signature appears with those of 11 other students as cosigners of Flaubert's protest letter of November 1839, *au proviseur du lycée Corneille,* the letter that led to his expulsion. Like Flaubert, Boivin was grieved by the premature death in 1848 of the young writer's close friend Le Poittevin, of which he wrote to Dumesnil.

More important is Flaubert's contact late in 1861 with Noel, around the time he was beginning to work on the *Education.* A letter from the novelist to "*mon cher Confrère*" of November 8, 1861, is a tantalizingly brief "*merci*" for something unspecified, with excuses offered "for the trouble I have caused you," and the equally obscure "One of these days I will go see you": to talk about what, precisely? All of this appears as loose sand, whose significance would probably be nil were it not for one unalterable fact. The very first reference in Flaubert's notebook to the lady who in the novel would become the madonna-like Mme. Arnoux, so vainly loved by the mother-complexed Frédéric, was a one-page fragment written within a few months after the letter announcing an imminent visit to Noel. It bore the title "*Le roman de Mme Dumesnil.*"

Which is not to say that it is either certain or even likely that Flaubert knew of, and integrated into his novel, the characters of Dumesnil's mother and her son and Noel. It does, however, seem to be a hypothesis worth looking at that there is a more than accidental connection between the maternal dependencies of Dumesnil and Noel and those in the *Education.*

Oehler's insight into Flaubert's novel places one aspect of Noel's identity, his problematic but unbreakable attachment to his mother, in a larger social and political framework. There is, however, another aspect of his identity and character that also needs comment: his peer relationship to Dumesnil and to others. For regardless of whether it is true that the mother complexes of Noel's generation stymied their chiliastic political aspirations, it is a certainty that the soil in which those aspirations flourished was the intimate ground of peer friendship characterized by the mutual friendship of Noel and Dumesnil, which, both men agreed in the years before 1848, was to be the model of the revolutionary fraternity to come (Mitzman, 1990b). Moreover, much of Noel's literary accomplishment as well as his character development grew directly out of his voluminous, half-century dialogue with his closest friend.

To sum up this tangled web of fact, theory, and supposition: The historian's approach to individual identity involves him in a simultaneous double investigation into relationships and motives, his own in approaching his subject and that of his subject in establishing his life history. In both sides of this inquiry, the convergence of object-relational theory with Bakhtin's notion of the dialogic imagination provides a useful point of departure. But the historian's sources must in the final analysis guide and justify both theory and introspection. I was fortunate in that my two friends were often explicit in their letters about their mutual interdependence, and aware of how important their relationship was for their creative identity. One of the clearest expressions of this was in a letter Noel wrote to Dumesnil in January 1845:

> Never will we be more valuable to any public than we are to one another. Others say: I will write this for the public, I will put this in my next work. We, we say: I will write it to Noel, I will say it to Alfred. Here is our true originality, it is to have done for each other what one ordinarily does for the entire world, for the future and for glory.[7]

Dialogue. Relation. Imagination. What the English novelist E. M. Forster was getting at when he wrote: "Only connect."

Notes

1. For a brief, clear presentation of the evolution of social history from a focus on long-term, unchanging structures to its present interest in the *événementiel,* see Revel (1989).

2. In a review article in the Dutch journal *Theoretische Geschiedenis,* Marleen Wessel provides a sympathetic critique of Ginzburg's epistemological distinction, which she views as too rigidly drawn (Wessel, 1991).

3. I am indebted to Joep Leersen for pointing out the applicability of this concept to peripheral ethnic cultures, such as those of the Breton and Irish peoples.

4. For the sake of brevity, I have simplified in this text an incredibly complicated process. Historians working with the concept realize that the relations between high and low are never one-way, that the way in which popular strata internalize the moral mandates of the elite inevitably affects the elite itself, that there are historical periods in

which the process appears to be suspended or even reversed (as in the assimilation by a modernizing elite culture of elements of the popular culture in French romanticism), and that one of the major examples of diffusion of "civilized" mores, the English, reveals the source of the new virtuousness to be not at the top, but in the middle of the social ladder: the Puritan middle class of the 17th century (Kruithof, 1980; Mitzman, 1986).

5. I have benefited considerably from discussions on this point with my assistant, Peter de Back, who has studied Hugo and Zola in the light of both Bakhtin and Elias. Bakhtin's notion of carnivalization, fruitful though it has been for historical and literary inquiry, requires and has received emendation. Stallybrass and White (1986) have noted the problems with its linkage to popular protest: As often as not, it is used to repress antiestablishment movements, which, themselves marginal, are derided with the use of grotesque humor by those adhering to the traditional morality and power structure. Such was the case in the suppression of Winstanley's Diggers in 17th-century England and in the recent antinuclear protests at Greenham Common. They propose the looser but broader concept of transgression, which is especially fruitful in analyzing literary examples of Bakhtin's ideas. Stephen Greenblatt (1982) has also broadened the applicability of Bakhtin's concepts. Several monographs by French social historians, though they do not discuss Bakhtin, can be viewed as emendations of his view of the carnivalesque and the scatological: Alain Faure (1978), Yves Marie Bercée (1976), and Alain Corbin (1986). A recently published monograph by Irish historian Dorinda Outram (1989) does interpret the French Revolution in the explicitly Bakhtinian terms of "a struggle between the 'closed body' of the bourgeoisie and the 'carnivalesque' body of the lower orders."

6. Demographers distinguish a traditional North French (and North European) from a South French (Mediterranean) family structure and mentality in matters regarding inheritance, cohabitation of generations, and economic and social solidarity (Todd, 1988).

7. Bibliothèque Historique de la Ville de Paris, Papiers Dumesnil, MS 1586, f.23V, 1-28-45.

9

Identity and Development

An Interdisciplinary View

TOBI L. G. GRAAFSMA
HARKE A. BOSMA
HAROLD D. GROTEVANT
DAVID J. DE LEVITA

The foregoing chapters clearly illustrate how the concept of identity is used in different ways, even within the same discipline. Sometimes the concept is used to indicate something about a core, whether that refers to the core of the individual (as in psychiatry and psychoanalysis) or to the characteristic features of a nation or ethnic group in which identity is considered to be representing its core (for example, as in historical studies of the Celtic identity or in sociological studies on nationalism and ethnicity). Here, core points to some valuable, esteemed character or essence to which one feels attached. At other times, however, as in the work of Erikson, the concept is used to refer to such core features in relation to the social and wider cultural context of the individual ("recognition by others," "embeddedness"; see Chapter 1). Then the interplay, the mutual regulation of social environment and individuality, is emphasized. Even better, the concept is used to stress an interactional perspective through the necessity of such mutuality. This is also expressed by authors who stress the importance of embeddedness or holding. In this relational view, identity refers to the coregulation of core and context characteristics. This core-context model of identity will be further elaborated in this chapter. Then the contributions to this volume will be discussed in terms of this model. However, first we want to make some remarks on the recent popularity of the concept of identity.

Identity, History, and Transference to Theory

The variations in the core-context balance point to the fundamental dependency and attachments of human beings. Individuality and autonomy are relative. Relative to what, one may ask. There seem to be constraints on autonomy coming from at least three sides: from the side of biological anatomy; from the side of unconscious, intrapsychic dynamics; and from the side of larger social and cultural factors. Obviously, both psychoanalysis and sociology point to the fact that identity is shaped and determined to larger degrees than one may want to believe by influences outside conscious individual control. Besides that, identity implies being attached both inwardly and outwardly. Without these attachments, uprootedness results. Erikson (1964) assumed that such uprootedness might be an explanation for the popularity of the concept of identity in recent decades.

Historians remind us, as does for example Mitzman, that the entire discourse on identity occurs at specific moments in Western history and under very specific conditions. Historians study these conditions. They investigate the large-scale historical networks and mentalities that produce collective identity. They even gradually become involved in the area of individual identity, as for example happens to Gay and Loewenberg, making use of psychoanalytic theory (see also Chapter 8).

Concepts sometimes reach peaks in popularity. For some time many phenomena are worded in language related to a certain concept, and then the use of that concept may decline. The pendulum swings from great expectations to great disappointments. Concepts and theories invested with expectations are embraced and discarded without regard to conceptual clarity. Psychoanalysts call this phenomenon *transference to theory.* Perhaps the vagueness itself contributes to the attractiveness of a concept, because so much can be projected in it. All this probably can be said of the use that was and is made of the concept of identity. The concept reached a peak in popularity by the mid-1960s (see also Gleason, 1983), when the term *identity* was used so widely and so loosely that in fact it began to cover up more than it clarified. Erikson, who played a key role in this process, commented in 1968:

> So far I have tried out the term identity almost deliberately—I like to think—in many different connotations. At one time it seemed to refer to a conscious sense of individual uniqueness, at another to an unconscious striving for a continuity of experience, and at a third, as a solidarity with a group's ideals. In some respects the term appeared to be colloquial and naive, a mere manner of speaking, while in others it was related to existing concepts in psychoanalysis and sociology. And on more than one occasion the word slipped in more like a habit that seems to make things appear familiar than as a clarification. (Erikson, 1968, p. 208)

This is his introduction to a further attempt to clarify the meaning of the concept, and a discussion of its relationship to other constructs.

Without going into detailed argumentation, it appears that the popularity of the concept of identity was caused in part by the cultural and social circumstances of the 1960s, years in which ideologies and values (indispensable for individual and cultural continuity and mutuality) in Western societies got uprooted—to use Erikson's terms (1964). The relation of the individual to society became more ambivalent than it had been for many years (cf. Habermas, 1988; Riesman, 1953). Identity as a term seemed useful in pointing to that changing relationship. Several sociologists even argued that the value Western societies put on autonomy, equality, and individualism implicitly reduced and complicated matters of communality and solidarity. Exactly this situation formed the crux of psychosocial identity theory for Erikson: Identity concerns the interaction and especially the confluence between the core of the individual and the core of his or her communal culture; identity concerns the dynamics of this confluence between historical times and the individual.

There is no reason to assume that scientific theories and models escape irrational idealizations or devaluations. Some are revered, others are fought against, devalued, or simply avoided. Scientific and theoretical schools come into existence. Within disciplines one can see much animosity and rivalry; between disciplines one can see the same. Not all causes working behind such attitudes reach our conscious awareness. In psychoanalytic terms, one would say indeed: Here is transference to theory at work. Rangell (e.g., 1982), who wrote much about the phenomenon of transference to theories, touched on this issue in Chapter 2.

Two reasons, we presume, why Erikson's identity theory was suitable for such transference investment were its apparent clarity and its promising, optimistic character. It differed from the more deterministic and thus painful character of psychoanalytic theory in general, to which Erikson's work added many insights. It did not seem to matter that it remained very difficult to pin down exactly what was meant by the concept of identity (e.g., de Levita, 1965).

Although many researchers based their definition of the concept on Erikson's definition, it probably did not matter to many of them what Erikson had meant with it himself. For some it may have only mattered that this psychosocial concept might be suitable to fight mainstream psychoanalytic thinking or main psychoanalytic discoveries, such as the painful discovery that the person is less master in his or her mind than one wants to believe.

Transference to theory may lead to creative theory formation; many scientific discoveries emerged out of work in which transference initially played a role. But transference to theory may also lead to theory formation, functioning as what psychoanalysis calls defensive screens: They may block painful insights and painful realities. This happens in particular—if we permit ourselves the extrapolation of a clinical finding—when one does not reflect on the phenomenon itself. Here one can see the wisdom of the adage that one is doomed to repeat one's history unless one reflects on and learns from the things done and the choices made. Thus, we see the importance of defining the concept of identity as precisely as possible.

An Interdisciplinary Model for Identity and Development

Identity and development are intrinsically related. As discussed in Chapter 1, identity may be considered in different ways: in terms of sameness, being an identifiable person, and also in terms of constancy in the midst of transformations. It is, of course, logically impossible to talk about remaining constant without addressing the fact of change. They are really two sides of the same identity coin. One cannot discuss the concept of identity without reflecting on development. Indeed, it is precisely the fact of development that provokes the question of identity.

We assert that the concept of identity is useful exactly and only here. Rather than considering identity some sort of static endpoint, we propose to use the concept when one studies the dynamic tension or balance between core and context in the midst of developmental change. In this volume we have presented perspectives on this dynamic tension or balance that range in scope from the intrapsychic to the historical.

Identity involves the balance between something that is core and something that serves as the context to that core. Attunement between these two guarantees the sameness or continuity over time that we think of as identity, a guarantee that for several reasons seems to be psychologically indispensable.

The developmental dimension underlying identity can range from the moment-to-moment adaptations that are made intrapsychically or within social interactions; to qualitative changes across developmental stages such as infancy, childhood, and adolescence; to generational and historical periods that can span decades and centuries. This may suffice to indicate that such attunement implies a demand for continual "identity work." Although this work continually needs to occur on several levels, it does not follow that such work is always very conscious or prominent.

Identity is thus at stake in a wide range of situations and over different scales of time, in which a need is felt to maintain the core-context balance. For example, social psychologists have identified the dimension of self-monitoring, which describes how willing individuals are to adjust their behavior or style of interacting to the feedback they receive from the partner with whom they are interacting. In a 10-minute interaction, persons low in self-monitoring might be likely to change their style of interacting or their way of presenting themselves very little, regardless of their interactional partner; whereas, an individual high in self-monitoring might modify his or her behavior quite dramatically. In adolescence as a developmental period, young persons must adapt to a whole range of biological, cognitive, and social changes. Yet although they change, they still feel they remain generally the same. Often this can work itself out only gradually, over several years (or decades). On a historical scale, the period of adolescence has only recently been viewed as a significant phase of identity development (Baumeister, 1986). Reciprocally, historical changes influence the issues around which the core-context attunement revolves (cf. Neubauer, Chapter 7).

These examples are all on the level of the individual person, but they can be extended both downward to more microlevel processes (e.g., the attunement of different intrapsychic processes discussed in Chapter 3) and upward to more macro ones (e.g., the relation between individual identity and ethnic identity, or the relation between national and regional identity, see Chapter 8).

From the perspectives of the chapters represented in this volume, it appears that the use of identity varies across different disciplines in at least two important ways. First, both core and context are defined differently. For example, core can refer to an intrapsychic core, to a national psyche, or the even the core of the writer or the subject of the writing. Likewise, context can refer to the intrapsychic context (through the interaction of id, ego, and superego) and to wider circles of contexts such as family, peer group, society, and historical time. Second, disciplines differ in how they focus on aspects of the model presented here. A short discussion of the perspectives represented in this volume may illustrate this.

Psychoanalysis tends to focus most clearly on the intrapsychic core (see Rangell, Chapter 2). For Rangell, identity is an enduring mental state, referring to individual conceptualizations about the self. These conceptualizations, Rangell states, are influenced by fantasies, by what one knows and wants to know about the self, by identifications (e.g., with expectations of parents), by a wish for uniqueness, by the impression one thinks one makes on others, and by evaluations of all of this. For Rangell, identity thus is a composition (like a piece of music), dissectable into many components; not an ultimate explanation, but result and cause of eventually unconscious choices made and directions taken by the individual ego for the self at certain moments in life. Within this perspective, identity is a composition based on the dynamics within the individual ego, that identity is influenced by some etiology and it leads the ego to choice and action; it is both outcome and starting point. Identity here is considered to be a subjective theory about the self in social interaction although it should be realized that that theory is first of all an affective theory. Rangell's views on identity make one think of the psychoanalytic theory on compromise formations, which also are partly conscious and partly unconscious compositions made by the individual ego in situations of internal and external conflict. Identity however seems to differ from compromise formations in general, because identity relates first of all to the self and the object world in interaction. Rangell's emphasis remains truly psychoanalytic: As he states at the end of his introduction, he tries to show how the human core (which consists of unconscious intrapsychic wishes and conflicts) motivates all choices and actions.

Graafsma (Chapter 3) also starts from a psychoanalytic point of view, but he puts less emphasis on the intrapsychic influences leading to some sense and conception of the self, to some identity. In fact, he proposes first to use the concept of identity very precisely, and second to use the concept of identity in two general ways. These ways can be summarized as consisting of two points of view on the dynamics of development. One concerns an interactional point of view and refers to the dynamics of the attunement between the self and environment, that is to the attunement work of the individual ego. The other concerns the (regular psychoanalytic and intrapsychic) dynamic point of view, with an emphasis on the unconscious ego in action. In that perspective, Graafsma's chapter is compatible with that of Rangell. He differs in that he uses the concept of identity in a less global, more microscopic sense as a (sometimes wanted, but also sometimes unwanted) outcome of what is called in psychoanalysis the organizing or integrating function of the ego.

The empirical study of identity in adolescence is discussed in Chapter 4. Marcia places his identity status model solidly within the framework of Erikson's theory of psychosocial development. Late adolescence is the first stage in the human lifespan in which an individual's identity is attained. The identity statuses Achievement, Moratorium, Foreclosure, and Diffusion are the behavioral outcomes of this process. Identity in late adolescence is a starting point, the challenges of the later normative crises can lead to thorough reformulations of the initial identity configuration. For Marcia, identity refers to a "coherent sense of one's meaning to oneself and to others within that social context" (Chapter 4). This definition is directly based on Erikson's work in the sense that it both refers to "feeling to be the same as I was" and "the recognition of that sameness by others." The behavioral measure used by Marcia, with the process variables of commitment and exploration as its core, neatly reflects this double meaning. The following quote from Bourne (1978, p. 227) illustrates this:

> Commitments can of course be of many kinds—vocational, avocational, social, marital, ideological, ethical. From an outside observer's point of view, an individual's commitments would include the domains in which he appears most engaged or involved. From the individual's own point of view his commitments are the matters which he characteristically cares about most or values. From either point of view, these commitments have a social significance and at the same time provide the individual with a definition of himself.

> [In other words] by my commitments I shall know myself and be known to others. (Bourne, 1978, p. 234)

Exploration refers to the experimentation with alternative possibilities of committing oneself, to whether the identity configuration is a self-constructed or an ascribed one.

Though Marcia's phrasing sometimes seems to reflect an inner core formulation of identity ("the initial identity . . . is not the last identity"; "A solid sense of self is a necessary, but not sufficient, condition for an identity"), the main variables in the measure, commitment and exploration, necessitate an interactional perspective on identity. They refer to the dynamic attunement of individual and context, to what could be called the identity process: attaining and maintaining some sort of identity between individual and contextual characteristics. And, of course, this identity needs reformulations whenever individual or contextual changes in the life span demand so. In this sense identity work never stops.

In Chapter 5 Josselson also stresses the need for a relational use of the concept of identity. However, according to her, empirical research on identity still has a male bias and, "as a result, our identity theory tends to expand in the directions of doing, of agency, of self-assertion and self-awareness, of mastery, values and abstract commitment." Her view is that identity has largely been equated with selfhood. She argues that next to being a separate and autonomous person (a lone self), identity can be described as continuity in relatedness, in having stable (but not static) connections with others, being embedded in sociocultural structures. Identity then is equated with relatedness, with connectedness as a continuous structure itself. "Although identity is, in part, distinct, differentiated selfhood, it is also an integration of relational contexts which profoundly shape, bound and limit, but also create opportunities for the emergent identity." In her contribution she next distinguishes eight dimensions that underlie the relational aspects of identity formation. These are holding, attachment, libidinal connection, validation, identification, mutuality, embeddedness, and care (see Chapter 5). The discussion of these dimensions serves to demonstrate how identity essentially emerges in the form of "being with." This is a truly relational approach to identity, that is, on the mutual attunement of core and context, which, at one place in Josselson's contribution, is effectively illustrated by Anderson's story of the ugly duckling.

In terms of the model we presented earlier, the dimensions Josselson proposes might be thought of as referring to different forms or aspects of an attunement process. One can also say that many of the dimensions refer to conditions—necessary, optimal, ideal—for identity to develop and remain. The "how" of such relatedness or attunement is still little explored. A static harmony might well predict future disturbances of development. An example of such a situation could be the steady state of identity foreclosure described by Marcia in Chapter 4. Although this is not the place for a thorough analysis of Josselson's suggestions in terms of the core-context model, it seems that the dimensions could be very helpful in a further specification of the model. For example, connections could be made to the different stages in the human life span (e.g., the attunement at infancy) or to the different aspects of the individual's context (e.g., in social contacts, in intimate relationships, in society).

The psychoanalytic contributions to this book (Part I) clearly have an intrapsychic focus. Marcia's chapter concerns identity on an individual level, and Josselson stresses the relational aspects of identity. Widdershoven's contribution (Chapter 6) provides a broader view, taking a philosophical perspective on identity and development within the context of modern life. His starting point is present-day philosophy and its focus on narratives. Within life-span developmental psychology the narrative approach is becoming more popular (which, in our opinion, does not necessarily imply better) as an alternative for the earlier mechanistic and organismic models. Widdershoven discusses different kinds of narrative approaches, depending on three types of narrative identity, the closed, the open, and the radically open. These types are thought to reflect differences in types of social order that form the context for the individual's identity. The closed type reflects a clear and stable social order, and the radically open type is characteristic of highly individualized societies.

This perspective points again to the interdependency of core and context. Widdershoven's contribution adds to the thought that different historical times have different identity scenarios available. The outcomes of attunement processes will vary accordingly, but the nature of these processes may remain the same. A further elucidation of the core-context model is necessary in order to be more explicit on these ideas.

In the contribution of Neubauer (Chapter 7) the core-context model seems applicable on three different levels, dynamically interrelated to one another. The widest level concerns historical changes and the conceptualization of adolescence in terms of an identity crisis. Within that particular context the so-called peer-group narrative convention is discussed, which, according to Neubauer, suggests that the primary context of the turn-of-the-century adolescent identity crises is the peer group. Lacretelle's book is presented as an example of this convention. This a story about the identity crisis of the protagonist and the narrator's identity crisis, which is conditioned through the friendship of the narrator and the protagonist. The interpersonal level is a second level where the core-context model is applicable. The book describes how Silbermann, a Jewish boy who is a newcomer to a school, makes the narrator, the central figure in the story, feel tempted to stand loyal to Silbermann when he became the target of anti-Semitic attacks, but ultimately to retreat to the unproblematic and permitted pleasures of some other friendship that might further his father's career. The entrance of a newcomer in itself is not to be called a development, because it lacks a structural character. It is better considered to be a change in the existing situation. But it presented the narrator with possible developments, which all implied conflict with core values and group solidarity. This brings us to the intrapersonal level. For the narrator anxiety proves to be too great in the end. Opportunism and conformity win. The narrator adapts by this solution: He rationalizes his choices, and not without difficulty, saying upon his return to the old, safe path: "This is very true to life." Which, by the way, again shows us the role self-deceit may play in any process of attunement (see also Chapter 3).

Lacretelle's book effectively illustrates the dynamics of identity maintenance, especially on the inter- and intra-individual levels. Modifications in core and/or context on whichever level require adaptations to maintain identity—or to put it in a different way, a certain "goodness of fit"—between core and context. The transactional character of this process is evident in Neubauer's contribution. In other chapters, especially in Josselson's chapter, similar processes are also described in some detail. However, there are still far more questions than answers concerning the nature of these processes on the various levels, and the interaction between the core-context balances of these levels.

In his contribution to the discussion of identity and development from history, Mitzman (Chapter 8) addresses the question of personal identity, the place of the individual in history. His scholarly review of the discussion on this subject between psychohistorians and social historians clearly illustrates the problems of linking different perspectives, in this case an intraindividual and a sociocultural perspective, and the need for a conceptual framework for linking perspectives from these different levels. According to Mitzman, an object-relational perspective helped clarify the mutuality of personal identity and historical conditions in 19th-century France. This very perspective also points to another important relationship, namely the relationship between the historian's own identity and that of his subject. Here the central question is formulated by Mitzman as "the extent to which one's own identity and values aid or hinder one's view of the subject: in analytic terms, the question of countertransference."

Again, the core-context model is clearly applicable in Mitzman's chapter; on the wider level of the relationship between individual and history, but also on the (intra-)personal level of the historian and his or her transference to the subject of study. Mitzman's suggestions and experiences might be of much help for a further study of these relationships. Mitzman shows what is well known in psychoanalytic technique: A thorough analysis of the complex of transference and countertransference promotes both clinical insight and scientific insight. According to Mitzman, the situation in the study of history (both on the level of the individual and history, and on the level of the historian and the subject of study) also illustrates a potential drawback of too much identity or the dangers of foreclosing, fixing the dynamic balance of core and context. True scientific progress could be blocked when the theoretical tools of the researcher are fixed and do not fit with the subject of study.

Concluding Remarks

In this volume, the concept of identity is used in a variety of ways. The heuristic model presented above is very useful in making clear that these variations are not mutually exclusive or unrelated, but that identity always refers to a relationship between a core and a context. This relationship can be seen on different levels. Thus, identity concerns an equality of two entities; it bridges, for example, states, persons, groups, or cultural structures. It also concerns development: structural change, which, paradoxically, leaves the object unchanged. Identity by definition implies an interactional point of view on development, individual, social, and historical. Therefore it may function in an interdisciplinary way: as an interface, for example, between individual personality and the character of social change.

By definition, identity refers to the tension between two opposing aspects—or to put it differently, has two poles to bridge—namely, being different and unique, and being similar and identical. Both are important aspects of identity. They are closely connected, and individuals as well as groups (for reasons we still do not completely understand) have a crucial need for some precise balance between the two. In our view, the proper subject of theoretical and empirical work in identity is how such a bridge is built and maintained. Given all of the different levels on which such a bridge can be discerned, identity also bridges disciplines. It presupposes an interdisciplinary approach.

As we draw to the end of this book, time and space prevent us from going into further detail about all of the disciplines that potentially could be involved in this interdisciplinary work. Given our own academic backgrounds (developmental psychology, psychoanalysis, child psychiatry) we will limit ourselves to some final remarks concerning personal identity.

For the individual, such a core-context balance may be experientially expressed as a sense of wholeness, comparable perhaps to what we can see already in infancy in the dual unity of mother and child, and what we can see on a larger scale in our close, intimate relation (although exactly as happens in mother-child relationships: with a lot of ambivalence) with our "motherland." We see the balance as dynamic: The wish for uniqueness and the wish for similarity mutually determine and influence each other. This mutuality might well be compared with a dance. The maintenance of identity might well be compared with the rhythm and culture of a dance.

In our view, identity points to the interface between two (or more) sides. However, it should be realized that identity is also an intermediate product. Some aspects of a child's identity, for example, are already determined in part before the child is born. It matters a great deal whether a child is born in the context of Western civilization (of which some of the participants in the Identity and Development conference said that it lived in the Century of Freud) or in circumstances of poverty in a Third World country. The emergence of identity is also influenced, also before a child is born, by the values and expectations parents have for their child and by their attitudes, their pride, their wishes, and their anxieties. The child has to identify itself with these parental expectations in order to fit in with his or her environment. Behind identity one can find the factors causing its emergence and dynamics. But identity works also as a cause itself; it leads to output, to actions, to moods, to attitudes. It may even lead to larger-scale changes and developments, as history and literature both inside and outside science amply demonstrate, for example, Erikson's biographies of Luther (1958) and Gandhi (1969).

This brings us back to the dynamics of identity formation and identity maintenance. Identity formation can and should be considered with regard to the ways individuals and groups meet expectations about them; with regard to the ways they identify themselves in order to achieve and maintain that precarious balance between distinctiveness and similarity, between holding on to some essential individual core and group acceptance.

No doubt, when a person lives in a generative harmony between self and environment, a subjective sense of identity scarcely emerges into consciousness. An optimal sense of identity, according to Erikson "is experienced merely as a sense of psychosocial well-being. Its most obvious concomitants are a feeling of being at home in one's body, a sense of 'knowing where one is going,' and an inner assuredness of anticipated recognition from those who count" (1968, p. 165). This applies probably to the identity of groups as well. But when someone doubts his or her own value and position and recognition in the surrounding world or in the development of the wider environment, feels "out of phase," so to speak, a painful self-consciousness can arise, and compulsive efforts to delineate a new identity can be stimulated. We hypothesize that in normal development such harmony is not a static form of congruence, but rather an affective mutual regulation, with a generative, development-promoting character, which, by some authors is nicely circumscribed as "attunement" (Stern, 1985) or "co-regulation" (Fogel, 1993). The importance of this mutuality for the recovery of patients with severe identity problems had been stressed long ago, for example by Searles (1959) and Winnicott (1965).

In each developmental stage the matter of identity must be addressed anew. However, identity formation has its nodal phases. Two crucial, decisive phases seem to be the separation-individuation phase of early childhood, and the phase of resolution of bisexual identifications in puberty. Although the preceding chapters have not focused specifically on these phases, it is necessary to note their importance, because they are both times during which gender identity and sexual identity become consolidated and integrated into one's overall psychosocial identity.

To conclude, we have conceptualized identity as a bridge between core and context. Simple as that statement appears, however, we must issue a warning. Unless we try to specify and unravel the dynamics of that mutual regulation, the dynamics of that dance, the dynamics of what happens on what we called a bridge, we run the risk of encountering the same situation the concept of identity has hit against so often: It is assumed that everybody understands what is meant without sufficient clarification.

To illustrate this closing point, we offer an excerpt from a discussion that took place during the Identity and Development conference in Amsterdam, which formed the basis for this book. It clearly underscores the need for further efforts to clarify the meaning and applicability of identity, but also the value of doing so.

Oppenheimer: I'm slowly getting angry. I've been listening now for almost 2 days to a group of people sitting together here from different disciplines whose reputations I value very highly. We have come in here and without any criticism have accepted the existence of a construct-like identity.

I have not heard from anybody here in this meeting what identity is actually all about, what it means, how to operationalize it, how to study it. We are all talking about identity. I haven't heard from my colleague philosophers whether it's a worthwhile concept, whether we should continue with this concept, or in whatever way we should deal with a concept like identity.

Marcia: If you did not hear a definition of identity and if you did not hear an operationalization of it, you were not listening. Now, you may have heard something that you did not like . . .

Oppenheimer: That's too simple.

Marcia: It's not simple. It was presented and it was presented fairly clearly, so either you heard it and did not like it or you did not hear it, but it would have been difficult not to hear it, having listened.

Oppenheimer: I don't agree. I have now heard the discussion. I have asked the question whether identity is a cultural problem. If we threw out the idea or the concept of identity, what would we be missing in psychology? Tell me.

Marcia: You would be missing a well-developed and organized psychosocial developmental scheme that will give some kind of order to human development, if in fact validity can be determined for the rest of that developmental scheme as well. You may not like that psychosocial developmental scheme, but if you throw out the concept of identity from it, then you will be missing a central part of it. That's what you will be missing.

Graafsma: I would like to add something to that, because identity theory led me to see the unconscious organizing function of the ego. Otherwise perhaps I would not have discovered the dynamics of the identity problems many of my adolescent patients speak about.

Oppenheimer: Yes, but why do we need the concept of identity then, if we can do it with the ego or the self or with personality? I mean what are we going to lose, except within a particular theory? If the theory's not that efficient, we take another one. What I have listened to now for a few hours is people talking on different levels, on different dimensions, one direction A, the other one the opposite direction. No communication is made. I'm sorry, I mean, some people may sense some communication here, I don't. I may be very stupid and naive, but I'm very ready to accept that. Still, I want to learn something about identity, and you are not teaching me anything. I'm very sorry, I mean that's what's left for me from this meeting. A very Babylonian mixture on terminology. And I had hoped—that was my expectation, and perhaps for some that happened—that we could sit here with a lot of people from different disciplines, with a lot of experience in working with the concept of identity, had to come up with some common type of definition, some common form of understanding: what is meant by identity, in the individual, in history, in philosophy, in psychology, in science.

Strayer: May I say something as another member of the listening audience? All I can do is respect how you feel and acknowledge your not having learned from the things you now express. But there are some of us who feel that we have learned something from different disciplines. Some of us were not seeking a common acknowledgment of a consensual type, but can use a perspectival view and say: When I shift from a particular view within a scientific domain, I can look with Marcia's view on identity, and I can look at your research on self and try to find some place where they may meet or, certainly as important, places where they cannot meet. And that informs me. I can also listen to the viewpoints brought up by people who have used different schemes in literature and history. I may not have the knowledge to assume their perspective, but I can for a moment share their perspective, looking upon the issue of identity and seeing how they can see it differently. This experience informs me in my own discipline about what needs further explanation and where I may go with it. So, I can see that I have learned a great deal, but I haven't sought the same criterion for showing me that I have learned as you have sought.

Oppenheimer: Thank you, I like that.

Neubauer: What can be concluded from an interdisciplinary project like this? It seems to me, it's a bit like traveling in a foreign country. Being exposed to other ways of seeing things will inevitably result in confusion, because it's another world, another way of talking about things. Sometimes you agree and sometimes you don't. Some people may conclude: I feel much better at home and I will stick to what I have. In my view, a better end result would be if somehow that foreignness, that otherness that you encountered, could in some way be integrated into your own way of seeing things in the future. So if people come away from here a bit confused, that's not necessarily bad. If you simply came to confirm what you already believed, then you didn't need to come anyway.

Glossary

TOBI L. G. GRAAFSMA
HARKE A. BOSMA

Since this volume addresses the issues of identity and development from different disciplines, and each discipline to some degree has its own vocabulary, some of the concepts with a highly technical or discipline-specific meaning are discussed here. Especially within the psychoanalytic part of the book a number of technical terms are used that probably are not familiar to a wider audience. Therefore, Graafsma wrote explanatory texts for these. Some other terms such as "identity" and "self" have different connotations within various schools of thought in psychology (and psychoanalysis). They were also added to this glossary. The explanatory text of these terms is—with permission of the author—almost completely derived from a glossary of Van der Werff (1990, in an appendix to a chapter about "The problem of self-conceiving").

Borderline personality disorder (psychiatry, psychoanalysis) A severe personality disorder, marked by chronic or episodic instability in the sphere of interpersonal relationships, self-image, identity, and affect. Borderline personalities can function quite a long time on a neurotic level, but suddenly they may cross the border with psychosis. Both intimacy and distance are difficult to tolerate: Both may lead to intense and overwhelming anxiety ("pananxiety"). Tolerance for anxiety is equally small. The disturbance is assumed to be rooted in the first separation-individuation phase of early childhood (see chapter 5), during which, for example, self- and object-constancy should be established. In borderline conditions, this is not the case.

Compromise formation (psychoanalysis) Term from the psychoanalytic theory of neurosis. Freud discovered that manifest dreams and certain symptoms consist of unconscious compromises between wishes on the one hand and defensive measures of the ego on the other. In general the ego feels in conflict and defends against those wishes (first of all: drive derivatives) out of fear related to moral prohibitions and ideals. Well known are parapraxes (happening in everyday life), conversions, and compulsive thoughts or actions that—though surely not always—often are the result of (neurotic) compromises.

Epigenesis (embryology, psychology, psychoanalysis) The gradual, step by step unfolding of organs and organisms in a fixed sequence of maturational levels. Each level has a specific time of ascendance and needs a particular environmental nutrition. Erik Erikson developed an epigenetic chart of psychosocial stages throughout the life cycle (see Chapter 4), in which the concept of identity was used to connect inborn potentialities with specific environmental actions and attitudes.

Identity (psychology, also used in various other disciplines) The concept refers, (1) in a general sense, to an individual's unique combination of personal, generally inalienable data, like name, age, sex and profession, by which that individual is characterized and distinguishable from any other person. This concept, which has a mainly public connotation, is also applied to groups or categories of persons (and to institutions and organizations, e.g. the identity of the Catholic Church).

Identity (2) in a psychological sense is a concept that has its roots mainly in ideas within personality and social psychology, e.g., ideas on the individual person's uniqueness, on personality dimensions distinguishing people, and, from the social side, ideas on images people have of each other. Identity in this sense refers to a person's unique personality structure and it is also used to refer to the images others have of that personality structure.

Identity (3) may also be used in a subjective, phenomenal sense, in which case expressions like "sense of identity" or "identity awareness" are preferable. Identity then refers to the individual's awareness of personal sameness, continuity, and uniqueness. Erikson (1968), and other authors, explicitly include a social-perceptual aspect: the awareness of being perceived by others in accordance with one's self-perception. The best-known operationalization with respect to adolescence was originated by Marcia (1966), who uses the presence of exploration and commitments as criteria of identity achievement. Other important perspectives do not tie identity achievement to adolescence. In humanistic psychology, it is part of a lifelong process of actualization of the potential true self, which is connected with an increasing awareness of really being oneself. In Sartrean existentialism, identity awareness cannot be anything else than convincedly and convincingly taking roles, as no authentic personal truth exists.

Identity crisis; identity problems (psychology, psychoanalysis, psychiatry) In a general sense these concepts include a state of serious questioning as to one's own essential personal characteristics, one's view of oneself, or the perceived views of others on oneself. The concept sometimes also includes doubts regarding the meaning and the purpose of one's existence. These descriptions are mainly associated with the Eriksonian tradition of theory and research on ego-identity development.

Latency (psychoanalysis) Developmental phase between the so called oedipal phase (4-7 years) and puberty (11-16 years). The term latency refers to the fact that the intense emotional concerns of the ("oedipal") child gradually fade away, until puberty brings back this intensity in, for adults, sometimes a much, more confronting way. Freud thought that the oedipal wishes of the toddler often became dynamically unconscious, latent, for several reasons (see also: "Oedipus complex"—this glossary). Latency is characterized by an upsurge in ego development, by consolidation of ego autonomy, and by the development of friendships with peers.

Metapsychology (psychoanalysis) The theoretical structure of psychoanalytic concepts and points of view. Sometimes also called the abstract theory of psychoanalysis. Metapsychology is the most abstract (distant from clinical observations and from what is called "clinical theory") dimension of psychoanalysis. Metapsychology concerns itself, for example, with the relationships between the more then five "points of view" on normal and abnormal psychic development. The three most known of those "coordinates" in psychoanalytic thinking are the dynamic, the structural, and the economic point of view. In the history of psychoanalytic theory formation, two other points of view, the adaptive and the genetic, gradually became more important. To these might be added an "interactional" point of view, which primarily concerns the psychoanalytic insights on object relations.

Narcissism (psychoanalysis) A term introduced in psychoanalysis by Freud. Narcissism in its most simple and common meaning concerns the libidinal counterpart of egoism. In general narcissism can be defined as the love invested in the image of oneself. Narcissism conceptualized this way is normal and necessary in healthy development. Freud assumed that already for the very little child, before the child is able to differentiate effectively between a self and others ("objects"), there exists a "primary narcissistic state," given the safety, continuity, and care of a stimulating and responding environment. Basically, this is not some selfish, independent state but a state of libidinal equilibrium comparable to the earlier intrauterine existence. The infant itself is unable to maintain this state. For that it is dependent on the presence and nursing care of the environment. Gradually, under the influence of maturation and experiences with painful aspects of inner and outer reality, this primary narcissistic state is injured and partly replaced by libidinal exchanges with the mothering environment. Loving and being loved is introduced. In part it is also replaced by what is called "secondary narcissism": conscious and unconscious efforts to rescue or to refind the original position of bliss and freedom of pain. Objects can be used for that. Idealizations and identifications often basically have such aim: They should restore self-love and self-esteem. Narcissism is considered to be pathological when it has a compulsive, defensive character and is not matched by pleasure in the joy of others. Behind narcissistic disturbances one always finds intense, though not necessarily conscious, anxieties. It might be said that the psychoanalytic theory of narcissism concerns itself with the self in conflict between dream and psychic pain.

Object cathexis (psychoanalysis) Technical term indicating that a subject invests an object energetically and effectively. Such investment originates from two sources. The first (that means historically described and investigated first) is a libidinal or aggressive drive. The drive investment may be manifest, but also may be defended against; for example, out of fear of rejection or loss. A subject (or better his or her ego) then may develop a "counter cathexis." In general, this happens unconsciously. But in combination with the influence of the superego and the ego ideal, the resulting attitude towards an object generally is consciously felt as intentional and wished for. The influence of the original tendencies shows itself in dreams, or by parapraxes, etc. A well-known example is the caring attitude of little children towards a newborn brother or sister, instead of violating it because it is an (because not asked for) intruder. Also the psychoanalysis of altruistic patients revealed that altruism in part may be fueled by a "counter cathexis" against sadistic wishes. The second, historically later investigated, source of object-investment, this time particularly affectively, stems from the primary mother-child unit. In this unit the (mutual) affect-investment has a major communicative, regulative and development-promoting function. Here, an object cathexis does not aim so much the possession of the object. Its aim is to get the object into a containing and generative position, The "object" thus is first of all important as a function for a child. Well-known in this regard is the term "transitional object," which refers to the use of some object (a person or some play material), with which a special affective relation is created, to prevent feelings of trauma and loss. The term cathexis originally belonged to the economic point of view in psychoanalysis but gradually became extended to an interactional point of view.

Oedipus complex (psychoanalysis) One of the most important discoveries of Freud. According to Freud, the Oedipus complex is a twofold complex, positive and negative, due to the psychological bisexuality of children. A boy not only has an ambivalent relation to his father (he loves him and considers him to be a rival in his affectionate wishes towards his mother), he also behaves like a girl and displays an affectionate, feminine attitude to his father and a correspondingly jealousy and hostility towards his mother. And so has a girl not only an ambivalent relation to her mother, she also behaves like a boy and displays masculine attitudes towards her mother, trying to make, so to say, her father superfluous. The Oedipus complex concerns an intense love affair in childhood. The shorthand notation "Oedipus complex" thus refers to a quite complicated set of conflicts. The Oedipus complex is considered to be the central intrapsychic developmental conflict of children between approximately 4 and 7 years and the nucleus of all neuroses. Indeed the psychoanalytic definition of a neurosis depends on the diagnostic assumption that the conflicts of the Oedipus complex unconsciously keep organizing and steering a person's life. The entrance into the Oedipus complex is different for boys and girls. Within the oedipal phase, several subphases are discerned. The course of the Oedipus complex depends to a large degree on what happens "preoedipal" and on the attitude of the parents towards the feelings of their child and on their wishes regarding the development of their child. The course of the child's oedipal conflicts tell much about how it is or was parented. Sometimes the Oedipus complex can be seen in the manifest behavior of a child. But in general, in more normal situations, the Oedipus complex remains for the most part unconscious. In part that is because of its painfulness: It is rooted in the dawning awareness of the child that it is small, not the most important person in the mother's or father's life, incapable to perform what father can (impregnate) or what mother can (giving birth to babies), so it feels impotent and excluded. In part the Oedipus complex is repressed because of the shame, guilt and anxiety it provokes: The rage, the envy, and the jealousy felt towards dearly loved objects evoke much anxiety, guilt, and shame. All this is also threatening the child's vulnerable narcissism. The child often prefers to negate the differences and (or) the sexes, and prefers to stress similarity and equality. As such, the Oedipus complex belong to one of the major calamities of childhood: The emotional discovery of the differences between the sexes and between big and small. One can get a glimpse of the dynamics of the unconscious Oedipus complex from the (internal) dynamics between the id, the ego, the superego, and the ego ideal. And formulated in psychosocial terms, the Oedipus complex sometimes is reflected in struggles with the older generation, in conflicts about big and small, about activity and passivity, and about the relation between the sexes. Here especially puberty and adolescence in general can be illuminating.

Primary process thinking (psychoanalysis) Certain type of thinking, characteristic for the immature (ego of the) child, in which a tendency to immediate gratification dominates, in which negatives, conditionals, and other qualifying conjunctions are absent and in which logical oppositions may coexist. Primary process thinking is thinking by wishful associations, by condensations (in which several ideas or images are represented by a single word or image), and by analogies. Concern with the logic of time is absent: Past, present and future are all one. Primary process thinking dominates in for example dreams, but it can be found also in jokes, cartoons, and poetry. The capacity to oscillate between primary and secondary process thinking is decisive in humor. In situations of intense anxiety and stress, primary process thinking tends to increase and may overrule secondary process thinking.

Screen experiences (psychoanalysis) Experiences in the sphere of memories, moods, affects, defenses, and even in identity formation that have important defensive purposes. Screen memories, for example, are compromise formations between the ego's wish to contend with some painful reality and the wish to avoid that. Partly revealing the truth may be a defense against the anxiety that the whole truth may come out. Something is offered to save some more essential, more painful truth. Well-known in psychoanalysis is the mechanism of defense "substitution with the same," a mechanism that is prominent in hysterical neuroses. Some affect is exaggerated to ward off the same but less intense affect to defend against painful reactions to the latter affect. Affect is defended against with the same affect; the manifest, defensive one is called the screen affect. Close to these matters lies the phenomenon of the inexact interpretation. Where repression fails because of contradicting wishes, screen experiences may come in.

Secondary process thinking (psychoanalysis) Type of thinking characteristic for the child with a mature ego. The ego here is able to delay, to abstain from direct gratification in the sphere of thinking. Secondary process thinking is ordinary, conscious, and logical thinking, in which verbal rules and the logic of time and causality are followed. Secondary process thinking is the more rational type of thinking, compared to primary process thinking. It is closely bound to maturation and to the ability of the child to refrain from immediate doing and wish fulfillment. Normally, the ego oscillates between secondary and primary process thinking, according to the circumstances of the moment. In play for example, there is more room for primary process thinking, in work secondary process thinking normally dominates.

Self (psychoanalysis) Term that basically refers to the own person. In psychoanalysis the self is considered to refer to what a person feels and thinks about him- or herself, the body included. So the term refers to a subjective and mental content, a product of the (system) ego. This implies that the self is no explanatory concept (although one may find authors who use the concept that way), nor a psychological structure like the ego, or the superego. Of this mental content, the self, one may love and favor certain aspects and hate and feel ashamed for other aspects. In part also, the self is unconscious, as are many feelings, fantasies, and thoughts. The construction of the self is influenced by the same conflicts, defenses, etc., as can be found in (for example) manifest dreams. About others, "objects," the ego equally develops such constructions.

Between the "self-representations" and the "object representations" exists an intrapsychic, dynamic relationship. Freud did not (yet) differentiate between the self and the ego. It was Hartmann (1939a) who clarified the difference. The self, as a mental content existing in the ego, is considered to be an important possession, prone to humiliation and loss. In this, psychoanalysis sees a parallel with the way children in the so called "anal" and "phallic" phase treat their possessions, the physical possessions (the body for example) included. Two serious mistakes can be made. One is, that the self is considered to be a mental structure itself, on a par with the ego or superordinate to the ego. Structure and content are here confounded. A second is that on the one hand the term self often is used carelessly and loosely, while on the other hand the self is considered to be a very important construct. In this, the term seems to be treated like people often treat money: highly important, but spent carelessly.

Self (psychology) (1) Self refers in an ontological sense to the essence of the individual person, to what is also described by means of expressions like the "inner core" of the personality system, the "very Me," or "the source of mental energy." Such a self cannot be anything else than a theoretical construct or an object of personal awareness, as no means exist to prove or to test its reality. Humanistic psychology suggests in the terminology it uses a belief in such a reality: Expressions like "true self" and "self-realization" suggest that some pre-existing potential core in a process of personal growth is to be actualized. In contrast, Sartrean existentialism fundamentally denies the possibility of such a core self. It sees self-realization in the humanistic sense as necessarily being self-deception: Such a "self" can be no more than a mask that keeps the personal vacuum concealed from other people's gaze.

Self (2) in a functional sense occurs in the ideas of authors who stress the "agent" or motivational aspects of the self construct. In many self psychologies since Calkins (1915), the self is the general force underlying an individual's various activities: Sometimes its function is more closely specified, e.g., it is said to avoid anxiety. In some authors' work, this self is not easy to distinguish from concepts like personality; according to one of Fromm's definitions, the self is "the personality with all its possibilities." In many cases, authors seem to use the concept of self to refer to some unifying principle that keeps an individual's activities integrated, in accordance with Calkins's original intentions. She saw psychology as being too atomistic, studying "elements" and ignoring the fact that these are perceptions, ideas, etc., "of a self, subject, mind, ego, call it as one will." Where the concept of self is defined as an "agent," or is associated with functions, especially unifying or integrating functions, it is hardly possible to differentiate it from the (neo-)psychoanalytical ego concept.

Self (3) in a phenomenal sense. Within an individual's phenomenal field of perceptions and concepts, some of these refer to the person himself. In its broadest sense, self indicates this part of a person's experience, including general self-awareness or a sense of self, as well as more or less structured images of one's own personality. In humanistic psychology, the expression self may have an "ontological" meaning self (1) but may also label these aspects of self-awareness and self-experience. In the empirical self-concept literature the term self is often used to cover the structured self-image or self-concept as operationalized, in most cases, by trait lists.

Self-actualization (psychology) This is an expression belonging to the tradition of humanistic psychology. It labels the continuous process of growth in which an individual's authentic and essential potential self is realized and also understood and accepted by that individual. The basic idea was originated by Plessner, who in his philosophical anthropology emphasized man's duty to realize what he essentially is. The concept must have some global relationship with what is called identity formation or identity achievement, which also refers to a process in which the individual is growing towards being himself. However, the two concepts originate from quite different schools of thought and, as a result, there are some essential differences. One is that the developmental psychology of ego identity does not suppose a potential true self to be realized, but stresses the individual's free choices in a crisis-like process of exploring the possibilities offered by his society. Another important difference refers to the time aspect. Self-actualization is a lifelong process that is essentially uncompletable: Identity achievement, in spite of Erikson's eight-stage theory, is connected with his fifth phase, and the expression itself does not suggest any reservations concerning the completeness of the acquired identity.

Self-concept (psychology) This concept can readily be defined as a person's view or mental representation of himself. Other expressions are also current, e.g. "perceived self" or "self-image." Strictly speaking, each of such terms should have a different meaning. Thus, a term like self-concept suggests more cognitive processing than is the case with perceived self. However, in the relevant literature the various labels are used to indicate concepts that are practically identical or that are not unanimously distinguished. Sometimes the term self is used in cases in which self-concept or self-experience is meant. Unlike the self in an ontological or a functional sense, this self-concept variant of the phenomenal self is accessible to empirical study. It is generally measured by analyzing self-attributions on trait lists and sometimes, by analyzing free descriptions of self. In the latter studies, in particular, various content categories have been distinguished, which can be taken as further specifications of James's (1890) tripartite division of the "empirical" self into the "material," the "social," and the "spiritual" self. In trait-list research, subjects are often asked to describe different self-perceptions: The most commonly used are the "real" or "actual" self, the "ideal" self, and "self as seen by others." Much attention in empirical studies has been paid to the evaluative aspects of the self-concept: self-esteem.

Self-esteem (psychology) Self-esteem may be defined as the evaluative aspect of the self-concept. It has attracted most attention from researchers in self-concept, much more, for example, than an area like the complexity of self-concept, or aspects of content. In operational terms, self-esteem is often the relative number of favorable self-attributions on trait lists. Sometimes it is measured by determining the difference between a person's ideal-self and real-self scores, an operationalization that takes account of the individual's own evaluation of the traits, as shown by the ideal-self scores. In the former, i.e., favorable, self-attributions, the criterion is defined at a general level, or by the researcher's own evaluation.

Self- and object-constancy (psychoanalysis, psychiatry) Terms that refer to the ability of a child, usually established within the first 36 months, to maintain continuous, positive, and distinct internal representations of itself and of important others ("objects"), independent of momentous affective states and wish fulfillment. The first of those objects usually is the mothering figure. A child should be able to tolerate ambivalent and contradictory feelings and wishes towards the self and towards important others. The concept is used in particular to differentiate between psychotic, borderline, and neurotic disturbances.

Signal anxiety (psychoanalysis) Refers to the conscious emergence of small quantities of anxiety, which alerts the ego. The ego then can take defensive measures, to confront or avoid some danger. The danger may be realistic, and the (signal) anxiety adequate, but the anxiety can also be the result of a memory or fantasy referring to a past, not an actual, danger. The memory or fantasy does not have to reach conscious awareness: One may feel anxious, without realizing what for. The danger may stem from external but also from internal sources, for example some forbidden drive. Signal anxiety thus refers to anxiety functioning as a signal. Not all anxiety does so.

Transference (psychoanalysis) In general: the mobilization of unconscious wishes, needs, conflicts, and special relationships within the psychoanalytic (treatment) situation. These wishes, needs, conflicts, and interactions basically are wishes and traumas out of the life history of the patient. They are not remembered consciously, but under the impetus and in the safety of the psychoanalytic situation, however, they become manifest again. First of all they become manifest in the form of inescapable resistances to the normal and realistic demands of the treatment, and secondly they become manifest in the revival of wishes, expectations, and needs basically belonging to persons from the past, but felt towards the analyst. Transference thus is a revival of the (until then repressed) past in the (psychoanalytic) present. Much of the psychoanalytic work consists of uncovering, interpreting, and working through the transference. The term transference often is used in a broader context, referring (in adults) not only to unconscious wishes, needs, and relationships stemming from the past (childhood and adolescence), but also to actual, age-adequate feelings that are repressed and unconsciously transferred into the treatment situation. And besides this extension, transference is considered to happen inside and outside the psychoanalytic situation, the only difference being that within the psychoanalytic setting transference can be and is explored systematically. In the development of psychoanalytic technique the complex of the transference feelings of a patient and their counterpart in the transference feelings evoked in the analyst, gradually have become an important focus of investigation and interpretation in the psychoanalytic situation.

References

Abeles, M., & Schilder, P. (1935). Psychogenic loss of personal identity: amnesia. *Archives of Neurology and Psychiatry, 34*, 587-604.

American Psychiatric Association. (1987). *Diagnostic and statistical manual of mental disorders* (DSM-IIIR). Washington, DC: Author.

Archer, S. L., & Waterman, A. S. (1990). Varieties of identity diffusions and foreclosures: An exploration of subcategories of the identity statuses. *Journal of Adolescent Research, 5*, 96-111.

Ariès, P. (1962). *Centuries of childhood.* New York: Vintage. (Original work published 1960)

Arlow, J. A. (1959). The structure of the déjà vu experience. *Journal of the American Psychoanalytic Association, 7*, 611-631.

Baumeister, R. F. (1986). *Identity: Cultural change and the struggle for self.* New York: Oxford University Press.

Bercée, Y. M. (1976). *Fête et révolte. Des mentalités populaires du xvie au xviiie siècle* [Feast and rebellion. Popular mentalities from the 16th until the 18th century]. Paris: Hachette.

Bertalanffy, L. von (1968). *General system theory.* Harmondsworth, UK: Penguin.

Berzonsky, M. D. (1988). Self-theorists, identity status, and social cognition. In D. K. Lapsley & F. C. Power (Eds.), *Self, ego and identity—Integrative approaches* (pp. 243-263). New York: Springer Verlag.

Binion, R. (1968). *Frau Lou, Nietzsche's wayward disciple.* Princeton, NJ: Princeton University Press.

Bion, W. (1961). *Experiences in groups.* New York: Basic Books.

Blasi, A. (1988). Identity and the development of the self. In D. K. Lapsley & F. C. Power (Eds.), *Self, ego and identity—Integrative approaches* (pp. 226-243). New York: Springer Verlag.

Blos, P. (1962). *On adolescence.* New York: Free Press.
Blos, P. (1967). The second individuation process of adolescence. *The Psychoanalytic Study of the Child, 22*, 162-186.
Blos, P. (1979). *The adolescent passage.* New York: International Universities Press.
Bosma, H. A. (1985). *Identity development in adolescence: Coping with commitments.* Unpublished doctoral dissertation, University of Groningen, The Netherlands.
Bosma, H. A. (1992). Identity in adolescence: Managing commitments. In G. R. Adams, T. P. Gullotta, & R. Montemayor (Eds.), *Adolescent identity formation* (pp. 91-121). Newbury Park, CA: Sage.
Bourne, E. (1978). The state of research on ego identity: A review and appraisal. Part I. Part II. *Journal of Youth and Adolescence, 7*, 223-251; 371-392.
Bowlby, J. (1969). *Attachment and loss* (Vol. I). New York: Basic Books.
Brazelton, T. B., Tronick, F., Adamson, L., Als, H., & Wise, S. (1975). Early mother-child reciprocity. In C. H. Waddington (Ed.), *The future as an academic discipline. Ciba foundation symposium.* Amsterdam: Elsevier.
Brenner, C. (1982). *The mind in conflict.* New York: International Universities Press.
Bruner, J. (1986). *Actual minds, possible worlds.* Cambridge, MA: Harvard University Press.
Buber, M. (1965). *The knowledge of man.* New York: HarperCollins.
Bühler, C. (1921). *Das seelenleben des jugendlichen* [The inner life of the adolescent]. Jena, Germany: Fischer.
Bühler, C. (1925). *Zwei knabentagebücher: Mit einer einleitung über die bedeutung des tagebuchs für die jugendpsychologie* [Two boys' diaries: With an introduction concerning the meaning of the diary for the psychology of adolescence]. Jena, Germany: Fischer.
Burke, P. (1978). *Popular culture in early modern Europe.* New York: Harper.
Calkins, M. W. (1915). The self in scientific psychology. *American Journal of Psychology, 26*, 495-524.
Camus, A. (1942). *L'etranger.* Paris: Gallimard.
Carr, D. (1986). *Time, narrative and history.* Bloomington: Indiana University Press.
Chodorow, N. J. (1986). Toward a relational individualism: The mediation of self through psychoanalysis. In T. C. Heller, M. Sosna, & D. E. Wellbery (Eds.), *Reconstructing individualism, autonomy, individuality, and the self in western thought* (pp. 197-208). Stanford, CA: Stanford University Press.
Christie, A. (1964). *And then there were none.* New York: Washington Square Press.
Christie, A. (1987). *Murder on the Orient Express.* London: Collins.
Clark, K., & Holquist, M. (1984). *Mikhail Bakhtin.* Cambridge, MA: Harvard University Press.
Collins, W. A. (Ed.). (1982). The concept of development: *The Minnesota symposia on child psychology, 15.* Hillsdale, NJ: Lawrence Erlbaum.
Cook, T. D., & Campbell, D. T. (1979). *Quasi-experimentation: Design and analysis issues for field settings.* Chicago: Rand McNally.
Corbin, A. (1986). *The foul and the fragrant, odor and the French social imagination.* Leamington Spa: Berg. (Original work published as *Le Miasme et la jonquille,* 1982)
Côté, J. E., & Levine, C. (1988). A critical examination of the ego identity status paradigm. *Developmental Review, 8*, 147-184.
Csikszentmihalyi, M. (1980). Love and the dynamics of personal growth. In K. S. Pope & Associates (Eds.), *On love and loving.* San Francisco: Jossey-Bass.
Davies, R. (1986). *What's bred in the bone.* Toronto: Penguin.
Davis, N. Z. (1975). The reasons of misrule. In N. Z. Davis, *Society and culture in early modern France* (pp. 97-123). Stanford, CA: Stanford University Press.

Davis, N. Z. (1983). *The return of Martin Guerre.* Cambridge, MA: Harvard University Press.

Davis, N. Z. (1988). On the lame. *The American Historical Review, 93*, 572-603.

De Blécourt, B.(1980). Psychoanalytische psychotherapie van de borderline patient [Psychoanalytical psychotherapy of the borderline patient]. In B. Frijling-Schreuder et al. (Eds.), *Psychoanalytici aan het woord* [Psychoanalytic therapists speaking] (pp. 237-248). Deventer, The Netherlands: Van Loghum Slaterus.

de Certeau, M. (1978). Psychanalyse (Histoire de) [Psychoanalysis (History of)]. In J. Le Goff, R. Chartier, & Y. Revel (Eds.), *La nouvelle histoire* [The new history] (p. 477). Paris: Gallimard.

de Certeau, M. (1986). Psychoanalysis and its history. In M. de Certeau, *Heterologies: Discourse on the other* (pp. 3-5). Minneapolis: University of Minnesota Press.

de Levita, D. J. (1965). *The concept of identity.* The Hague: Mouton.

Demos, J., & Demos, V. (1969). Adolescence in historical perspective. *Journal of Marriage and the Family, 31*, 632-38.

Deutsch, H. (1942). Some forms of emotional disturbances and their relationship to schizophrenia. *Psychoanalytic Quarterly, 11*, 301-321.

Doyle, A. C. (1894). *The memoirs of Sherlock Holmes.* London: Newnes.

Duby, G., & Lardreau, G. (1980). *Dialogues.* Paris.

Eco, U. (1983). *The name of the rose.* San Diego: Harcourt Brace Jovanovich.

Erikson, E. H. (1950). *Childhood and society.* New York: Norton.

Erikson, E. H. (1956). The problem of ego-identity. *Journal of the American Psychoanalytic Association, 4*, 56-121.

Erikson, E. H. (1958). *Young man Luther. A study in psychoanalysis and history.* New York: Norton.

Erikson, E. H. (1959). Identity and the life cycle. *Psychological Issues* (Monograph 1). New York: International Universities Press.

Erikson, E. H. (1964). *Insight and responsibility.* New York: Norton.

Erikson, E. H. (1968). *Identity, youth and crisis.* New York: Norton.

Erikson, E. H. (1969). *Gandhi's truth.* New York: Norton.

Erikson, E. H. (1971). On the nature of psycho-historical evidence: In search of Gandhi. In B. Mazlish (Ed.), *Psychoanalysis and history* (pp. 181-212). New York: Grosset.

Erikson, E. H. (1974). *Dimensions of a new identity.* New York: Norton.

Erikson, E. H. (1978). *Life history and the historical moment.* New York: Norton.

Erikson, E. H. (1982). *The life cycle completed.* New York: Norton.

Erikson, K. T. (Ed.) (1973). *In search of common ground: Conversations with Erik H. Erikson and Huey P. Newton.* New York: Norton.

Evans, R. I. (1969). *Dialogue with Erik Erikson.* New York: Dutton.

Fairbairn, W.R.D. (1954). *An object relations theory of the personality.* New York: Basic Books.

Fairbairn, W.R.D. (1957). Freud, the psychoanalytic method and mental health. *British Journal of Medical Psychology, 30*, 53-62.

Faure, A. (1978). *Paris carême-prenant. Du carnaval à Paris au xixe siècle* [Paris in Lent: Carnival in Paris in the 19th century]. Paris: Hachette.

Feigl, H. (1958). The "mental" and the "physical." In H. Feigl, M. Scriven, & G. Maxwell (Eds.), *Minnesota studies in the philosophy of science* (pp. 370-497). Minneapolis: University of Minnesota Press.

Fenichel, O. (1945). *The psychoanalytic theory of neurosis.* New York: Norton.

Fenichel. O. (1946). *The psychoanalytic theory of neurosis.* London: Routledge.

Flaubert, G. (1870). *L'education sentimentale: Histoire d'un jeune homme*. Paris: Levy.
Fogel, A. (1993). *Developing through relationships. Origins of communication, self, and culture*. New York: Harvester Wheatsheaf.
Ford, D. H., & Lerner, R. M. (1992). *Developmental systems theory. An integrative approach*. Newbury Park, CA: Sage.
Fournier, A. (1966). *Le grand meaulness* [The great adventure]. Harmondsworth: Penguin. (Original work published 1913)
Freeman, D. (1983). *Margaret Mead and Samoa: The making and unmaking of an anthropological myth*. Harmondsworth, UK: Penguin.
Freud, S. (1900). The interpretation of dreams. *Standard Edition, 4, 5*. London: Hogarth.
Freud, S. (1920). Beyond the pleasure principle. *Standard Edition, 18*, 7-64. London: Hogarth.
Freud, S. (1926). Address to the society B'nai B'rith. *Standard Edition, 20*, 273-274. London: Hogarth.
Freud, S. (1936). A disturbance of memory on the Acropolis. *Standard Edition, 22*, 237-248. London: Hogarth.
Friedman, L. (1988). *The anatomy of psychotherapy*. Hillsdale, NJ: Analytic Press.
Frondizi, R. (1954). *The nature of self*. New Haven: Yale University Press.
Gadamer, H-G. (1960). *Wahrheit und methode* [Truth and method]. Tübingen: Mohr.
Gay, P. (1984). *The bourgeois experience, Victoria to Freud: Vol. 1: Education of the senses*. New York: Oxford University Press.
Gay, P. (1985). *Freud for historians*. New York: Oxford University Press.
Gay, P. (1986). *The bourgeois experience, Victoria to Freud: Vol. 2: The tender passion*. New York: Oxford University Press.
Gergen, K. (1987) Toward self as relationship. In K. Yardley & T. Honess (Eds.), *Self and identity: Psychosocial perspectives* (pp. 53-63). New York: John Wiley.
Gestrich, A. (1988). Einleitung: Sozialhistorische biographieforschung [Introduction: Social-historical biography research]. In A. Gestrich, P. Knoch, & H. Merkel (Eds.), *Biographie—sozial-geschichtlich* [Biography—social-historical]. Göttingen, The Netherlands: Vandenhoeck & Ruprecht.
Gide, A. (1973). *The counterfeiters*. New York: Random House. (Original work published 1925)
Gilligan, C. (1977). In a different voice—Women's conceptions of self and of morality. *Harvard Educational Review, 47*, 481-517.
Gilligan, C. (1982). *In a different voice*. Cambridge, MA: Harvard University Press.
Gilligan, C., Lyons, N. P., & Hammer, T. J. (Eds.). (1990). *Making connections*. Cambridge, MA: Harvard University Press.
Gillis, J. (1974). *Youth and history: Tradition and change in European age relations 1770-present*. New York: Academic Press.
Ginzburg, C. (1980). *The cheese and the worms: The cosmos of a sixteenth-century miller*. London: Routledge & Kegan Paul.
Ginzburg, C. (1980). Morelli, Freud, Sherlock Holmes: Clues and scientific method. *History Workshop, 9*, 5-36.
Gitelson, M. (1951). Psychoanalysis and dynamic psychiatry. *Archives of Neurology and Psychiatry, 66*, 280-288.
Gleason, P. (1983). Identifying identity: A semantic history. *Journal of American History, 69*(4), 910-931.
Glenham, M., & Strayer, J. (in progress). *Integrity and identity*. Burnaby, BC, Canada, Simon Fraser University, Department of Psychology.

Glover, E. (1955). The therapeutic effect of inexact interpretation. In *The technique of psychoanalysis* (pp. 353-366). New York: International Universities Press.
Goethe, W. (1949). *The sorrows of young Werther.* New York: Holt, Rinehart & Winston. (Original work published 1774)
Goffman, E. (1963). *Stigma. Notes on the management of spoiled identity.* Englewood Cliffs, NJ: Prentice Hall.
Graafsma, T. (1992). Enkele gedachten over de integratieve funktie van het ego in de adolescentie [Some thoughts about the integrative function of the ego in adolescence]. *Tijdschrift voor Kinder—en Jeugdpsychotherapie, 19,* 10-26.
Graafsma, T., & Bosma. H. A. (1991). *De ontwikkelingspsychologische en psychodynamische betekenis van psychosociale bindingen in de adolescentie* [The developmental and psychodynamic meaning of psychosocial commitments in adolescence]. Unpublished research report, Pedologisch Instituut, Amsterdam.
Greenblatt, S. (1982). Filthy rites. *Daedalus, 3,* 1-16.
Greenson, R. R. (1954). The struggle against identification. *Journal of the American Psychoanalytic Association, 2,* 202-217.
Greenson, R. R. (1958). On screen defenses, screen hunger and screen identity. *Journal of the American Psychoanalytic Association, 6,* 242-262.
Grotevant, H. D., & Cooper, C. R. (1985). Patterns of interaction in family relationships and the development of identity exploration in adolescence. *Child Development, 56,* 415-428.
Grünbaum, A. (1984). *The foundations of psychoanalysis. A philosophical critique.* Berkeley: University of California Press.
Habermas, J. (1988). *Nachmetaphysische denken* [Postmetaphysical thought]. Frankfurt/ Main: Suhrkamp.
Hall, G. S. (1904). *Adolescence: Its psychology and its relations to physiology, anthropology, sociology, sex, crime, religion and education.* New York: Appleton.
Hardy, B. (1968). Towards a poetics of fiction: An approach through narrative. *Novel, 2,* 5-14.
Hartmann, H. (1939a). *Ego psychology and the problem of adaptation.* New York: International Universities Press.
Hartmann, H. (1939b). Psychoanalysis and the concept of health. *International Journal of Psychoanalysis, 20,* 308-321.
Hartmann, H. (1964). *Essays on ego psychology.* New York: International Universities Press.
Hauser, S. T. (1991). *Adolescents and their families.* New York: Free Press.
Havighurst, R. J., & Taba, H. (1949). *Adolescent character and personality.* New York: John Wiley.
Hearn, S. (in progress). *Development and validation of a measure of Eriksonian Integrity.* Burnaby, BC, Canada: Simon Fraser University, Department of Psychology.
Hesse, H. (1970). *Demian.* New York: Bantam. (Original work published 1919)
Histoire et sciences sociales: Un tournant critique? [History and social sciences: A critical turning point?] (1988). *Annales Economies Sociétés Civilisations, 43,* 291-293.
Hoshmand, L., & Polkinghorne, D. E. (1992). Redefining the science-practice relationship and professional training. *American Psychologist, 47,* 55-66.
Hugo, V. (1862). *Les misérables.* Paris: Nelson.
Jacobson, E. (1953). Contributions to the metapsychology of cyclothymic depression. In P. Greenacre (Ed.), *Affective disorders* (pp. 49-83). New York: International Universities Press.

Jacobson, E. (1957). Normal and pathological moods. *Psychoanalytic Study of the Child, 12*, 73-113.

Jacobson, E. (1964). *The self and the object world.* New York: International Universities Press.

James, W. (1890). *The principles of psychology.* New York: Holt.

James, W. (1966). *The awkward age.* Harmondsworth, UK: Penguin. (Original work published 1899)

Jelavitch, P. (1982). Popular dimensions of modernist elite culture: The case of theater in fin-de-siècle Munich. In D. Lacapra & S. L. Kaplan (Eds.), *Modern European intellectual history, reappraisals and new perspectives* (pp. 220-250). Ithaca, NY: Cornell University Press.

Josselson, R. (1980). Ego development in adolescence. In J. Adelson (Ed.), *Handbook of adolescent psychology* (pp. 188-210). New York: John Wiley.

Josselson, R. (1987). *Finding herself: Pathways to identity development in women.* San Francisco: Jossey-Bass.

Josselson, R. (1992). *The space between us: Exploring the dimensions of human relationships.* San Francisco: Jossey-Bass.

Joyce, J. (1977). *A portrait of the artist as a young man.* Harmondsworth, UK: Penguin. (Original work published 1916)

Kaufman, S. R. (1986). *The ageless self: Sources of meaning in late life.* Madison, CT: International Universities Press.

Kaufmann, W. (1980). *Discovering the mind.* New York: McGraw-Hill.

Kernberg, O. F. (1975). *Borderline conditions and pathological narcissism.* New York: Bronson.

Kernberg, O. F. (1984). *Severe personality disorders.* New Haven: Yale.

Kett, J. (1977). *Rites of passage: Adolescence in America 1790 to the present.* New York: Basic Books.

Kinser, S. (1984). Chronotypes and catastrophes: The cultural history of Mikhail Bakhtin. *The Journal of Modern History, 56*, 301-310.

Kipling, R. (1982). *Stalky & co.* London: MacMillan. (Original work published 1899)

Kipling, R. (1987). *Kim.* Harmondsworth, UK: Penguin. (Original work published 1901)

Kobak, R. R., & Sceery, A. (1988). Attachment in late adolescent: Working models, affect regulation and representations of self and others. *Child Development, 59*, 135-146.

Kohut, H. (1966). Forms and transformations of narcissism. *Journal of the American Psychoanlytic Association, 14*, 243-272.

Kohut, H. (1971). *The analysis of the self.* New York: International Universities Press.

Kohut, H. (1977). *The restoration of the self.* New York: International Universities Press.

Kohut, T. A. (1986). Psychohistory as history. *The American Historical Review, 91*, 336-354.

Kowaz, A. H., & Marcia, J. E. (1991). Development and validation of a measure of Eriksonian industry. *Journal of Personality and Social Psychology, 60*, 390-397.

Kruithof, B. (1980). De deugdzame natie. Het burgerlijk beschavingsoffensief van de maatschappij tot nut van 't algemeen tussen 1794 en 1860 [The virtuous nation: The bourgeois civilizing offensive of the society for the benefit of the community between 1794 and 1860]. *Symposion, Tijdschrift voor maatschappijwetenschap, 2*, 22-37.

Lacapra, D. (1984). Is everyone a mentalité case? Transference and the "culture" concept. *History and Theory: Studies in the Philosophy of History, 23*(3), 296-311.

Lacretelle, J. de. (1983). *Silbermann.* Paris: Gallimard. (Original work published 1922)

Ladame, F. (1991). Adolescence and the repetition compulsion. *International Journal of Psychoanalysis, 72*, 253-275.
Lampl-de Groot, J. (1962). Ego ideal and superego. *The Psychoanalytic Study of the Child, 17*, 94-106.
Larbaud, V. (1979). *Fermina Márquez*. Paris: Gallimard. (Original work published 1911)
Lasch, C. (1979). *The culture of narcissism*. New York: Norton.
Laufer, M., & Laufer, M. E. (1984). *Adolescence and developmental breakdown*. New York: Yale.
Lazarus, R. S., & DeLongis, A. (1983). Psychological stress and coping in aging. *American Psychologist, 38*, 245-254.
Levi, G. (1989, November-December). Les usages de la biographie [The uses of biography]. *Annales, 44*(6).
Lichtenstein, H. (1977). *The dilemma of human identity*. New York: Jason Aronson.
Lifton, R. J. (1968). *Death in life: Survivors of Hiroshima*. London: Weidenfeld & Nicolson.
Locke, J. (1954). Essay concerning human understanding. Section II, XXVII. In R. Frondizi, *The nature of self* (p. 36). New Haven: Yale University Press. (Original work published 1894)
Loewenberg, P. (1983). *Decoding the past. The psychohistorical approach*. New York: Knopf.
Lorenz, C. (1987). *De constructie van het verleden, een inleiding in de theorie van de geschiedenis* [The construction of the past, an introduction in the theory of history]. Amsterdam: Boon.
MacAdams, D. P. (1985). *Power, intimacy and the life story*. New York: Gilford.
MacIntyre, A. (1981). *After virtue*. London: Duckworth.
Mahler, M., Pine, F., & Bergman, A. (1975). *The psychological birth of the human infant*. New York: Basic Books.
Malory, T. (1906). *The book of King Arthur and his knights of the round table*. London: Dent.
Mann, T. (1981). Tonio Kröger. In T. Mann, *Gesammelte werke in einzelbänden: Frühe erzählungen* [Complete works in single covers: Early stories]. Frankfurt/Main: Fischer. (Original work published 1903)
Marcel, G. (1962). *Homo viator: Introduction to a metaphysic of hope*. New York: Harper.
Marcia, J. E. (1966). Development and validation of ego-identity status. *Journal of Personality and Social Psychology, 3*, 551-558.
Marcia, J. E. (1982). Identity status in late adolescence. In H. A. Bosma & T.L.G. Graafsma (Eds.), *De ontwikkeling van identiteit in de adolescentie* [The development of identity in adolescence] (pp. 50-64). Nijmegen, The Netherlands: Dekker and Van de Vegt.
Marcia, J. E. (1986). Clinical implications of the identity status approach within psychosocial developmental theory. *Cadernos de Consulta Psicologica, 2*, 23-35.
Marcia, J. E. (1988). Common processes underlying ego identity, cognitive/moral development, and individuation. In D. K. Lapsley & F. C. Power (Eds.), *Self, ego and identity—Integrative approaches* (pp. 211-226). New York: Springer Verlag.
Marcia, J. E. (1989). Identity diffusion differentiated. In M. A. Luszcz & T. Nettelbeck (Eds.), *Psychological development: Perspective across the life-span*. Amsterdam: Elsevier.
Marcia, J. E., Waterman, A. S., Matteson, D. M., Archer, S. L., & Orlofsky, J. (1993). *Ego identity: A handbook for psychosocial research*. New York: Springer Verlag.

Markova, I. (1987). Knowledge of the self through interaction. In K. Yardley & T. Honess (Eds.), *Self and identity: Psychosocial perspectives* (pp. 65-80). New York: John Wiley.

May, K. (1893). *Winnetou*. Freiburg im Breisgau, Germany: Fehsenfeld.

Mazlish, B. (1971). Introduction to the revised edition. In B. Mazlish (Ed.), *Psychoanalysis and history* (p. 19). New York: Grosset.

Mazlish, B. (1975). *James and John Stuart Mill: Father and son in the nineteenth century*. New York: Basic Books.

McCullers, C. (1946). *The member of the wedding*. New York: Houghton Mifflin.

Mead, M. (1928). *Coming of age in Samoa*. New York: Morrow.

Mendel. G. (1968). *La révolte contre le père*. Paris: Payot.

Mendousse, P. (1909). *L'ame de l'adolescent* [The soul of the adolescent]. Paris: Alcan.

Miller, J. B. (1976). *Toward a new psychology of women*. Boston: Beacon.

Mink, L. O. (1987). *Historical understanding*. Ithaca, NY: Cornell University Press.

Mitzman, A. (1986). The civilizing offensive; mentalities, high culture and individual psyches. *Journal of Social History, 20*, 664-688.

Mitzman, A. (1990a). *Michelet, historian: Rebirth and romanticism in 19th century France*. New Haven: Yale University Press.

Mitzman, A. (1990b). Les amis d'Alfred Dumesnil: Sociabilité juvénile et fraternité révolutionnaire à la veille de 1848 [The friends of Alfred Dumesnil: Juvenile sociability and revolutionary brotherhood on the eve of 1848]. *Le "Bulletin" de la Société d'histoire de la Révolution de 1848 et des Révolutions du XIXe siècle: 1848, révolutions et mutations au XIXe siècle, 6*, 65-76.

Monas, S. (1983, October 8). *Verbal carnival: Bakhtin, Rabelais, Finnegan's Wake and the Growthesk*. Paper presented at the International Bakhtin Conference, Queen's University, Kingston, Ontario.

Muchembled, R. (1978). *Culture populaire te culture des élites dans la France moderne (XVe-XVIIIe siècle)* [Popular versus elite culture in modern France (15th-18th century)]. Essai. Paris: Flammarion.

Muchembled, R. (1988). *L'invention de l'homme moderne. Sensibilités, moeurs et comportements collectifs sous l'ancien regime* [The invention of modern man: Susceptibilities, morals and collective behaviors during the ancient system]. Paris: Fayard.

Musil, R. (1966). *Young Törless*. New York: New American Library. (Original work published 1906)

Neubauer, J. (1992). *The fin-de-siècle culture of adolescence*. New Haven: Yale University Press.

Oehler, D. (1980). L'echec de 1848. *L'Arc, 79*, 65.

Outram, D. (1989). *The body and the French revolution. Sex, class and political culture*. New Haven: Yale University Press.

Overton, W. F., & Reese, H. W. (Eds.). (1973). Models of development: Methodological implications. In J. R. Nesselroade & H. W. Reese (Eds.), *Life-span developmental psychology: Methodological issues* (pp. 65-86). New York: Academic Press.

Phinney, J. S. (1989). Stages of ethnic identity development in minority group adolescents. *Journal of Early Adolescence, 9*, 34-49.

Piaget, J. (1968). *On the development of memory and identity*. Barre, MA: Clark University Press.

Prince, M. (1906). Miss Beauchamps. *Journal of Abnormal Psychology, 15*, 67-135.

Rangell, L. (1960, November 11). *Anxiety, discouragement and uncertainty—The "little" problems in daily living*. Paper presented at symposium on Psychological Problems in

Medical Practice, University of California, Department of Continuing Education in Medicine, and External Division of the San Francisco Psychoanalytic Institute, San Francisco.

Rangell, L. (1967). Psychoanalysis, affects and the "human core." *Psychoanalytic Quarterly, 36*, 172-202.

Rangell, L. (1969). The intrapsychic process and its analysis. *International Journal of Psychoanalysis, 50*, 65-77.

Rangell, L. (1971). The decision-making process. *Psychoanalytic Study of the Child, 26*, 425-452.

Rangell, L. (1973). On the cacaphony of human relations. *Psychoanalytic Quarterly, 42*, 325-348.

Rangell, L. (1974). A psychoanalytic perspective leading currently to the syndrome of the compromise of integrity. *International Journal of Psychoanalysis, 55*, 3-12.

Rangell, L. (1976). Lessons from Watergate. A derivative for psychoanalysis. *Psychoanalytic Quarterly, 45*, 37-61.

Rangell, L. (1978). On understanding and treating anxiety and its derivatives. *International Journal of Psychoanalysis, 59*, 229-236.

Rangell, L. (1980). *The mind of Watergate*. New York: Norton.

Rangell, L. (1982). The self in psychoanalytic theory. *Journal of the American Psychoanalytic Association, 30*, 863-891.

Rangell, L. (1987). A core process in psychoanalytic treatment. *Psychoanalytic Quarterly, 56*, 222-249.

Rangell, L. (1988a). The future of psychoanalysis: The scientific crossroads. *Psychoanalytic Quarterly, 57*, 313-340.

Rangell, L. (1988b). Roots and derivatives of unconscious fantasy. In H. P. Blum, Y. Kramer, A. Richards, & A. D. Richards (Eds.), *Fantasy, myth, and reality: Essays in honor of Jacob A. Arlow*. Madison, CT: International Universities Press.

Rangell, L. (1989). Seventeen. In R. A. Nemiroff & C. A. Colarusso (Eds.), *Frontiers of adult psychiatry* (pp. 3-25). New York: Basic Books.

Rangell, L. (1990). *The human core*. Madison, CT: International Universities Press.

Rapaport, D. (1958). The theory of ego autonomy. *Bulletin of the Menninger Clinic, 22*, 13-35.

Rapaport, D. (1960). The structure of psychoanalytic theory. *Psychological Issues* (Monograph 6). New York: International Universities Press.

Reese, H. W., & Smyer, M. A. (1983). The dimensionalization of life events. In E. Callaham & K. A. McCluskey (Eds.), *Life-span developmental psychology: Non-normative life events*. New York: Academic Press.

Revel, J. (1989). L'histoire au ras du sol [History from below]. In G. Levi, *Le pouvoir au village. Histoire d'un exorciste dans le Piémont du XVIIe siècle* [Power of the village: History of an exorcist in 17th-century Piedmont] (pp. 1-18). Paris: Gallimard.

Richardson, S. (1962). *Clarissa*. Boston: Houghton Mifflin. (Original work published 1747-1748)

Ricoeur, P. (1983). *Temps et récit, I*. Paris: Seuil. (Published as *Time and narrative* by Chicago University Press)

Ricoeur, P. (1990). *Soi-même comme un autre*. Paris: Seuil. (Published as *Oneself as another* by Chicago University Press)

Riesman, D. (1953). *The lonely crowd*. New York: Anchor.

Rogers, C. R. (1942). *Counseling and psychotherapy*. Boston: Houghton Mifflin.

Rosen, V. H. (1955). Strephosymbolia. *The Psychoanalytic Study of the Child, 10*, 83-99.

Rosenfeld, S. K., & Sprince, M. P. (1963). An attempt to formulate the meaning of the concept "borderline." *The Psychoanalytic Study of the Child, 18*, 603-636.

Sarbin, T. R. (Ed.). (1986). *Narrative psychology: The storied nature of human conduct.* New York: Praeger.

Sartre, J-P. (1971/1972). *L'idiot de la famille.* Paris: Gallimard.

Searles, H. (1959). *Anxiety concerning change.* Paper presented at the winter meeting of the American Psychoanalytic Association, New York.

Simenon, G. (1963). *Maigret et le clochard.* Paris: Presses de la Cite.

Spacks, P. (1981). *The adolescent idea: Myths of youth and the adult imagination.* New York: Basic Books.

Spitz, R. A. (1945). Hospitalism. *The Psychoanalytic Study of the Child, 1*, 53-74.

Spranger, E. (1924). *Psychologie des jugendalters* [Psychology of adolescence]. Leipzig: Quelle.

Springhall, J. O. (1986). *Coming of age: Adolescence in Britain 1860-1960.* Dublin: Gill.

Stallybrass, P., & White, A. (1986). *The politics and poetics of transgression.* Ithaca, NY: Cornell University Press.

Stephen, J. E., Fraser, E., & Marcia, J. E. (1992). Moratorium-achievement (MAMA) cycles in lifespan identity development: Value orientations and reasoning system correlates. *Journal of Adolescence, 15*, 283-300.

Stern, D. (1985). *The interpersonal world of the infant: A view from psycholanalysis and developmental psychology.* New York: Basic Books.

Stevenson, R. L. (1886). *The strange case of Dr. Jekyll and Mr. Hyde.* London: Longmans & Green.

Stone, L. (1981a). Family history in the 1980s. *Journal of Interdisciplinary History, 12*, 51-87.

Stone, L. (1981b). *The past and the present.* London: Routledge & Kegan Paul.

Sullivan, H. S. (1953). *The interpersonal theory of psychiatry.* New York: Norton.

Tinker, C. B., & Lowry, H. F. (Eds.). (1950). *The poetical works of Matthew Arnold.* London: Oxford University Press.

Todd, E. (1988). *La nouvelle France* [The new France]. Paris: Seuil.

Torch, E. M. (1981). The depersonalization syndrome: An overview. *Psychoanalytic Quarterly, 53*, 249-258.

Van der Werff, J. J. (1985). *Identiteitsproblemen. Zelfbeschouwing in de psychologie* [Identity problems: Perceptions of self in psychology]. Muiderberg, The Netherlands: Coutinho.

Van der Werff, J. J. (1988). Zelfconceptie in ontwikkelingspsychologisch perspectief. [Self-conception from a developmental perspective]. In W. Koops & J. J. van der Werff (Eds.), *Overzicht van de empirische ontwikkelingspsychologie, 3* [Overview of the empirical developmental psychology, 3] (pp. 156-190). Groningen, The Netherlands: Wolters-Noordhoff.

Van der Werff, J. J. (1990). The problem of self-conceiving, appendix. In H. A. Bosma & A. E. Jackson (Eds.), *Coping and self-concept in adolescence* (pp. 13-33). New York: Springer Verlag.

Van der Werff, J. J. (1991). *Identity and development: Identity scientists build their own Babel tower.* Unpublished paper, Department of Psychology, University of Groningen, The Netherlands.

Van Haaften, A. W., Korthals, M. (Eds.). (forthcoming). *Philosophy of development.*

Vovelle, M. (1982). *Idéologies et mentalités* [Ideologies and mentalities]. Paris: François Maspero.

Waelder, R. (1962). Psychoanalysis, scientific method and philosophy. *Journal of the American Psychoanalytic Association, 10*, 617-637.

Wallerstein, R. S. (1988). One psychoanalysis or many? *International Journal of Psychoanalysis, 69*, 5-21.

Waterman, A. S., & Archer, S. L. (1993). Identity status during the adult years: Scoring criteria. In J. E. Marcia, A. S. Waterman, D. M. Matteson, S. L. Archer, & J. Orlofski (Eds.), *Ego identity: A handbook for psychosocial research* (pp. 241-270). New York: Springer Verlag.

Wedekind, F. (1969). *Spring awakening*. London: Calder. (Original work published 1891)

Weinstein, F., & Platt, G. (1969). *The wish to be free: Society, psyche and value change.* Berkeley: University of California Press.

Wessel, M. (1991). Van sporen en vormen: Carlo Ginzburg en de geschiedenis [About traces and shapes: Carlo Ginzburg and history]. *Theoretische Geschiedenis, 18*, 155-162.

White, H. (1981). The value of narrative in the representation of reality. In W.J.T. Mitchell (Ed.), *On narrative*. Chicago: University of Chicago Press.

Widdershoven, G.A.M. (1988). Models of development. *Schweizerische Zeitschrift für Psychologie, 47*, 129-134.

Widdershoven, G.A.M. (1991). The image of man in phenomenology, hermeneutics and deconstruction. In J. van Nispen & D. Tiemersma (Eds.), *The quest for man* (pp. 94-97). Assen, The Netherlands: Van Gorcum.

Widdershoven, G.A.M. (1993). The story of life: Hermeneutic perspectives on the relation between narrative and life history. *The Narrative Study of Lives, 1*, 1-20.

Widdershoven, G.A.M. (1994). Models of development. In A. W. van Haaften & M. Korthals (Eds.), *Philosophy of development*.

Winnicott, D. W. (1965). *The maturational processes and the facilitating environment.* New York: International Universities Press.

Woods, J. M. (1987). Some considerations on psycho-history. In G. Cocks & T. L. Crosby (Eds.), *Psycho/history* (pp. 109-120). New Haven: Yale University Press.

Wylie, R. (1974). *The self concept: Vol. 1. A review of methodological considerations and measuring instruments* (rev. ed.). Lincoln: University of Nebraska Press.

Wylie, R. (1979). *The self concept: Vol. 2. Theory and research on selected topics* (rev. ed.). Lincoln: University of Nebraska Press.

Name Index

Subject Index

About the Contributors

Harke A. Bosma has worked since 1972 at the Department of Psychology at the University of Groningen, where he received his Ph.D. in 1985 on a thesis titled "Identity Development in Adolescence, Coping with Commitments." In the same year he was appointed senior lecturer in adolescent psychology. His main research interests include adolescent coping and identity development and adolescent development in the family context. He has published several articles and some books in these areas. Among these are *Ontwikkeling tot volwassenheid* (*Development Toward Adulthood*, 1975, with J. Baltink) and *Coping and Self-Concept in Adolescence* (1990, with A. E. Jackson).

David J. de Levita studied medicine in Amsterdam and was trained in psychiatry and child psychiatry in Utrecht. He received his doctorate at the University of Utrecht with his thesis "The Concept of Identity" (1965). He is a training analyst of the Dutch Psychoanalytical Association. His appointments include full professor of Child Psychiatry at the Erasmus University of Rotterdam in 1969, full professor of Child Psychiatry at the University of Amsterdam in 1974, special professor of Child Psychiatry in the faculty of Education of the University of Amsterdam in 1987, and special professor of transgenerational sequelae of war at the Catholic University of Nijmegen in 1990. He is a member of diverse national and international committees and boards and an advisor of the Johannes Wier Foundation for the Protection of Human Rights.

Tobi L. G. Graafsma, psychologist and psychoanalyst, works at the Child and Youth Psychiatric Hospital of the Free University of Amsterdam. He also has a private practice. In 1975 he received his Ph.D. at the University of Groningen with his thesis "Identity Conflicts in Adolescence." His main interests are in the areas of child and adolescent psychopathology and in the area of psychoanalytic theory and technique. His publications comprise several articles in these areas and a book titled *Identiteitsontwikkeling in de Adolescentie* (*Identity Development in Adolescence*, 1982, with H. A. Bosma).

Harold D. Grotevant is Professor and Head of the Department of Family Social Science at the University of Minnesota. He completed his undergraduate work in psychology at the University of Texas at Austin and his doctoral degree at the University of Minnesota's Institute of Child Development. He taught at the University of Texas in Child Development and Family Relationships from 1977 to 1989 and began his work at Minnesota in 1990. His research publications focus on the development of children and adolescents within their families, particularly those in adoptive families. Much of his work focuses on the development of ego identity in the family context. His research has resulted in many articles published in professional journals and also several books: *Adolescent Development in the Family* (with C. R. Cooper, 1983); *Emotional Disturbance in Adopted Adolescents: Origins and Development* (with R. G. McRoy, 1988); *Openness in Adoption: New Practices, New Issues* (with R. G. McRoy, 1988); and *Family Assessment: A Guide to Methods and Measures* (with C. I. Carlson, 1989).

Ruthellen Josselson is a professor of psychology at Towson State University. She received her Ph.D. in 1972 from the University of Michigan in clinical psychology. The recipient of a Fulbright research scholarship, she has published many articles on normal development in adolescence. Her first book, *Finding Herself: Pathways to Identity Development in Women* (1987) focused on female development. Her recent book, *The Space Between Us: Exploring the Dimensions of Human Relationships* (1992) attempts to extend the theory of relational development. Professor Josselson has also served on the faculties of Harvard University and The John Hopkins University.

James E. Marcia is a professor of Psychology at Simon Fraser University, Vancouver, Canada. He received his Ph.D. at the Ohio State University in Clinical Psychology, completed his internship at Massachusetts Mental Health Center in Boston, and then taught at the State University of New York at Buffalo. He directed the Psychological Clinics at both Buffalo and Simon Fraser. He has a private practice in psychotherapy and his research interests include construct validation of psychosocial developmental theory. Most of his published research has been in the area of ego identity.

Arthur Mitzman attended the Juilliard School of Music before taking a Bachelor's and Master's Degree in History at Columbia University. He received his Ph.D. from the program in history of ideas at Brandeis University in 1963 and taught at Brooklyn College, Goddard College, the University of Rochester, and Simon Fraser University before being invited to occupy the chair in modern European history at the University of Amsterdam in 1971. He was a fellow at the Netherlands Institute for Advanced Studies in 1982-1983 and a guest professor at Rutgers University in 1986. He has written *The Iron Cage: A Historical Interpretation of Max Weber* (1970), *Sociology and Estrangement: Three Sociologists of Imperial Germany* (1973), *Michelet, Historian: Rebirth and Romanticism in 19th Century France* (1990), and numerous articles in scholarly journals in North America and Europe. For one of these, "The Unstrung Orpheus: On Flaubert's Youth and the Psycho-Social Origins of Art for Art's Sake" (Psychohistory Review, 1977), he was given the William L. Langer Award by the Group for the Use of Psychology in History, a division of the American Historical Association.

John Neubauer is professor of comparative literature at the University of Amsterdam. He received his education in the United States and taught at various American universities before coming to Amsterdam. His publications include *Symbolismus und sybolische Logik* (1978), *Novalis* (1982), and *The Emancipation of Music from Language* (1986). He has also been editing Goethe's scientific writings.

Leo Rangell was twice President of the American and the International Psychoanalytic Associations. He is Clinical Professor of Psychiatry at UCLA and UC San Francisco. His publications comprise some 300 scientific articles on psychoanalytic theory, on such subjects as anxiety, conflict, psychic trauma, integrity, friendship, and the unconscious roots of the decision-making process. His books include *The Mind of Watergate: An Exploration of the Compromise of Integrity,* and a two-volume work *The Human Core: The Intrapsychic Base of Behavior.*

Guy A. M. Widdershoven is an Associate Professor of Philosophy and Head of the Department of Health Ethics and Philosophy at the University of Limburg, Maastricht, The Netherlands. His research concerns philosophy of health and philosophy of the humanities. He wrote a dissertation on the relation between action and rationality in phenomenology and hermeneutics (1987) and edited several books on philosophical hermeneutics and the foundations of the human sciences.